IKHNATON: *legend and history*

F. J. GILES

# IKHNATON

*legend and history*

RUTHERFORD • MADISON • TEANECK
FAIRLEIGH DICKINSON UNIVERSITY PRESS

*IKHNATON.* © *F. J. Giles 1970.* *First American edition published 1972 by Associated University Presses, Inc., Cranbury, New Jersey 08512*

*Library of Congress Catalogue Card Number:* 76-37800

DT
87.4
.G5
1972

*ISBN: 0-8386-1077-3*

*Printed in the United States of America*

# CONTENTS



ALMA COLLEGE
MONTEITH LIBRARY
ALMA, MICHIGAN

2/28/74 Scot Shop

# ILLUSTRATIONS

*Between pages* 204 *and* 205



*Line drawings*

# ACKNOWLEDGEMENTS

The author would like to express a debt of gratitude to his first teacher of Egyptology, the Rev. Professor R. J. Williams, as well as to the late Professor F. M. Heichelheim, both of the University of Toronto, and also wishes to thank Professor Walter B. Emery, C.B.E., and Dr. R. O. Faulkner, both of University College, for their encouragement during the period of his research in the University of London.

The author wishes to acknowledge with thanks permission to reproduce photographs of items in the British Museum; the Egyptian Museum in Cairo; the Staatliche Museen, Berlin; and the Metropolitan Museum of Art, New York. The perspective drawings of Akhetaton (pl. XV, XVI) are reproduced by kind permission of the Egypt Exploration Society from J. D. S. Pendlebury *The City of Akhenaten* (1951), vol. III, pl. II and IX; illustrations from the tombs at Akhetaton are reproduced from N. de G. Davies *The Rock Tombs of El Amarna,* Egypt Exploration Society (1903–8), Part One, Tomb of Meryre, pl. XXII (p. 110) and pl. XI (pl. XVI), Part Two, Tomb of Meryre II, pl. XXXVIII (pp. 216–17) and pl. XLI (pp. 218–19), Part Three, Tomb of Huy, pl. III (p. 205), IV (pp. 206–7), VI (pp. 208–9), VIII (pp. 210–11), XIII (pp. 212–13), XVI (p. 214), XVIII (p. 215), and Part Six, Tomb of Ay, pl. XXXVIIa and XXXVIIIa (pl. XII) and pl. I (pl. XII); the aerial photograph of the site of Akhetaton is reproduced by courtesy of the Air Force of the United Arab Republic; and the drawings of Amenhotep III and Tiy enthroned (p. 220) and the details of the throne decoration (p. 47) are taken respectively from *Annales du Service*, vol. 42 (1943), Ahmed Fakhry 'A Note on the Tomb of Kheruef at Thebes', pl. XXXIX, and J. Leibovitch 'Une nouvelle représentation d'une sphinge de la reine Tiy', figs. 11 and 12. The photographs of the mask and wooden statuette of Ikhnaton (pl. I and II), the caricature relief (pl. IV), the relief of Amenhotep III (pl. V), and of Smenkhkare and Meritaton (pl. IX) are by Walter Steinkopf; those of Queen Tiy's sepulchral canopy (pl. VI), her portrait head and canopic vase (pl. VII) are from Theodore M. Davis *The Tomb of Queen Tiy* (1910); and those of the mummies of Queen Tiy's parents are from Theodore M. Davis *The Tomb of Iouya and Youiyou* (1907).

# AUTHOR'S NOTE

In addition to its ordinary use in parentheses, I have throughout the text used the round form of bracket to indicate the presence of a cartouche—the oval ring enclosing the name and title of an Egyptian king—so that ( ) is rendered (Tutankhamen). The cartouche on many occasions contains an epithet as well as a specific name, in this case (*ḥḳꜣ 'Iwn rsy*) 'King of Southern Iwn' and the whole name would be read 'Tutankhamen is the King of Southern Iwn', but throughout this book—unless the epithet has some significance in the argument—it will not be translated or transliterated, where the name is one by which the king is usually called, as in this case Tutankhamen. Unfortunately, it is impossible to be either consistent or, without the use of a number of diacritical marks, entirely accurate in the spelling of names. In addition certain inaccurate spellings have become traditional. Square brackets are used to indicate words inserted by me as explanatory of the text under discussion, or as an indication of restorations.

# Introduction

It was while engaged in specialised research at University College in the University of London some ten years ago that I first conceived the idea of a book which would enable the non-specialist reader interested in Egyptology to come to grips with the real problems of the history of the Armarna Age. Since 1960 my work has been in an entirely different field, and during the preparation of this volume I have had neither the leisure nor the opportunity to examine publications relating to matters discussed here. However, whatever material has come to my attention from time to time during these last ten years in Australia does not indicate the discovery of new facts which would force me to alter my conclusions here.

The study of Egyptology is not more than 125 years old as a serious discipline. It has, however, in this short span of time been widely practised by scholars in numerous countries. Expeditions from many lands over the years have excavated the ancient sites of Egyptian culture. The objects discovered by these excavations have been distributed all over the world and the publication of their results, when they exist at all, have been in numerous periodicals in divers languages issued since roughly 1860.

Since debris from the Amarna period was scattered throughout Egypt and Nubia, and perhaps Palestine-Syria as well, individual objects and sites of the period were uncovered from the earliest days of this study up to the present time by various excavators. Any person then who wished to make a comprehensive study of the history of Amarna and its personalities would have to engage himself first of all in an exhaustive search to assemble as many of the pieces of the puzzle as he was able before he could even begin to interpret it as a picture. Since—as I have said—relevant data were hidden in many obscure publications printed in English, German, French and Italian, this task occupied me for a long time. Important facts were even buried in defunct periodicals some of which always seemed to be lacking in whatever library I used. Because of these circumstances individual pieces of important material could easily have been missed, though I am not aware of any large body of information omitted from close scrutiny.

The conclusions which I have drawn produce many historical

interpretations at variance with the accounts which appear in most current publications. For this I take full responsibility. I can only say that a careful study of all the evidence which I could obtain has led me to believe that the story of the latter part of the Eighteenth Dynasty does not greatly resemble the history books.

I have believed for many years that the co-regency between Amenhotep III and his son was a matter of fact, not conjecture, but some of the results of my research were frankly surprising. For example, it had never occurred to me that Tutankhamen's queen had reigned for a fairly substantial period after her husband's death, though this very fact is indicated by the evidence.

There is a great need for further excavation in the area of Akhetaton. It is quite probable that if such work were accomplished the extent of our knowledge of these remote but fascinating pages of human history might be considerably enlarged.

2

My own concern with ancient history in general and Egyptology in particular arose very early in my life. So early in fact that I find it impossible to trace its origin to any one particular cause, but it may have arisen from the world-wide interest resulting from the epic discovery which Howard Carter and Lord Carnarvon made in 1922 in the Valley of the Kings, namely the tomb of Tutankhamen. It is difficult now, when the between-wars period seems almost itself to be ancient history, to appreciate exactly how great a sensation this was. For years it was written about, read about, and talked about, and it was, I think, in this climate of general interest that my own preoccupation with the period began.

To be sure, every child has some romantic idea of what he will be when he grows up. Some want to be policemen, and others engineers, cowboys or pilots. I wanted to be an archaeologist. This idea did not persist because as I grew older my interest turned away from the actual process of digging up history rather towards piecing together the material which the archaeologist had unearthed. It was this fascination which directed my studies.

Tutankhamen and his relatives had always attracted me. While I was still in my teens I combed libraries searching out books bearing on the period. When I became an undergraduate at the University of Toronto, however, I began to take a critical interest in Amarna but there were, even in that great library, only enough books and periodicals about the period to be tantalising rather than enlightening. It was not till several years after I left school, I thought for good, that the establishment of the Canada Council for the Arts and Sciences granted me enough money to pursue the study. This delay was perhaps a good thing, for by 1958 the war-inspired hiatus in such esoteric studies as Egyptian history had long passed and the backlog of material whose publication the war had delayed was in print. As well my own grasp of the necessary tools of the trade, the Egyptian language especially, was much better fitted to the task at hand.

3

The difference between events as they really happened and how men have described them in their later written works has always intrigued me. Our own law courts every day illustrate how eye-witnesses of an accident or crime can produce accounts of the happening at which they were present which bear no resemblance to each other, even though each may be telling the truth to the best of his recollection. This fact, which is very important in everyday life, becomes of much greater significance when the more remote past is involved, since every person who writes about the past has his own point of view and hence his own unconscious bias which colours all his writing.

The effect of this, for example, among the Greeks and Romans was that quite respectable historians permitted themselves to say what they liked about the past of their own culture without any particular concern for its truth or falsity. It is difficult to tell, for instance, how much of Roman history before the time of the first Punic War is a record of actual events and how much concocted by later historians, such as Livy. Julius Caesar, who was, generally speaking, a very pragmatic person, liked to believe that his family was descended from the goddess Venus. It is impossible to avoid the idea that the Greeks or Romans may have valued a good story more than a close attention to the actual course of events.

In Egyptian history the situation is somewhat different. The various priesthoods undoubtedly kept copious records of certain aspects of the past, such as the names of kings and the dates of their coronations and deaths, but apart from this chronological skeleton of history and the dates of festivals, they probably had no specific interest in the detail of events. Once, a complete Egyptian king list was discovered, now known as the Turin papyrus. The gentleman who found it first of all packed it in a box with insufficient protection, and sent it on camel back to the coast and then by ship across the Mediterranean to Italy in a particularly rough season. As a result of the jolting of the camel and the rolling of the sea, the papyrus, dry and brittle from thousands of years of burial, shattered into a great many fragments and a quantity of dust. Ever since learned gentlemen have been playing a rather amusing intellectual game, trying to put Humpty Dumpty together again without much agreement or many noteworthy results.

The one Egyptian historian of Egypt of whom we have any knowledge was a priest named Manetho who wrote in Ptolemaic times. His own work was not preserved, but we have some extracts from it and a précis of certain parts of it in the works of other authors. Unfortunately, in many respects these accounts differ and in any case Manetho may well have had the customary classical habit of filling up the gaps in personal investigation by invention.

To the Greeks and Romans alike Egypt was the symbol of the distant past, and classical writers generally, when they wished to establish the extreme antiquity of some custom or event, connected it with Egypt. Thus the spell of Egypt exercised a certain power even in the Roman Imperial time. Did not Antinous, the young favourite of the Emperor Hadrian, drown himself in the Nile, sacrificing himself as a substitute for the emperor, to fulfil the terms of an Egyptian priest's prophecy? Hadrian, in an orgy of grief unprecedented in his time (or even this), set his favourite among the gods and ensured his immortality by mummifying his body in the Egyptian fashion.

Modern Western interest in Egypt has been fostered by our intense preoccupation with biblical history, especially during the nineteenth century. For, after all, it was Egypt from which the Children of Israel made their exodus. The desire to see the setting of this important event led travellers to visit Egypt and created a profound interest in its past. As a result, a great traffic in Egyptian antiquities arose and whatever could be purchased or stolen that was not too large to put on board ship was sent off to Europe, thus forming the nuclei of many modern museum collections.

It was not until Napoleon invaded Egypt close to the beginning of the nineteenth century, in the course of his projected expulsion of the British from India, that any scientific approach to the study of Egypt's past became possible. Indeed, Napoleon, perhaps in imitation of Alexander the Great, had brought scholars and scientists with him, probably to ensure that all his achievements might be assured of permanent record. At any rate, these people produced the first scholarly description of the country and its antiquities.

It was during this expedition that the Rosetta stone, inscribed in three scripts—hieroglyphic (the pictorial sacred engraved writing), demotic (the popular, very simplified version of hieroglyphic writing) and Greek—with the details of an unimportant decree concerning religious matters, was discovered, thus providing the essential clue to the translation of the Egyptian language. Despite the terms of the peace, under which the stone itself went to London, it was the French scholar Champollion who first succeeded in reading the language from a copy of the inscription which had been obtained by the Louvre.

Since then both private persons and educational institutions of various kinds have sent numerous expeditions to Egypt, and from the results of these our knowledge has been so increased that at the present time it is possible for me to write a book of considerable length about a period of less than three-quarters of a century, occurring more than three thousand years ago.

4

'More nonsense has been written about the Amarna period than any other in Egyptian history,' wrote Dr. Margaret Murray—and with a good deal of justice.

There have been many different causes for this state of affairs, but undoubtedly the most important factor in confusing the issue so badly has been the persistent intrusion of modern religious speculation into ancient history. This has ended in creating a wholly legendary Ikhnaton, a kind of pre-Christian Christian in whose life and teaching scholars have found the germ of ideal Western morality. The facts that survive regarding the period have either been obscured or even deliberately neglected or distorted, so that the image of an ancient Egyptian plaster saint might not be destroyed. It was the contrast between the facts that I could ascertain and the highly circumstantial narrative of the king's career, based on little discernible evidence, that first led me to doubt the Ikhnaton legend.

Ikhnaton's actual reign lasted no longer than seventeen years, of which scarcely half could have been spent in residence at his new city Akhetaton, now called Tell el Amarna. But his reign cannot be considered in isolation, and—for my purpose—the Amarna period will include the reign of his father Amenhotep III, and the reign of his successors Tutankhamen and Eye, an era of approximately sixty years.

5

Some three hundred miles north of Thebes was the location which Ikhnaton chose for his new city. There, where the cliffs rising along the eastern side of the Nile Valley retreated a little and left a small semi-circular bay of level ground, the king set out his boundary markers and built his city. At the height of its splendour it must have created an impression of jerry-built magnificence, the royal architect having evidently changed his mind on more than one occasion. At any rate, in the new city the king established in full the apparatus of his belief. Several Aton temples were erected and numerous palaces and official buildings as well as a great number of private dwellings, large and ornate for the nobles and the king's favourites, and small and cramped for the majority of the inhabitants. As well the city contained all the workshops and business premises necessary to carry on its life. Then, too, in the hills behind Akhetaton the king and some of his nobles began the construction of tombs, and the ordinary people of the town, rich and poor alike, established also a plot of ground in which to bury their dead. (See the map p. 38.)

Ikhnaton's city was never destroyed. His successor, Tutankhamen, abandoned it, and left it to rot. Sometime later Haremhab and his successors, to whom Ikhnaton was anathema, quarried out its stone for re-use in their own buildings and left on the site only heaps of debris. And so largely it remained while more than thirty centuries passed, and all memory of the king, its founder, failed. Never again did anyone establish a major settlement on its site, though during early Christian times some ascetic hermits lived in the tombs. In short, here was an entire ancient city left almost miraculously to modern archaeologists, so that a thorough scientific study might be made and a segment of society of such a remote time brought to life. It was an archaeologist's dream, but it turned into a nightmare.

Tourists had visited the sites of the tombs in early days and scratched their names here and there, and the cooking fires of the Coptic inhabitants had in some cases blackened the tomb walls, but it was the nineteenth-century souvenir hunters who began the practice of carving pieces out of the visible tomb reliefs and carrying them away so that, in most cases, they disappeared for ever. So severe was the damage to these tombs that many of the details are now entirely lost, and one must refer to old copies of the reliefs (notably those of Lepsius, a German scholar, made about 1845) to gain a more accurate impression of the scenes. This work, of Lepsius, too, is unfortunately quite unreliable in matters of detail, because in many cases, whereas Lepsius drew the reliefs as they actually appeared in the tombs, his publishers touched them up in the interests of beauty.

Lepsius was not the only travelling nineteenth-century scholar to visit the tombs, but he was the first to have his work published. Serious excavation on the site, however, only started as a consequence of the discovery of the Tell el Amarna letters (to be discussed later) towards the end of the nineteenth century, when scholars belatedly recognised the value of the tablets as historical documents. From this time onward, various expeditions pursued desultory efforts at Amarna until the eve of the Second World War.

Among the difficulties which hampered work in Egyptian archaeology most effectively was the French control of the Department of Antiquities which was established during the Khedival administration and continued after the British occupation of the country, partly as a sop to French nationalism to prevent diplomatic difficulties between the French and British over the seizure of the country, and partly, I am certain, because administrators and politicians have always found it difficult to take scholars or scholarly affairs seriously. Archaeologists of other nationalities naturally objected, both on the grounds of the French officials' incompetence and of the importation of French nationalism into Egyptian archaeology, and William Matthew Flinders Petrie—the greatest archaeologist of his era and one of the greatest of any era—carried on a running feud with the Antiquities Department for much of his career.[1]

Petrie came to Amarna in 1891, having obtained a concession to dig in the town only over the protests of French officials of the department who had reserved the tombs for their own expedition. Shortly after beginning work on the site of Ikhnaton's palace he came across large sections of painted floor—some 250 sq. ft. in all—and arranged for them to be enclosed in a building open to tourists. Unfortunately, the authorities failed to have a proper path made to it through the surrounding fields and the local people hacked the paintings to pieces to prevent the tourists trampling their crops. The style of the work can now only be judged by study of Petrie's monograph, or by a visit to Oxford's Ashmolean Museum where the one fragment of paintwork which he managed to remove survives in a dark corner.

Petrie also tells how, when working at Amarna, he was joined by Howard Carter—later the discoverer of the tomb of Tutankhamen—who was searching for antiquities on behalf of Lord Amherst, the great English collector. Carter discovered during his work on the Aton temple site some broken statues of Nofretiti, Ikhnaton's queen, and very carefully collected even the smallest chips of stone so that the statues could later be restored. However, when Amherst died, although the statues were sold at high prices, the fragments were thrown away as valueless.

During Petrie's excavations in the city the official departmental expedition concentrated on the so-called royal tomb of Ikhnaton. Before the local Arabs sold the secret of its location to the government they had removed everything of obvious value, and were still allowed to rake over the debris unsupervised while the excavation was in progress, so that Petrie managed to buy from them some shawabtis (magical statues of servants to serve the dead in the next world) after the expedition had left. All the official party actually achieved was the publication of the inscriptions on the one tomb, and it was not until early in this century that the British scholar Norman de Garis Davies copied and published a number of others. In 1894 the French found more painted pavement in the southern part of the city, and this was taken into the charge of the Department of Antiquities and eventually displayed in the Cairo Museum.

Just before the First World War the Germans mounted a major expedition. Since, however, only a preliminary report has ever been published, the only important discovery we know to have been made was of the workshop of the chief royal sculptor, Thutmose, though many other important data must have been found by this expedition. This studio with its numerous models and plaster casts of various persons, including some of members of the royal family, was most important. Among the rest was the complete or nearly complete bust, which was identified as being that of Nofretiti, a work of art which ranks as one of the greatest masterpieces of any age. Under the terms of their agreement with the Egyptian authorities the excavators were bound to hand over any unique finds or outstanding works of art to the Cairo Museum, but the bust was smuggled out and has been for almost fifty years in Berlin. The story of how this was achieved varies. One anonymous doctor's wife claimed that her husband concealed it in a basket of vegetables; others claim that it was encased in plaster of paris to make it look like an ordinary block of stone; and yet others that it was actually placed among the spoils to be divided between the Egyptian Museum and the Expedition, but that a deliberate covering of mud and debris led the Museum officials to ignore it. Whether the learned gentlemen used fraud or outright theft to remove this particular bust the Egyptian government never forgot or forgave the outrage, and the consequences in subsequent governmental interference with foreign field workers in Egypt have been grave.

However, during the 1920s and 1930s the Egypt Exploration Society, which has its headquarters in London, gained permission to send a reasonably well-equipped expedition to dig at Akhetaton. Its members over the years included all England's great Egyptologists, and in the latest period, just before the Second World War, it was headed by J. D. S. Pendlebury, a young archaeologist of remarkable gifts.

The three volumes of the Society's reports so far published deal largely with architectural detail.[2] The cemetery or cemeteries which must exist in the area were not found, and neither were the tombs Petrie reported before the turn of the century as being in the cliffs near the city. Except for the rather meagre effort by F. W. Fairman of Liverpool University as editor of the third volume, no conclusions were drawn regarding the history of the period and even this inadequate material had to wait until the 1950s for publication.

This third volume was to have been produced by Pendlebury, but his interest in Cretan studies, and knowledge of the island and its people, led him to become a leader of the 'underground' there after the Nazi invasion. He achieved considerable success, but was eventually so seriously wounded that a doctor was essential and the German authorities discovered his whereabouts. With customary despatch and brutality, they marched Pendlebury out of the hut where they found him and shot him on the spot. This ended any hope of a satisfactory report of the Amarna excavations.

Fairman did attempt to marshal the data bearing on the disputed question whether Ikhnaton and his father were joint rulers, but did not use all the evidence available, so that his account merely prolonged discussion of a point which one could reasonably have expected settled years ago. Pendlebury must obviously have made copious notes while working on the site and I had hoped to draw from them an idea of his own conclusions, but, although I have made exhaustive inquiries, I am still unable to say whether these notes are still extant.

6

My plan in this book has been to make a compromise between a work of scholarship and a popular book. I am not unmindful of how my own interest came to be awakened in these matters, and I venture to think that others as well who have no specialist preoccupations with this period might gain some amusement from a kind of antiquarian detective work. Nevertheless, since a lot of material is of some technical interest I could not in conscience present a piece directed purely to the general reader.

I have attempted to achieve this double-barrelled aim by presenting first an account of what I have called 'The Ikhnaton Legend' as it appears in most of the histories which were current in the libraries in the recent past, and regrettably still exist in most of those in the libraries of the present. I have followed this section by presenting a short account of the period as I see it in order to simplify matters for the general reader. Finally in the main sections of the book I have detailed the evidence and the interpretations which cause me to change the first picture into the second.

# PART ONE
# The Ikhnaton legend

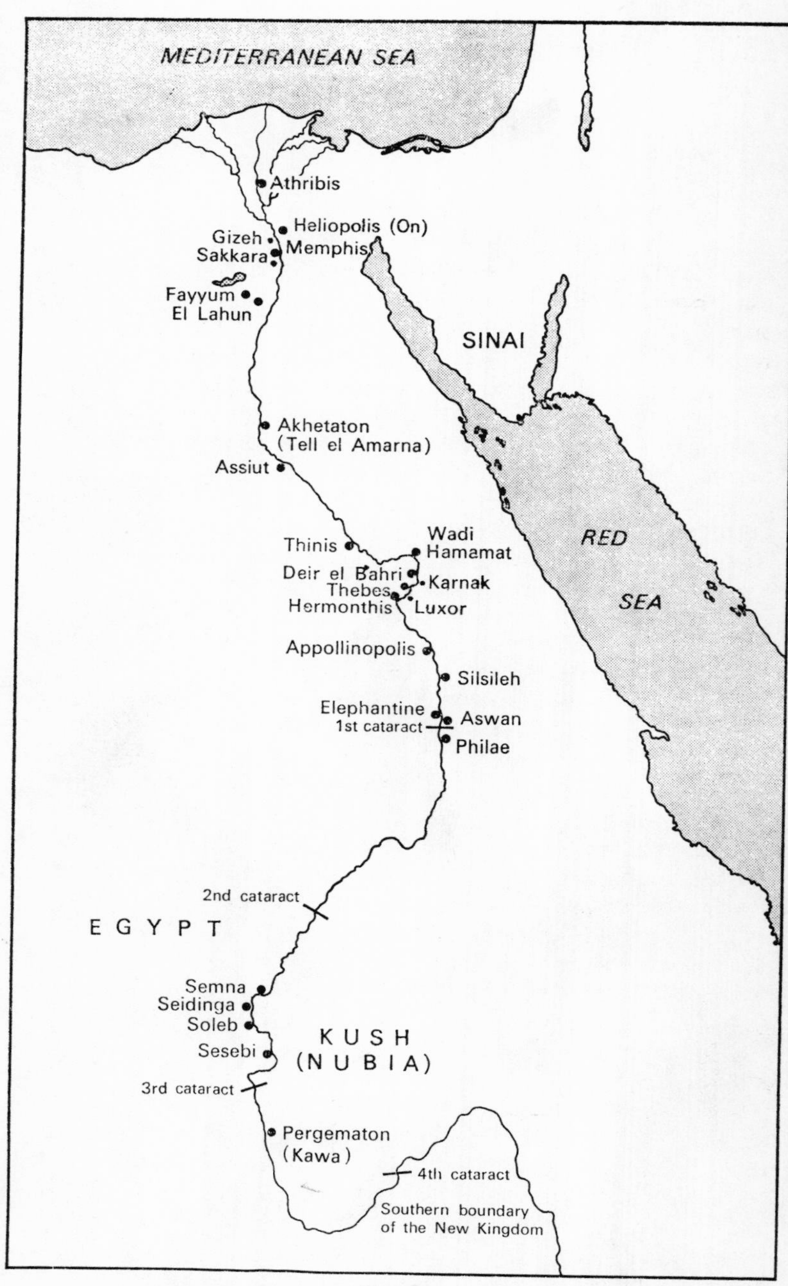
MEDITERRANEAN SEA
Athribis
Heliopolis (On)
Gizeh
Memphis
Sakkara
Fayyum
El Lahun
SINAI
Akhetaton
(Tell el Amarna)
Assiut
Thinis
Wadi
Hamamat
RED
SEA
Deir el Bahri
Karnak
Thebes
Hermonthis
Luxor
Appollinopolis
Silsileh
Elephantine
Aswan
1st cataract
Philae
2nd cataract
E G Y P T
Semna
Seidinga
Soleb
K U S H
(N U B I A)
Sesebi
3rd cataract
Pergematon
(Kawa)
4th cataract
Southern boundary
of the New Kingdom

*Egypt*

# ONE: Youth

The legend of the life and beliefs of Ikhnaton which was evolved at the end of the nineteenth century is a beautiful story. It portrays a man of the highest ideals struggling against heaven and earth in his pursuit of truth, beauty, and god. A man in whom the spirit burned more fiercely because his body was infirm, and who stood, virtually alone, hundreds of years in advance of his age, striving to bring to the world those ideas of morality to which our own era aspires in vain. Like the story of Prester John, it is one which has to be told of distant times, or very remote places, because the hero is so much larger than life.

Romanticism was such an integral part of the nineteenth-century approach that it is unfair to blame Breasted, Baikie, or Weigall—to cite only a few scholars of the period—who produced this new saga from the scanty facts in their possession.

Amenhotep III is credited with starting the whole affair. Like many despots with territories in a quiet state of subjection, he is supposed to have had little to occupy himself except the pursuit of pleasure. Becoming lazy and lethargic, he no longer bothered even to keep up appearances at court, and, though a mystic, had not sufficient character to initiate a religious reformation. His wife, Queen Tiy, had him under her thumb from an early period in the reign, and portraits of this remarkable woman appear on monuments to a far greater extent than those of any previous queen consort: in Nubia she even had her own temple.

After thirty years of rule Amenhotep had lost all interest in the exercise of power, and was plagued by poor health. The skull of his mummy reveals that he had very bad teeth and a number of abcesses must have made his life a misery, and from the Amarna letters we learn that Tushratta, king of Mitanni, sent a statue of the healing goddess Ishtar to visit Egypt in the hope of effecting his cure.

As the *de facto* ruler of Egypt, Queen Tiy used her influence to promote the cult of Re, the sun-god, and started to work against the power of the Amen priesthood. The heir to the throne as the reign drew to a close was the only living son of the royal couple, a boy of ten or eleven, already developing grave physical peculiarities which made it doubtful if he would live very long. To ensure the succession, the king felt that he had to marry him off as soon as possible to a suitable princess in the hope that a physically stronger heir might be produced. The chosen bride was the daughter of the king of Mitanni, who on her arrival in Egypt was re-named Nofretiti. Since she was still only a child, she did not have immediate relations with the prince, but was put in the charge of another Tiy, the wife of the nobleman Eye, who was later to seize the throne.

Soon after the contraction of this alliance the king died. His son being too young to rule, the queen-mother assumed the regency, as a letter written to her by the king of Mitanni shortly after her husband's death shows. Just as she had influenced her husband in religious matters, Tiy had had full control of her son's education and had imbued him from earliest youth with her own ideas: the influence of her son's young bride was also probably exerted in the same direction.

Consequently, at the very time when Egypt most needed an able and sensible ruler, it got a woman with a strongly mystical streak guiding two children, one a foreigner, and the other weak, sickly, and completely unworldly. From the outset the young king made a habit of avoiding the duties of his office, and turned more and more to religious matters. At first his mother encouraged him, but as his fanaticism grew, she tried in vain to hold him back. In particular the king was opposed to war and made no attempt to protect his ancestors' hard-won conquests in near Asia.

Weigall wrote: 'One may now imagine the Pharaoh as a pale and sickly youth; his head seemed too large for his body, his eyelids were heavy; his eyes as one imagines them were wells of dream. His features were delicately moulded, and his mouth in spite of a somewhat protruding jaw is reminiscent of the best of the art of Rossetti. He seems to have been a quiet studious boy whose thoughts wandered in far places, searching for that happiness which his physical condition had denied to him. His nature was gentle, his young heart overflowed with love. He delighted, it would seem, to walk in the gardens of the palace, to hear the birds singing, to watch the fish in the lake. . . . There was a grave dignity in his gait, or the artists have lied, and his words were already fraught with wisdom. . . . Already he was so much beloved by his subjects that their adherence to him through the rough places of his future life was assured.'[1]

The king's mystical outlook would also have been reinforced by his being an epileptic, subject to hallucinations and hearing voices which would appear to him divine revelations.

# TWO: Religious ideas

By the Eighteenth Dynasty religious thought in Egypt had reached immense complexity, and the involvement of the Amen cult with that of Re shows that syncretism was not unknown. The idea that one god is but an aspect of another is a step along the road that leads to monotheism.

The Re cult was the oldest powerful system of worship in Egypt, and its priests may well have resented the primacy of Amen, and the perhaps forced connection of the Re cult with that god. In any case, Amenhotep III had by the end of his reign felt that the Amen cult was becoming too powerful, and had ceased the practice of appointing members of its hierarchy to secular offices, such as the premiership or vizierate, and of making the high priest titular chief of all other priests in Egypt. In this spirit also he tolerated Tiy's interest in a new god (at least in name), and permitted her education of their son in her beliefs.

Tiy may have been of Asiatic origin, which would suggest a connection between the god Adon, well known in near Asia, and the new cult of Aton. Be this as it may, the Aton name was involved in Egypt with the cult of Re—in particular with the god name Re Harakhte, which was for a time almost another title for the Aton.

Brought up in the new cult from childhood, the young king felt far more strongly about it than either of his parents, developing the fanatical streak which worried his mother. Tiy may have seen her god as one of a large pantheon, a concept which would have given no offence to leaders of other cults, but it was soon apparent that her son did not concern himself with the pretensions of mere priests, and perhaps even welcomed the opportunity to destroy their power.

From the beginning of his reign Ikhnaton took, or was given, the title of high priest of Re Harakhte. This put him, or those who ruled through him in those early years, in control of the development of the new religion and a king's party grew up which owed adherence to the new god, and which was activated by the hope of personal gain.

As the king grew older his concept of the nature of his god grew more philosophical. The extent of the empire under his nominal control led him to see his deity as exercising a similar universal power, and he eventually came to believe that his god was the only one to be worshipped.

Near the start of his reign, however, Ikhnaton or his regents had a temple dedicated to the new cult erected in Thebes. The site was one already consecrated to Amen, between Karnak and Luxor, but even the name of the whole city was changed to the city of the Brightness of Aton. The Amen priesthood was greatly annoyed, yet at this stage the king did not make any overt move against their cult itself. In reliefs the king is still shown worshipping Amen, but it was at this time that official support of the Amen cult ceased, and the money and royal gifts of estates previously devoted to Amen were diverted to establishing the Aton worship on a sound economic basis.

The king felt that everything about his god should be new, and adopted a novel symbolism for portraying the god in temple reliefs—the sun's disc, with rays emanating from it and each ending in a hand. This was a new departure altogether, since Egyptian gods had previously been portrayed as either human or animal, or a combination of both, e.g. the falcon-headed man commonly used in the Re cult. The Aton symbol, however, was an abstraction, a divorcing of deity from the physical world. The human beings who served the god were also to be portrayed after a new fashion, naturalistically and with a freedom of line that broke entirely with old conventions. A new school of artistic expression was established.

The maturing of the king's religious ideas was marked by his adoption of the name Ikhnaton 'Spirit of the Aton', instead of the style Amenhotep which he had used in the early years of his reign, and shortly afterwards he founded the new city of Akhetaton, 'the horizon of Aton', as a centre from which the new cult might spread throughout his empire. Aton cities were later established in Nubia and probably also in Syria.

Weigall wrote of this period: 'Sometimes the thoughts he voiced came directly from the mazes of his own mind; sometimes he perhaps repeated the utterances of his deep-thinking mother, and sometimes there passed from his lips the pearls of wisdom which he had gleaned from the wise men of his court.' It had been the boy's desire to listen to the dreams of the east, to receive into his brain those speculations which ever meander so charmingly through the lands more near the sunrise. At his behest the dreamers of Asia related to him their visions; the philosophers made pregnant his mind with the mystery of knowledge; the poets sung to him harp-songs in which echoed the cry of the elder days; the priests of strange gods submitted to him the creeds of strange people. To him was made known the sweetness of the legends of Greece. The laughter of the woods rang in his ears, though never in narrow Egypt had he felt the enchantment of great forests. He had not seen the mountains, and the wooded slopes which rise from the Mediterranean were sights but dreamed of, and yet it was the flute of Pan and the song of the Nymphs in the mountain streams which set the thoughts dancing within his mis-shapen skull. He had not walked in the shadow of the cedars of Lebanon, nor had he ascended the Syrian hills; but nevertheless the chants of Baal were as familiar to him as were the solemn chants of Amon-Ra. The rose gardens of Persia, the incense groves of Araby, added their philosophies to his dreams, and the haunting lips of Babylon whispered to him tales of far-off days. From Sardinia, Sicily, Crete, and Cyprus there came to him the doctrines of those who had business in great waters; Libya and Ethiopia disclosed their mysteries to his eager ears. The fertile brain of the pharaoh was thus sown at an early age with the seeds of all that was wonderful in the fields of thought.'[1]

Soon Ikhnaton decided on even more radical measures. It was not enough to separate himself physically and mentally from the old beliefs, and withdraw his court from the unwholesome Amen worship of Thebes. Positive action must be taken against the further misleading of the minds of his people, and Aton must be sole god in fact as well as in theory. He began his onslaught on Egypt's religious system by closing the temples of other gods and dismissing priests from their livings. Crews of workmen were despatched to hack the names of the gods from monuments throughout the country. Not even inscriptions inside the tombs of the dead were safe, for he had these broken open and their walls mutilated. Even his own father's name was erased in many places, because it contained that of Amen. Even the plural of the noun 'gods' received attention.

This campaign against all religious beliefs except his own engendered ill-feeling, and as Thebes became increasingly hostile he pressed on the more swiftly with the building of his new city, taking up residence there in the eighth year of his reign and vowing never to leave it. He recorded his beliefs and intentions on large inscriptions set out at the limits of the city area, 'the domain of Aton', which was now intended to be the real capital of his empire. Here Ikhnaton developed his theology, and had recorded on its temples and palaces, and also on the walls of the tombs of his nobles, the articles of his belief.

In every monument of the new city, the real subject of its inscriptions was the relationship of the king and his god, the wording—including the two great hymns to Aton, being almost certainly the king's own work. Breasted wrote: 'Either for temple service or personal devotions the king composed two hymns to Aton, both of which the nobles had engraved on the walls of their tomb chapels. Of all the monuments left by this unparalleled revolution these hymns are by far the most remarkable and from them we may gather an intimation of the doctrine which the speculative young pharaoh wished to disseminate.'[2] 'In this hymn the universalism of the empire finds full expression and the royal singer sweeps his eye from the far off cataracts of the Nubian Nile to the remotest lands of Syria.'[3] Unlike his contemporaries, the king wrote of his god as applying his natural morality to the creation of the world, and saw him as the benign ruler of his creation. From the highest to the lowest, man or beast, all were in his care. Thus, declared Breasted, Ikhnaton became the first prophet and the first individual in history.

His teaching contained the germ of Christian morality, and his doctrines are far closer to those of Christ than the beliefs of early Judaism from which Christianity evolved. Ikhnaton's god found and showed his power in love, and was no god of battles rejoicing in the number of the slain and revelling in the blood of prisoners sacrificed by his chosen worshippers. There was no destructive or evil element in this creed, the new god was pacificist, and the idea of war among his creatures was anathema to him.

Ikhnaton hoped that his new religion would sweep through Egypt, touching the hearts of all his people, and that it would replace the cults of their thousand gods, even of Osiris himself, whom the majority of the common people worshipped in the hope of an afterlife in his kingdom of the dead. Unfortunately, his lofty concept of deity left his subjects far behind, and their inability to rise to the level of his own beliefs was a constant pain to him.

The king's desire to communicate with the mass of his people in terms they could understand was the moving impulse behind his adoption of a free, naturalistic style in art. He wanted the home life of the royal family to be depicted realistically, showing them as people, not semi-divine beings. This led to the 'show-me-with-my-spots' attitude of the Amarna portraits. It is certain that Ikhnaton's physique was in some respects abnormal, but that he was so fantastically mis-shapen as he is often shown seems improbable. In an excess of freedom, the artist may have enlarged the king's blemishes, giving them a complimentary extension in his depictions of Nofretiti and their daughters, and also of other people, but except for this circumstance Amarna art became so naturalistic in its approach that it resembles in this respect the highest type of Greek art.

# THREE: The last days of Ikhnaton

Such absorption in religion and ethics had unfortunate results. The popularity with which Ikhnaton had started his reign was exhausted by his religious adventure. The members of the former priesthoods, their livings snatched from them, undoubtedly hated him, especially those of the Amen cult. Deprived of their former leading position, as well as of wealth and lands, they represented an organised and bitter enemy incessantly working to undermine still further the king's position in the hearts of his people and ruin his policies. The military were also in opposition, for he had thrown away in a few years the far-flung empire built by the patient work of generations of warrior kings.

Ikhnaton became more and more depressed with the passing years. Worn down by affairs of state, his health precarious since youth, he found the situation intolerable, and sensed his feeble hold on life was slipping away. Most terrible of all was the lack of a successor. He was monogamous both in feeling and practice and the wife he had chosen, who had been portrayed with him on monuments countless times, the beautiful Nofretiti, had borne him nothing but girls. There was no one to carry on the great religious reform he had initiated, and as time passed he bitterly realized that even should his wife now bear a son it was too late. He would never see the baby reach boyhood, much less become a man. As the next-best thing, he married his two oldest surviving daughters, Meritaton and Ankhsenpaaton, to two young nobles of his court, Smenkhkare and Tutankhaton; his second daughter, Meketaton, by this time had died.

By the fourteenth year of his reign his health had so worsened that he found himself unable to reign alone, and so nominated his son-in-law Smenkhkare as co-regent, which he duly became in the fifteenth year of Ikhnaton's reign. The throne, however, continued to be very shaky, for all the enemies the king had made were gathering in anticipation of his death, which would lead to the accession of two almost-children.

All those who had joined the Aton cult to curry royal favour saw the turn events were taking, and made haste to disassociate themselves from the king. As he sank towards death, the king saw treason everywhere. The country was in semi-revolt, with the army and the priesthood on the alert to take advantage of his weakness, and a Hittite army was at the very gates. Tribute from abroad, once the chief source of royal income, had dwindled to nothing, and the king's feeble co-ruler succeeded to a throne threatened from within and without, and to an empty exchequer.

Not long after Ikhnaton was buried in his tomb in the cliffs near Amarna, his chosen successor disappeared from history. The boy-king pushed into his place was Tutankhaton, his second son-in-law. To him fell the melancholy task of liquidating the heretic king's work, but since he had been put on the throne by those who were to some extent friendly to Ikhnaton's memory, the policies of his reign were initially moderate. However, before his short reign was half over, he was forced to return to Thebes, the old capital, and place himself under the tutelage of the Amen priests while Akhetaton, the city founded with so much hope, was abandoned to wild beasts and thieves. As a symbol of his acceptance of the triumph of Amen, the king had to change his name to Tutankhamen, and it is under this title that he was buried in the little tomb, found almost intact by the Carnarvon-Carter expedition, excavating in the Valley of the Kings near Thebes.

Yet, Tutankhamen and those for whom he was the figurehead had some reverence for Ikhnaton's memory, for they brought his body with them from Amarna and formed a resting-place for it in another small tomb in the Valley of the Kings. Indeed, Tutankhamen had buried in his own tomb quite a number of keepsakes of Ikhnaton, Smenkhkare, and even Amenhotep III and Tiy.

Tutankhamen died when he was about twenty, and his successor was the last person who had any connection with Ikhnaton's great reformation. Eye was the husband of Nofretiti's nurse when the young princess first came to Egypt, and his reign is too obscure for much to be said: it was at any rate short, and Harem-hab, who succeeded to the throne, was probably a usurper. In the new reign the enemies of Ikhnaton gained power, doing everything possible to obliterate all traces of the existence of that 'criminal of Akhetaton'. Even the king's tomb in Amarna was invaded, and any objects bearing his name were ruined, and his named erased in all inscriptions. The Egyptians believed that, in order to achieve immortality, a man's name and preferably his body had to be preserved, so that Ikhnaton's enemies were exacting a revenge which went beyond the grave and hoped to blot him out of the after-life.

# FOUR: Foreign policy

Ikhnaton's attitude to Egypt's hard-won empire in Asia probably earned him as much, if not more, hatred than his religious reforms. In his father's reign the situation was already difficult, for although the troops maintained in the area could cope with the intrigues of Egypt's vassal princes, they were insufficient to meet in addition the simultaneous threat of a southward movement by the Hittites and an invasion of desert nomads, called Habiru, from the south. The failure of Amenhotep III to campaign in Syria himself had suggested a lack of interest in the area which must have weakened Egyptian influence with the local rulers.

Ikhnaton and his regency council consequently inherited a dangerous position, but were initially too concerned with religious reformation to spare much time for Asia. Matters did not improve as the king grew older, for he became less inclined to make war for any reason, and finally developed into a strongly convinced pacifist.

Immediately on his accession, certain disaffected Syrian princes began plotting war against loyal Egyptian vassal princes, and even rebellion against Egypt itself. The Tell el Amarna letters give many details of the lengthy struggle between the parties, and show that the king and his advisers often simply did not wish affairs in Syria brought to their notice. The chief rebels, Abdi-Ashirta and his son Aziru, the kings of the Amorite domain in northern Syria, and Aitugama, the ruling prince of Kadesh on the Orontes, were making hay while the Aton shone, and sought and received help from the king of the Hittites, who was always anxious to magnify his own power at the expense of Egypt. Most persistent in opposing the rebels, both on the field of battle in Syria and by letter to the Egyptian court, was Ribaddi, ruler of the north Syrian port of Gubla (Byblos).

Time after time Ribaddi begged the king to help his Syrian subjects, and his letters over a period of many years warned the Egyptians of the piecemeal destruction of their empire. Ikhnaton, however, in the midst of his devotions at Akhetaton, could not spare time and trouble for such a remote area as north Syria, and left these complaints, warnings, and entreaties unanswered, or sent a merely perfunctory reply.

The climax came in north Syria when Sumur (Simyra) was attacked. Ribaddi repeatedly warned Ikhnaton against the possible loss of this city, and after its fall continually urged its reconquest. He obviously regarded it as the most important stronghold in the area, and feared that its surrender endangered his own city. In this he was right, for shortly before the close of the correspondence, he met the reward of his own long and faithful adherence to Egypt when his own people ousted him from power.

Ikhnaton's attitude to Ribaddi influenced other vassal princes in the area. If this miserable fate was the reward of so much faithful service they would do better to look elsewhere, and the internal rot in the fabric of Egyptian control consequently spread ever wider as the reign drew to a close.

The Hittites, always ready for trouble, were well aware of Egyptian difficulties, and took every opportunity to profit from them. They intrigued constantly with Egyptian vassals in open revolt in the north, and also with other nominally loyal princes who were beginning to realise the little support they were likely to receive from Ikhnaton. In this way people like Zimrida, the prince of Sidon, came to make an alliance with the arch-rebel Aziru.

Another foreign danger was the invasion of Egyptian-held territory by nomadic bands, the Habiru, in southern Palestine. In a somewhat analogous position to that of Ribaddi was the governor of Jerusalem, Abdi Hiba, and his letters to the court included the same pleas for help and apparently received the same kind of response, for we find no evidence that the king sent substantial aid.

The situation demanded a full-scale expedition led by the king himself, for the Egyptian auxiliary forces in the area were obviously unable to contain the trouble. But the king was too busy with theology, and so the position in Asia worsened rapidly until finally the Hittites, who must have been watching the Egyptians giving away their empire with some surprise, decided that the apparent collapse was real and launched a full-scale attack which shattered the trembling structure of Egyptian power.

As Breasted wrote: 'At Akhetaton the new and beautiful capital the splendid temple of Aton resounded with hymns to the new god of the Empire, while the Empire itself was no more.'[1]

By the close of Ikhnaton's reign the Hittites and the nomads were at Egypt's gates, and civil strife and economic breakdown ruled within the country—this was the accomplishment of the man who has been called the first individual in history, the founder of a faith as advanced as any before the advent of Christianity. Centuries ahead of his time, he came into a world unprepared for his advanced teaching, so that high and low, even those close to him, rejected him and his beliefs. His reign was a complete failure.

# FIVE: The historical situation

In the preceding chapters I have briefly sketched the story of the life and times of Ikhnaton as seen through the eyes of Breasted and Weigall who represented, in quotation, the views of two or three generations of scholars regarding this period. I have said the picture is in its own way beautiful, as is any account of human heroism whether it succeeds or fails. Unfortunately, many of the heroes in whom humanity has been encouraged to believe are shadow figures and their alleged achievements mythical, stemming more from their apostles' minds than the records of history. The same can be said, I think, here.

Is it not often the case that when an historian comes across a person of another age with whom he feels either an intellectual or emotional sympathy, he cannot help but be influenced by this in his reconstruction of events in which that historical personage was involved? When indulged to a slight extent, such a sympathetic bias may produce only a small distortion in the historian's point of view, but the more it fastens itself upon him, the more disastrous its effects on his work. Impetuous foolishness becomes in his hero bravery; vacillation and indecision, a judicious all-round view; and wholesale bloodlust, an attention to the minutiae of justice. The historian may even feel he knows a character so well that he is able to reproduce his hero's thoughts and motivation where no written or oral evidence for them exists.

This is particularly the case with Ikhnaton. We have no written works by him, or purporting to be by him, and without a work of self-conscious explanation we can have no evidence of his state of mind at any stage of his so-called religious reformation. Everything to be said of this period must rest on data which is not easily interpreted, for the original creators of the artifacts and writings we now possess undoubtedly assumed that the same cultural background would be possessed by anyone who would be dealing with these materials. They were not made for archaeologists.

From this it can be seen that any long discussion of the motives of Ikhnaton, his family, or his associates, passes inevitably into fiction, and that even a surmise as to the attitude or intention any of them adopted concerning any single specific event or idea must be very cautiously made.

With these reservations clearly in mind I want to paint another picture of the life and times of Ikhnaton and his relatives, a picture which I think is historical and which I will attempt in the rest of this book to justify by the evidence.

During the Eighteenth Dynasty, Egypt attained the apex of its power and influence as a great nation. From the end of the reign of Thutmosis III, Egypt's hegemony in Palestine and nearer Syria was assured, and the vassal kings in the area were accustomed to control by Egypt. By the beginning of the reign of Amenhotep III even the necessity for a show of force was largely formal.

For the most part Amenhotep lived in amicable relationship with the kings of the other great powers around, and conducted his foreign policy by making matrimonial alliances with their families and subsidising them with gold, a substance in which Egypt was exceptionally rich. He had made formal treaties with the kings of Mitanni and Hatte which protected his northern sphere of influence, and the treaty with the king of Mittani probably provided that in return for a gold subsidy the king of Mittanni guaranteed to protect Egypt's northern frontier area militarily. Since the Egyptian 'Empire' was more of a loosely held hegemony of client states than a system of centrally administered provinces, a certain amount of fluctuation in the sphere of influence in the extreme northern sector was probably quite normal and accepted by the Egyptians. Within the area more definitely held by Egypt, the king maintained control by playing on the desires and the jealousies of his vassals, and by the threat of Egyptian force rather than its exercise.

This essentially quite flexible and sensible policy maintained Egypt's control over its sphere of influence throughout Amenhotep's long reign, and permitted him to devote most of his energy to Egypt.

Amenhotep III was one of the most remarkable sovereigns of Egypt of whom we have record. He was a man of tremendous energy who undertook great works of construction and development in all parts of the country. He was also a man who shared, as other men in positions of great power have done, the weaknesses of such a driving and energetic nature. He was an extremely wilful man who set no limits upon his desires and who rarely worried about the consequences of his decisions. This much is certainly evident from his behaviour.

He came to the throne as a young man, but nevertheless as a man old enough to hold supreme power in his own hands, for before he had been on the throne for two years, he took in marriage a woman who was of noble not royal birth and made her his principal queen. This woman, Tiy, is shown by the side of her husband throughout his long reign and, even after his death, still with her full title she dedicated offerings to her husband's divinity.

Right at the outset of his reign Amenhotep thus struck his claim to independence from tradition and custom. These decreed that the principal Queen of Egypt should be descended from royalty on both sides of her family. This Tiy was not.

Amenhotep's affection for his wife was so strong that he naturally wished their son to be his successor. This problem was one which must have given him some difficulty in its resolution. Tiy was by no means his only wife. The king of Egypt had a large number of women in his personal household. His harem contained many concubines from Egypt's better families, indeed more than a few wives of the king were royal princesses in their own right, any one of whom would be regarded as more fitting to be the mother of the next king than was Tiy.

In order to establish the succession according to his own desires, while he was still in the full vigour of his manhood, Amenhotep made the eldest son of his and Tiy's marriage co-regent with himself. The king planned to live long after he had made his son co-ruler, and he did so, for the co-regency lasted about twelve years. Here also Amenhotep defied custom, for such a co-regency, although not infrequent in the Middle Kingdom had not been the practice among the ruling family of the Eighteenth Dynasty.

Amenhotep III was also concerned with religious matters. Egypt had a multiplicity of gods, mostly divinities closely attached to an individual shrine or city. Some gods, however, had become in time important enough to be worshipped throughout Egypt. Among these were Osiris, Amen, the Re group (Re Horus, Atum, etc.) and Ptah. Originally Amen was the local god of Thebes but when in the Eleventh and Twelfth Dynasties some hundreds of years previously Thebes had become the centre of royal power, the status of its god also had vastly improved until the importance of the Amen cult was as great as that of any other god in the land. This remained true in the Eighteenth Dynasty whose kings raised many temples to the great gods of Egypt and especially Amen. Amenhotep III was particularly active in this respect, and as only one of his constructions for this god he built the great temple at Luxor near Thebes perhaps the largest temple to Amen erected in Egypt by one king up to that time. (Karnak, of course, was much bigger, but it had been built by a long succession of monarchs over a considerable time.)

Amenhotep's construction of religious buildings was by no means limited to the cult of Amen. His temples to many other gods are known. Among the rest he also constructed shrines for the worship of Re and the other sun-gods. From all of this it might be concluded that Amenhotep was a man of surpassing piety.

During the Eighteenth Dynasty the name of one of the sun-gods had become increasingly prominent, and this cult—the rite of the Aton—particularly appealed to Amenhotep III and his family.

Amenhotep named his royal barge *Teḥen Aton* (The Aton Gleams) and later he called a part of Thebes itself the city of Teḥen Aton. Numerous persons during his reign held offices of obscure meaning connected with this worship. But in particular his son and co-ruler, who had like his father taken the throne name of Amenhotep IV, had become totally fascinated by the Aton. The fixation of Amenhotep IV on the Aton became so important to him that he developed a kind of religious mania. While resident in Thebes, he went so far as to change his throne name from Amenhotep (Amen is Satisfied) to Ikhnaton (The Spirit of the Aton.)

The Egyptians, in view of their plethora of divinities, must have been a people who practised a great deal of religious tolerance, perhaps in the light of the circumstances as a form of self-protection. The rise or fall of a given rite in importance was probably largely a matter of politics or royal favour, since it was the king directly who held the control over the purse strings of temple construction and the payment of endowments to established religious foundations. Thus it would be a simple matter for the ruler to increase or diminish the importance of any religious community in Egypt simply by a change in his policy of donations. Certainly Amenhotep III devoted vastly increased benefices to the Aton cult during his reign, but it must be emphasised that in no apparent manner did he reduce his expenditure on the establishments of Amen; rather, compared with other reigns, he increased it.

It must have been a source of considerable surprise and regret to the old king when he noted the increasing preoccupation of his co-ruler with religious matters. It may well have appalled him that his son, instead of playing a carefully impartial role in religious matters, had begun to make a personal identification with the Aton cult, something which would offend the worshippers of all the multitude of Egyptian gods.

In addition to this Amenhotep III must have been aware that the apparent physical peculiarities of his son had, as well, mental parallels. Accordingly when the suggestion to build a new capital far from the heavily inhabited centres of Egypt was advanced by (or forced upon) Ikhnaton, the senior monarch agreed with perhaps a sigh of relief. There in a sort of mini-kingdom the young king could practise his religious revolution while in the rest of Egypt business went on much as usual.

Amenhotep continued in the normal manner of an Egyptian king and in his thirtieth year celebrated his 'Heb-Sed festival' or jubilee, and subsequently celebrated two further jubilees before his reign's end. He continued to build temples to Amen and the other gods and conducted his foreign policy as usual. He did not neglect his son and co-regent, however, but rather on occasion he and his wife Tiy visited their son in his new city, where as time passed he was becoming still more involved with his religious beliefs. All in all, Amenhotep III ruled almost four decades, and then the shadows of history enveloped him. We do not know where he died or where he was buried. The mummy which most scholars have accepted as his is actually that of a much later king.

The succession of Ikhnaton to his father's throne apparently was not without incident, for there appears to be an interval when for some obscure reason Amenhotep's queen Tiy exercised a regency on behalf of her son. This period could not have lasted any considerable length of time and shortly after the death of his father, Ikhnaton gained secure possession of the throne.

From the time of Amenhotep's death, the restraint controlling Ikhnaton's religious fanaticism lapsed, and the new king initiated a campaign to destroy the cults of gods other than the Aton. In this regard he had crews of workmen in all parts of Egypt effacing the names and figures of the god, perhaps in particular Amen, from monuments and inscriptions.

Probably the Egyptian public were only prepared to take a certain amount of this kind of behaviour even from a divine king, for evidence exists that these practices had stopped before the reign closed. Indeed those people who wished to control Ikhnaton's religious frenzy probably forced him to accept his son-in-law (perhaps his son) Smenkhkare, as co-ruler before the end of his fifteenth regnal year. This young man married Ikhnaton's eldest daughter, Meritaton, and about the same time his third daughter may well have married Tutankhaton.

In the latter part of his reign Ikhnaton's wife. Nofretiti, is no longer in evidence and, since her name is replaced on certain inscriptions in the city of Akhetaton by that of her daughter Meritaton, it seems likely that she had died.

Within a relatively short time after Smenkhkare's accession as co-regent, Smenkhkare, or those whose puppet he was, made strong efforts to remedy the effects of Ikhnaton's religious frenzy, for Smenkhkare himself went to Thebes and made gestures of reconciliation to the various priestly factions who must have been entirely disaffected by the treatment they had received at Ikhnaton's hands. Smenkhkare's efforts, however, were not particularly successful, since apparently both he and Ikhnaton died or were murdered not long after, in the seventeenth year of Ikhnaton's reign. Where Ikhnaton was buried remains unknown, but the hasty burial of Smenkhkare was made in the Valley of the Kings near Thebes in a small uninscribed tomb with borrowed funerary equipment.

Smenkhkare's and Ikhnaton's successor was the famous

Tutankhamen. He was a boy of about eleven years of age at the commencement of his nine-year reign, who could not have exercised power in his own right. Perhaps the abandonment of Akhetaton and Atonism was presided over by one of the men who succeeded Tutankhamen—Eye or Haremhab. At any rate, before he was twenty-one the young king died and was buried in the little tomb in the Valley of the Kings, the discovery of which almost intact by Carnarvon and Carter amazed the world.

As far as foreign matters are concerned, the sources show that Ikhnaton continued his father's policies in Palestine-Syria with much the same results, and that the much-discussed loss of the Empire never took place. There was, however, campaigning in the Western Area during the reigns of Tutankhamen and his successors.

# PART TWO
# Egypt during the Amarna period

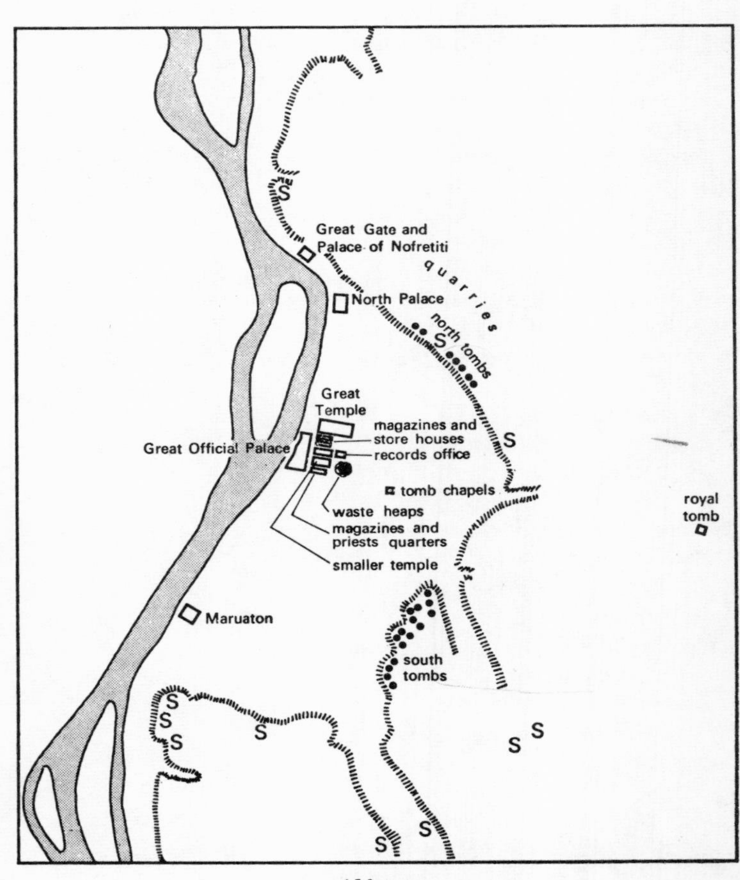

S
Great Gate and
Palace of Nofretiti
quarries
North Palace
north tombs
S
Great
Temple
magazines and
store houses
Great Official Palace
records office
S
tomb chapels
royal
tomb
waste heaps
magazines and
priests quarters
smaller temple
Maruaton
south
tombs
S
S
S
S
S
S
S
S


*Akhetaton*

# ONE: Two mummies

Let us begin with a companionable conversation about a couple of corpses.

As we have seen, the reconstruction of the early Amarna period depends largely on the idea that Amenhotep III was naturally indolent and easy-going, both as a father and a ruler. Granted that the surviving records of his foreign campaigns are few, the sole *positive* fact quoted to support this belief is the condition of his mummy. The severe abcesses about its jaws must in life have been agonising, that is so far true, but have we any evidence that this is actually the mummy of the king?

Egypt's halcyon days continued some generations after the Amarna age, but decay eventually set in, perhaps during the later years of the over-long reign of Ramesses II (*c.* 1300–1230 B.C.). At each new accession Egypt's rule in Asia was a little less secure, and the internal administration of Egypt itself became less well controlled. Ramesses III (*c.* 1200–1175 B.C.) was forced to battle by land and water right at the borders of Egypt proper with the marauding bands of the so-called Sea Peoples, who had destroyed the Hittites almost in one blow. His victory was won with the greatest of difficulty, and he was not strong enough to prevent the defeated enemy from settling on the south coast of Palestine where they gave their name to the whole region: in the Bible we meet them as the Philistines.

After the death of the third Ramesses shadow kings flitted one by one across the scene. Seeing Egypt's fast-failing power, barbarians—mostly from Libya—were making raids right into the heart of the country. Even the temples of the gods were forced into service as fortresses with their priests as garrisons, the attackers being sometimes not only the foreign enemy but dissident Egyptians envious of their wealth.

By the end of the Twentieth Dynasty in 1100 B.C. the central administration had largely collapsed, so that the kings maintained but little control even in the area of Thebes itself. It was at this period, and under such conditions that the great tomb robberies occurred.

Grave robbing was a time-honoured profession in Egypt, as would be expected in a land where a rich man attempted to take much of his wealth with him to set up house in the next world.

Practitioners of this trade were not limited to the professional or the poverty-stricken, for many important tombs were robbed very shortly after an interment by people who must have been in on the secret. However, this was different, the robberies were now undertaken on a much grander scale, and the royal tombs were in particular danger. As a preventive measure, the priests of the royal burial ground took many of their charges to secret caches, where they might be more carefully watched. If a tomb had already been robbed, and the mummies broken open to get at any jewelry actually on their persons, the priests re-wrapped the broken mummies, repaired the coffin or other equipment, and endeavoured to preserve the relic as best they could.

As a matter of fact, the spoilers missed hardly any of the royal burials of the Eighteenth Dynasty, only Tutankhamen having survived to fall into the hands of a modern and slightly different kind of grave robber, the archaeologist.

Naturally, the original tomb of Amenhotep III was thoroughly robbed, but a mummy found in one of these caches is considered by modern scholars to be that of Amenhotep III. Elliot Smith,[1] who examined it, found it to be severely damaged when he unwrapped it. The robbers had broken off the head, staved in the whole front wall of the torso, and broken the spine across at the loins, evidently to take out any precious amulets placed inside the body cavity; for good measure, they had also broken off the right leg. Litter left inside the body cavity included a chicken bone and a human big toe.

Most important of all, Smith noticed that a resinous mass had been packed under the skin of the legs, arms and neck, and perhaps other parts as well. On hardening, this material preserved the original contours of the body, and the mummy was in effect a kind of statue covered with skin. This technique was unknown in the Eighteenth Dynasty, though frequently practised in the Twenty-first and Twenty-second. Smith commented: 'In no mummy earlier than Amenhotep III is there any evidence to indicate or even to suggest that any such curious procedure was put into practice, and as I have examined the mummies, not only of Amenhotep's immediate predecessors, but also of his wife's parents . . . without finding any trace of stuffing in the limbs, it is safe to conclude that this addition to the embalmer's technique was invented at or near the close of the reign of Amenhotep III when the spirit of change was rife in Thebes, and the old conventions in the arts as well as worship were being overthrown. Whether or not the bodies of the Eighteenth Dynasty successors of Amenhotep III were submitted to this strange process of packing it is now impossible to say, because nothing but the skeletons have come down to us.' [We now have the mummy of Tutankhamen, the last but one king of the dynasty, discovered in the 1920s, and this technique is not used.] 'But we do know that none of the royal mummies of the Nineteenth or Twentieth Dynasties was so treated and it was not until the close of the Twentieth Dynasty or the beginning of the Twenty-first Dynasty that the practice was revived and became part of the regular routine of mummification.'

The true explanation, which Smith failed to grasp, is simply that this mummy belongs, not to the Eighteenth, but to the Twenty-first or Twenty-second Dynasty. It was at this point in my investigations that I unearthed some comments by anatomist Professor Derry[2] denying the attribution of this mummy to Amenhotep III. These remarks occur in an appendix to Volume II of Howard Carter's *Tomb of Tutankhamen* dealing with the examination of the mummy of Tutankhamen, so that I came across them more or less by accident. Difficulty in location of important data is one of the bedevilments of Egyptology.

Pursuing the matter further, we find that the badly broken mummy was rebound by the mortuary priests, and the new shroud was lengthily and rather illegibly inscribed in hieratic to the effect that this had been done in the year 12 of the high priest Panegem. On the coffin itself another inscription reads: 'The Osiris, King (Usermaatre Merykheper), the Son of Re, the Lord of Diadems [the reading of the following name is difficult].' The opening 'The Osiris', a term denoting the dead and deified monarch, indicates that the person named was the original owner of the coffin, and the form of the cartouches proves that this ruler lived after the time of Ramesses II. The name of the Osiris Ramesses III, the first king of the Twentieth Dynasty, is clearly legible inside the coffin, the very garbled names on the outer lid may also refer to that king.

The ascription of the mummy to Amenhotep III resulted from the presence beside the vertical coffin lid inscription (written horizontally in hieratic) of the single name Nebmaatre, which occurs again on the shroud. This is indeed the praenomen of Amenhotep III, still the fact that other kings possessed the same praenomen renders such an argument valueless. Ramesses VI, a king of the latter half of the Twentieth Dynasty, is one of them and the mortuary priests probably thought it was his mummy with which they were dealing. Judging by the technique, however, even the date of Ramesses VI would be slightly too early.

What a tangled situation! Here we have a coffin which may belong to Ramesses III, containing a mummy thought by the priests to be Ramesses VI (though perhaps it is not), and claimed by modern Egyptologists to be that of Amenhotep III merely because of the similarity in praenomina between the two kings.

We can conclude, however, that whatever name the mummy bore in life it was not Amenhotep III, and that there is consequently no positive evidence at all that Amenhotep III was a negligent or lazy ruler, and no justification for any theories concerning his wife and son which rest on that idea. We are left with the negative evidence of the paucity of records of foreign campaigns of this king, and in considering this must remember that the odds against the survival of such records of campaigns are long. Moreover, there is every possibility that after so many decades of subjection Asia required no large-scale personal campaigns to ensure continued quiet and delivery of tribute on schedule. The Tell el Amarna correspondence shows a constant interest and activity in foreign affairs.

The confusion which may arise from the careless attribution of any royal mummy rescued by the mortuary priests, and then rebound and preserved outside its original tomb, is further illustrated by what happened in the case of the mummy of Thutmose IV. Amenhotep III's father is known to have had a short reign, the highest year shown on his monuments being 8,[3] but there is no suggestion that his son was not of age, or close to his majority, at his accession. Here, too, the mummy had been badly damaged: both feet were broken off, the right leg being broken again at the knee, but the priests rescued the mummy, rewrapped it, and traced the king's name across the chest in large hieratic signs drawn in blue ink. Unhappily for this identification, Smith noted in his examination that the body was of a man not more than twenty-five, though the figure might be pushed to twenty-eight if it suited the historians better.[4] If Amenhotep had been sixteen on his accession, the minimum age at which he could have ruled alone, then his father would have been between eight and eleven at the time of his conception. Even in a country such as Egypt, where maturity comes early, this seems ridiculous. Hence, it is extremely probable that the mummy re-labelled by the priests as that of Thutmose IV is also in reality the body of someone else.

It follows from this that any arguments which depend on physical appearance, or family resemblance, adduced from the mummies of Amenhotep or his father, are extremely suspect.

# TWO: Amenhotep III and Tiy

What then do we know about Amenhotep III and his family, and particularly of the relationship between the king and his wife?

In discussing the position of Queen Tiy, the English Egyptologist T. E. Peet[1] once maintained that the honours heaped upon her were unusual but not remarkable. On the other hand, Kees,[2] a German scholar, believes the royal marriage to have been one stage in a power struggle between the crown and the Amen priesthood, and that the king was trying to break its stranglehold on the administration of the country. As part of this break with tradition, he married a commoner, Tiy, who could not be the divine wife of Amen—a somewhat obscure position usually held by the king's most important wife. Instead of keeping the misalliance quiet, he publicised it as widely as he could, the wedding scarab he issued being an instance of this. (Scarabs were gems of carnelian, obsidian, and so on, in the form of the scarab beetle, having on the flat underside some design or inscription: they were issued occasionally in large quantities to mark a notable event, rather as a modern state issues commemorative stamps.) In addition, he announced the queen's parentage openly and awarded her mother and father, members of the minor nobility, a tomb in the Valley of the Kings; and when he built a temple to his own divine essence at Soleb in Nubia, also built one there for Tiy at Seidinga. In the view of Kees, therefore, Tiy became a pawn in the struggle between King and Church.

Such an interpretation would gloss over the real power of the queen and presupposes a quarrel between Church and State which would have come to its climax at the very period when we know that Amenhotep III was building Luxor,[3] a great temple to Amen. Moreover, since the king was quite young at his accession, his marriage to Tiy would have been highly imprudent if undertaken simply to flout tradition at a time when power could hardly have been securely in his hands, and it would have been lunacy if entered upon during a power struggle already in progress when he came to the throne. The whole matter of religion will be considered later,[4] but we can already see that Tiy's position is not to be explained so easily.

Turning from theories to facts, we find that the marriage of Amenhotep III and Tiy took place very early in the reign, since the bull hunt scarab[5] the king issued in his second year bears both their names. He ruled thirty-nine to forty years,[6] and when we take into consideration that the reign of his father, Thutmose IV, was probably no longer than nine years[7] we may conclude that Amenhotep III was quite young at his accession, although there is no indication that he was not of age. On the contrary, we know the parents of Queen Tiy from their tombs in the Valley of the Kings,[8] and since they were neither royal nor of high rank in the nobility,[9] the marriage of Amenhotep III and Tiy must have taken place after he was old enough to make his own decisions. Iuya and Tuya, the parents of Tiy, must have lived long enough to have known their grand-daughter Sitamen fairly well, for some mementoes of her childhood were found in their tomb.[10] It was this princess, his daughter by Tiy, whom Amenhotep married sometime before his first jubilee in the year 30, by which time she had presumably reached maturity. She must have been the eldest surviving daughter of Tiy and himself, and so the royal heiress, otherwise such a marriage would have been pointless.

When she married Amenhotep III—an event which might have taken place even before his accession, since this was surely a love match—Tiy would have been at least sixteen or perhaps a few years older. Child marriages were frequent in Egypt at this period and the sexual maturity of women was reached at about fourteen, but we can assume that a young man marrying for reasons of affection not political expediency, and already having a harem stocked with daughters of Egypt's best families, would select someone a little beyond the absolute minimum child-bearing age. That it was a love-match is confirmed by the way in which the personality of the queen shortly made itself felt, and by the second year of his reign the king was associating the name of this young woman of non-royal origins with his own in inscriptions. For a pharaoh to associate a queen's name with his own was unusual in normal circumstances, and it was a unique honour for someone with Tiy's comparatively plebeian background.

From this point their names appear linked until the end of the reign. Amenhotep III had other wives, the most honoured of these being Sitamen, his daughter by Tiy. The rest included two

Mitannian princesses, a daughter of Sutarna[11] whom he married in his tenth year and a daughter of Tushratta[12] who became his bride towards the close of the reign, but these and other royal wives who are known to be probably of this reign are mere names compared with Tiy. Her relatives shared in her glory, for not only were her parents honoured by a tomb in the Valley of the Kings, but her only known brother was appointed 'chief of seers', i.e. high priest of Amenre at Hermonthis.[13] This is evidence enough to establish that the queen had real power and was not a mere pawn in the political game.

Tiy's achievement is an anomaly in Egypt's long history. A queen consort whose parents were unimportant people, she was the wife of an absolute autocrat, the visible incarnation of a god. Despite the king's possession of a large harem, all of whom would have been in competition for his favour, she captured and held the king's affection not only during her youth, but when she became older.

The queen of Egypt occupied a rather peculiar position. Traditionally the succession passed through the female line, yet power generally passed into the hands of a man who must marry the royal heiress—which, of course, Tiy had never been. The system led to many brother and sister marriages, and the occasional father-daughter marriage, but there were very few queens regnant, even though in theory the right to rule travelled along the female line. In the Eighteenth Dynasty Hatshepsut took power by means of a regency during the minority of her daughter and son-in-law, and neglected to give up power when her son-in-law attained his majority, but usually the queen was a very shadowy figure who appeared only occasionally beside the pharaoh. Of most Egyptian queens we know little more than their names. Not so Tiy.

When Amenhotep III married a princess of Mitanni in the tenth year of his reign, he placed not only Tiy's name but those of her parents on the scarab he issued to commemorate the event.[14] The next year he issued another scarab to mark the occasion of the completion of an ornamental lake for the queen.[15] In the last two lines of the wedding scarab mentioned earlier,[16] he says of her: 'She is the wife of a powerful king whose southern

*Detail (left) of the decoration of Tiy's throne, as shown in the tomb of Heruef at Thebes. Shown as a female sphinx, she tramples down a Syrian and a Nubian woman. The presentation is exactly similar to that of her husband, Amenhotep III, on another throne (right) recorded by Lepsius from the tomb of Khaemhat.*

boundary is as far as Kary and whose northern is as far as Naharin.' Such scarabs are indeed significant.

In the tombs of royal officials the queen is often depicted at the king's side.[17] In that of Heruef at Thebes a relief shows her in the form of a sphinx trampling female enemies, the inscription reading: 'The principal royal wife, his beloved (Tiy) may she live, may she endure, may she flourish every day, who crushes every foreign land.'[18] She also appears with her husband on the reliefs from Soleb,[19] and naturally on those of her own temple at Seidinga.[20]

This queen of humble origins apparently took a much more active role in the affairs of the kingdom than the vast majority of queens of impeccable royal birth. Certainly her influence on policy though we can not gauge its exact extent must have been considerable. Her influence or example may have led to the rise of many other people of obscure birth to important posts, and she obviously retained her power after her husband's death, since Tushratta, king of Mitanni, wrote to her directly[21]. The letter is no mere friendly exchange of courtesies, and indicates besides that the power of Queen Tiy in Egypt was well known as far away as Mitanni. There is no contemporary mention of any other Egyptian queen consort after her husband's death, and Tushratta's letter points to Tiy having become regent for her son, probably only for a short time but long enough for other nations to be aware of it. The theory is supported by the inscribed offering table Petrie found at Gurob, which was dedicated to the Osiris Amenhotep III (this form of the name indicating her husband was dead):[22] the queen dedicated this monument in her own name and still preserved the cartouche used only by a reigning king or queen. A similarly inscribed wooden stele, showing the royal pair in an embrace, was also found at Gurob and had been set up by Tiy.[23] The offering table has inscribed on its underside: 'The principal royal wife (Tiy). She made [it] as her monument for her beloved husband (Nebmaatre).' On the left and right sides are offering formulae ending in this phrase: '(N.M.R.) for the Ka of the Osiris (Nebmaatre).' The upper side of the wooden stele reads: '(Tiy), the royal wife, his beloved [of, or for] (Nebmaatre)' and the lower: 'A boon which the king gives [for] Osiris Wenennefer the great lord of the red land. May he give an oblation [consisting of] wine, milk and every good and pure thing . . . for the ka of the Osiris king (Nebmaatre) the son of Re (Amenhotep is ruler of Thebes) deceased. The king's principal wife, his beloved, the lady of the two lands (Tiy). She made [it] as her monument for her brother, her beloved.'

Besides their interest as evidence for Tiy's retention of power when widowed, these documents also show how Amenhotep III would have been named after his death.

The discovery of the cartouche of Tiy, followed by the two names of Ikhnaton,[24] on a wall of rock *en route* to the quarries of the Wadi Hamamat and the presence of the queen's unaccompanied cartouche[25] in the quarry north of the main town of Akhetaton is so remarkable that it leads inescapably to the conclusion that Tiy held power for a short but definite period after her husband's death. Subsequently she retired to a palace at the mouth of the Fayyum, and probably lived on there into the reign of Tutankhamen.[26] She did not outlive him since a lock of her hair was found in a nest of little anthropoid coffins in his tomb, the innermost of which was inscribed with her name and titles, to which the words *mꜣʿ-ḫrw* deceased' were added[27]. The attitude of the ordinary well-to-do Egyptian to the royal pair is illustrated by a stele set up by a man named 'Kay'[28] requesting that praise may be given to the Osiris and Isis, Amenhotep III and Tiy so that they may grant him a beautiful burial after old age. For him the king and queen were a pair of gods after their death.

# THREE: Ikhnaton and his family

Before approaching the major historical problems of the era, it is useful to turn for a moment to Ikhnaton himself and his environment.

We know him to have been the son of Amenhotep III and Queen Tiy from inscriptions on the Theban tomb of the official Heruef and from the funerary shrine which he presented to his mother. Probably he was their oldest son, and though it could be that an elder brother had died in childhood, it is more likely that he was from his youth the crown prince and heir to the throne of Egypt. This is in itself somewhat unusual, since Tiy could not have been the royal heiress, that is, the daughter of the preceding king.

Ikhnaton was apparently raised in Thebes and was extremely influenced by and interested in religious questions, especially the worship of the Aton, a cult which was increasing in importance during his formative years.

As soon as he was old enough he married a woman of uncertain origin named Nofretiti, and by his ninth regnal year had six daughters by her. His wife stood in the same relationship to him as had Tiy to Amenhotep III. She is shown at his side on all kinds of state occasions, her name was very frequently inscribed alongside his, and intimate scenes of their life together—at meals, enjoying their leisure, on journeys, and in company with their children—are depicted on the tombs of the Akhetaton necropolis to such an extent that these form far more a record of the existence of the royal family than of their owners.

Of the royal princesses the eldest, Meritaton, married Smenkhkare, the heir to the throne; the second, Meketaton, died before the end of her father's reign; and a third, Ankhsenpaaton, married Tutankhamen, possibly the next in line of succession to Smenkhkare. Nothing definite is known of the other three.

A series of wall reliefs enables us to calculate the approximate date of Meketaton's death. In the twelfth year of her father's reign she was still alive, since she is shown in reliefs of a celebration dated to that year on the Amarna tombs of Huya and Meryre II,[1] two high court officials. Yet she must have died before her elder sister's marriage to Smenkhkare,[2] because in the funeral scenes of her tomb chambers at Amarna we see her sister still wearing the sidelock of hair which was left uncut in ancient Egypt as a kind of mark of juvenility. Turning once again to the tomb of Meryre II, we find that besides the reliefs showing Meritaton as a child there is also one which shows her with Smenkhkare, both she and her husband wearing the royal regalia. This relief is entirely different in style and artistically much cruder than the rest, and is obviously of later date. Since Meritaton is often shown as a child in the other reliefs of this tomb, and since she is still shown as a child in Meketaton's funeral scenes while Meketaton is shown still living in a relief from this same tomb portraying a great celebration, it is certain that the scene depicting Meritaton as a queen must follow both the celebration shown in the year twelve, and the subsequent death and funeral of Meketaton. Therefore, Meketaton died at some time between her father's twelfth and fifteenth regnal years, the latter year being the most probable date of Meritaton's marriage to Smenkhkare.

This wedding also enables us to find the approximate age of Ikhnaton at his accession, and so ascertain whether he could possibly have come to the throne as a child, as those who framed the legend would have us believe. At the time of her marriage Meritaton would be either adult, or nearly so, and if she were sixteen in her father's fifteenth year of rule, we can assume that her father must have been sixteen or even older when he came to the throne, and hence at least in his middle thirties at the time of his death. Surviving sculptures of the king, if we can consider them reliable in this respect, certainly depict a middle-aged man and one much older in appearance than thirty-five. This should not be pressed too far, but it would be reasonable to assume that, since Ikhnaton's parents were married by the second year of a reign of almost four decades, there would be only an exceedingly remote possibility of the heir of such a union being still a child at his father's death. For us it is sufficient that, by Egyptian standards, Ikhnaton was at his accession either mature, or almost so, a married man, at least once and perhaps twice a father, and certainly not a boy.

In the light of this the religious innovations he is alleged to have made are no longer impossibly precocious. Ikhnaton would then not have been the only young ruler who attempted to meddle with the religion of his people.

Unfortunately for Ikhnaton's reputation as a monogamist, the name of another wife, other than Nofretiti, was recently discovered on two calcite pots, one in the Metropolitan Museum and the other in the British Museum. This woman, Kia,[3] is called the 'great beloved wife' of Ikhnaton, but we know nothing further of her. However, it would be only natural that the king should have a harem of many wives and concubines, for this multitude of female consorts was a feature of life among the upper classes and royalty, not only in Egypt but throughout the Near East.

It is also said that, just as Amenhotep III married his daughter Sitamen, so Ikhnaton took to wife his third daughter, Ankhsenpaaton, as she was then known. This theory rests on the discovery by Helmut Brunner at Hermopolis,[4] a site not too far from Akhetaton, of some broken, inscribed Amarna blocks. The surviving portions of the inscriptions read:

I 1 'The king's daughter of his body, his beloved Ankhsenpa – – – – – – – – – – –'
2 'born to the king's daughter of his body Ankhsenpa – – – –'
3 '(Neferkheperure – – – – –) given life – – – – – f – – – – – – '
II 1 '– – – – – – – – – – – – – – – – – – – – – – – – – – – f Ankhs.'
2 '– – – – – – – – – – (female determinative) may she live.'
3 '– – – – – – – – – – – – – – – – – – – – – – – – – – tf Ankhsen.'
4 '– – – – – – – – – – – – – – – (Little or younger) – – – – – – – – –.'
III 1 – – – – – – 'lord of the circuit of the Aton – – – – – – – – –.'
2 'the sunshade – – – – – – – – – – – – – – – – – – – – – – – – – – –.'
3 '– – – – – – – – – – – the daughter of body – – – – – – – – – – –.'
4 '– – – – – – – – – – – enpaaton.'
5 '– – – – – – – – – – – enpaaton.'

Brunner wishes to restore the second inscription to read: '[The king's daughter of] his [body], Ankhs [enpaaton], may she live, [the king's daughter of his body], his [beloved], Ankhsen [paaton] the younger.' He restores the third similarly to an inscription regarding the sunshade or shrine of Tiy depicted in the tomb of Huya at Amarna: '[Live the Aton, great lord of Hebseds, lord] of the whole circuit of the Aton [lord of heaven lord of earth in],

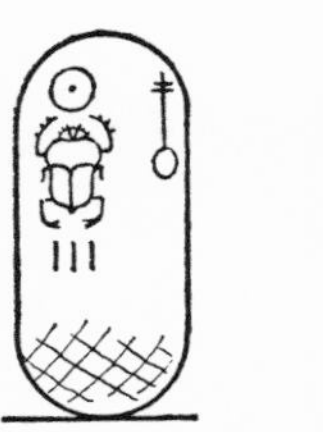
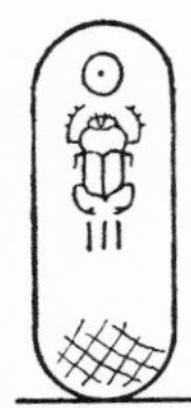

the sunshade of [Re of the king's] daughter of his body [his beloved Ankhs], enpaaton – – – – – – – – – – – [Ankhs] enpaaton.'[5] These are large restorations. The restoration of inscription number three, however, contributes nothing to the case, since the Ankhsenpaaton to whom it twice refers could very well be the same person. Number two contains more restoration than text, and the restoration is at best conjectural, so that it is inscription number one by which the theory stands or falls.

The photograph of this first inscription, which is written in vertical columns, clearly shows that it is broken and may continue some distance on the next lower block in columns two and three. In column one it seems likely that the inscription would soon be broken off by an enlargement of the scene appearing below, hence it seems that Ankhsenpaaton may have borne a child. Brunner hazards the conjecture that the words ' begotten by' should be restored after the name of Ankhsenpaaton in column two. However, as noted above, this column might well continue downward on to the next block. The cartouche in column three is read by Brunner as illustrated above left. This is a very peculiar arrangement of signs, and one wonders whether the reading might be in error. I have not seen the original but the photograph is obscure, for the ☉ Re sign is definitely in the middle of the cartouche and the (kheper) sign seems to be directly under it, and I can see no traces of the (nefer) sign. Another possible reading from the traces visible in the photograph is shown above right, the praenomen of Tutankhamen who was in any case the lady's husband. The reproduction also makes it uncertain that there was sufficient space in the ring of the cartouche to have allowed the rest of Ikhnaton's name to be inscribed without crowding, and, in any case, the (nefer) sign usually preceded the (kheper) sign.

To summarise: the first inscription is the vital one as regards the supposed marriage of Ikhnaton and his daughter, since the third gives no evidence either way, and the second is too fragmentary to be of use. Yet this first inscription requires an uncertain restoration to establish that the man named was the father of the child mentioned, and even if we do this we cannot be at all sure that the name which originally stood in the cartouche was that of Ikhnaton.

If Tutankhamen should be the father of Ankhsenpaaton junior, then we are at first sight left with the six daughters of Nofretiti as the only children of Ikhnaton, but there is a considerable body of evidence indicating that he had others, some of them sons. In the Tell el Amarna letters[6] we find that all Ikhnaton's royal correspondents, except Assur-Uballit of Assyria who mentions that he has never previously written to Egypt, refer in the salutation of their letters as a matter of course to 'your sons'. When Tushratta writes to Tiy after her husband's death, he refers to 'your son' in his salutation—certainly meaning Ikhnaton—and when he comes to write to Ikhnaton himself he speaks of 'your sons' or 'your children'. The king of Alashia (Cyprus), in letters certainly written to Ikhnaton, mentions the words 'your son' three times. These kings must have had some degree of knowledge of the people to whom they were writing, and it would have been ludicrous for them to have asked after the health of non-existent royal children.

Besides shattering the idea of the monogamous relationship of Ikhnaton and Nofretiti, the discovery of the existence of the 'great and beloved' royal wife Kia makes it necessary to reconsider the possible relationship of Smenkhkare and Tutankhamen to Ikhnaton. The whole question of the wives and children of the king has until now been obscured by the quite extraordinary, from the Egyptian viewpoint, portrayals of his daughters by Nofretiti. Even the depiction of the queen beside her husband is by no means a common feature of Egyptian art, and such a treatment of the children is unique. With many pharaohs it is even difficult to establish the names of some of their children, and since it was the common Egyptian practice for the royal heiress (the eldest daughter of the king and his principal wife) to marry the son whom the king wished to succeed him, we have no reason to suppose that Meritaton and Ankhsenpaaton did not marry their half-brothers when they married Smenkhkare and Tutankhamen. Since the Tell el Amarna letters make it quite clear that Ikhnaton did have male children, the burden of proof would rest on those who believe that neither of the king's successors were his sons.

2

At his accession the young king was known as Neferkheperure (Uanre usually present) Amenhotep the Divine King of Thebes, but by the fifth year of his reign he had changed his name to Neferkheperure Uanre Ikhnaton, by which he is generally known to us and which he retained until the end of his reign.

Ikhnaton was intimately concerned with the Aton cult as it developed during his lifetime, and a number of the strange features of the belief may have been his own idea. In particular, the god Aton is the only Egyptian deity who seems consistently to be treated like a king. From the outset the formal name of the god is almost invariably written in a cartouche in the same manner as that of a king, and—again like a king—the Aton celebrates the Heb-sed festival or jubilee.

The name of the Aton also suffers a change on the monuments dating from about the ninth year of the reign. The early Aton name reads (Live Re-Harakhty rejoicing on the horizon) (in his name of the Shu which is in the Aton) and the later (May Re who rules the two horizons, live, rejoicing on the horizon) (in his name of Re the father who comes as Aton). These name changes of the king and his god allow events to be approximately dated according to which combination of names is used. Some scholars even maintain that the various titles of the Aton relating to the Heb-sed festivals can be used for more precise dating of events, but the evidence for this is insufficient.[7]

The very significance of these festivals is obscure. Perhaps originating as a symbolic renewal of the power of kingship after a thirty-year tenure of the throne, the Heb-sed festival was celebrated by the time of the Amarna period by kings who had not achieved a reign of this length. Ikhnaton had three of these jubilees, and probably conjointly with these ceremonies, the Aton also celebrated jubilees. What thirty-year period could have been involved in any of these cases is unknown. It has been suggested that the period concerned was the lapse of time since Ikhnaton became crown prince, or since the formal establishment of the Aton cult, but no real evidence exists to support either theory. However, it is more than possible that these celebrations were adjuncts to similar festivals of Amenhotep III, who had reigned thirty years.

3

In the fourth year of his reign, as he declared on the boundary stele set up to mark the city limits, Ikhnaton began to build his new capital of Akhetaton. It was not ready for permanent occupation until four more years had passed, which perhaps explains the relatively few uses of the early form of the full name of the Aton in the city. Here the king lived out the major remaining portion of his reign. Here he built his tomb, here he sought to be buried, and here he still may lie in a tomb yet undiscovered.

Varied scenes of life in the city during its brief heyday are shown on the wall reliefs in the tombs of the nobles of the court. We see the great temple of Aton, open to the rays of the sun, the great court filled with offering tables, and we stand, as if among his subjects, looking up at the great window of appearances from which the king with his family would reward his servants.

We also know some of the important courtiers from their tombs in the necropolis. Among the most interesting are Eye, who was later to become king, and his wife Tiy; Huya, the steward of the House of Queen Tiy at Amarna; Tutu, the court chamberlain whom we find mentioned in the Tell el Amarna letters as Dudu; Meryre (I), the high priest of the Aton; and another Meryre (II), the chief steward of the royal household. From Petrie's account we can understand that there may well be other tombs hidden in the rugged hills behind the city, but not even the fragments of a burial are preserved in any of those known to us, and possibly all, with the exception of Huya's, were incomplete when the city was abandoned.

The plan of the major buildings of Akhetaton may well have altered from time to time as its royal creator's ideas evolved, and the atelier of the royal sculptor would certainly have been kept busy producing enough decorative statuary and relief to keep up with the royal building.

Much has been written about the so-called revolutionary art style of Amarna. True, Egyptian art had always maintained a stiff and rigid canon of conventions—in which the peculiar Egyptian notion of perspective is important—when portraying the human figure, but we must at the same time remember that by far the greater part of their surviving pictorial art was originally designed for use in tomb or temple, and hence had a religious significance. Even at a very early period the portrayal of animals had always been more natural than that of the human figure, and it is just this treatment of human beings which is to a certain extent changed in the Amarna style. In the paintings, statuary and relief of Akhetaton, and to a very limited extent outside the city proper, the royal family, and once in a while members of its entourage, are depicted naturalistically. In pose they are relaxed, they lounge and lean and slouch; all of this is anomalous in religious or semi-religious art. The person of the king is specially treated: the usual portrayal is more or less distorted and at time verges on a malignant caricature, as in the case of the colossal statues from Karnak. His head is enlarged and he is shown with a long, hanging jaw. His belly is pendulous and bloated, and his thighs very fat and feminine, and the lower part of his legs spindle-shanked. If Egyptian art has any historical value whatever, as I am sure it has, then this strange portrayal of Ikhnaton must have some origin in his actual physical condition. The art work, however, tends to exaggerate. This is shown particularly because this series of deformities is, as it were, catching. Nofretiti and her daughters are shown in a similar fashion, as is Smenkhkare. Such a great concatenation of gross malformity is a genetic absurdity, and stems from a kind of honorific transposition, whereby it is regarded as desirable for a subject to resemble his monarch even in that which is loathsome.

The use of the term revolutionary to describe this style is misleading. Remembering the shortness of the period, it is incredible to suppose that such mastery of the materials and techniques of the new style could be so perfectly realized as to produce one of the world's most beautiful masterpieces, namely the bust of an Egyptian queen now in the Berlin Museum. Egyptian tombs and temples were built mostly of stone, so that the religious art to some extent survived the ravages of time in one way or other, and was preserved through the 2000 to 6500 years which separates the Egyptian creative period from our own day. The secular pictorial art of Egypt, existing as it did in the less robust palaces and houses built mainly of sun-dried brick, has vanished almost completely, but it is most probably there that we should seek the antecedents of Amarna art.

We know the names of two of the master sculptors of the era, Auta, who was active about the twelfth year of Ikhnaton's reign and who is shown working in his studio on a statue of Beketaton (daughter of Tiy and Amenhotep III), in a relief from Huya's tomb, and Thutmose, whose atelier was discovered by the German expedition to Amarna. The workshop of the latter contained many plaster masks or models, presumably of the important figures of his time, together with other pieces of statuary. It was closed when Akhetaton was abandoned, with its equipment intact, as if the sculptor and his staff were uncertain whether or not they would return and take up their work once again. The plaster masks, whether taken from life or death, indicate that the artist was interested in preserving an exact likeness of his subject. The beauty of his portraiture is obvious in the bust of an Egyptian queen—usually identified as Nofretiti—and shows a complete mastery of technique, even though as a general rule the Egyptians preferred full size statues, and this bust is in any case unique. The fact that it is incomplete at the shoulders suggests to me that it was perhaps made to be set into the top of a pillar.

This masterpiece presents a problem. Despite its being known to the world as the bust of Nofretiti, there is some question about this attribution. The latest contemporary inscription which refers to Nofretiti is one occurring in the tombs of both Huya and Meryre II at Amarna, incorporated in a scene which shows the king and queen in procession, and dating from the year 12 of Ikhnaton. No later representations of the queen which can be dated have been found. Huya's tomb also has among its smaller reliefs a picture of a chief sculptor at work in his studio, and whereas this artist is named Auta, it was in the workshop of Thutmose, active in the middle of the reign of Tutankhamen, that the 'Nofretiti' bust was found. We have to bear in mind, too, that two of the queen's daughters ruled after her in Akhetaton—Meritaton, the wife of Smenkhkare, and Ankhsenpaaton (later Ankhsenamen) the wife of Tutankhamen.

Since the city was abandoned by the court only in the middle of the reign of Tutankhamen, when he had ruled some four years, and Nofretiti is last mentioned in an inscription of the year 12 of Ikhnaton, a period of nine years at least had elapsed between this latest reference to the queen and the date at which the sculptor closed his studios. If Smenkhkare reigned for any length of time by himself, this period can only be lengthened, and if we add to this the possibility that the person who held the office of chief sculptor in or about the twelfth year of Ikhnaton's reign may not have been the same man as the person in whose studio the German expedition found the bust, the situation becomes more difficult. The most likely explanation is that the sculpture was in process of completion at the time the artist shut up shop in Amarna and prepared to leave. If this is true, then it must represent Ankhsenamen, the wife of Tutankhamen, the reigning king. It is also just possible that the bust in question could have been made for Meritaton at the time that she was queen. What is least likely is that the bust is really of Nofretiti and dates from Ikhnaton's reign, so that it would have been standing on a shelf in the studio for a decade more or less.

The frequently mentioned likeness between the bust and various other depictions of the queen is no argument for the attribution of the piece, since we are here concerned with a mother and her daughters, and a similar likeness—as far as can be told from the remaining depictions of the members of the royal family—is also apparent there between parent and children.

Nofretiti herself is an enigmatic figure. From the beginning of the reign to its twelfth year, when she is last shown in dated inscriptions on the tombs of Huya and Meryre II, she appears constantly with her husband and family, but is thereafter so far as we know never depicted again. It has been commonly held because of this that Nofretiti was disgraced sometime after the year 12, support for this theory being assumed from the replacement of her name on the walls of the Maruaton, a building in the southern part of Akhetaton, by those of her daughter Meritaton, the wife of Smenkhkare.[8] Some time ago, Pendlebury suggested that Nofretiti might even have lived on with Tutankhamen in the north suburb of the city, because his expedition had found some objects bearing her name together with a considerable number bearing that of Tutankhamen.[9] Since all of these were small portable objects, however, there is nothing convincing in this argument. We have no evidence indicating anything specific about Nofretiti's actions after the year 12 of Ikhnaton, but the most obvious deduction from the known circumstances would be that she died soon after the year 12, and that her special position in the Maruaton was transferred to her daughter. There is some indication that a beginning was made to prepare the royal tomb for her burial, since there is a single coffin niche cut in the floor of the main tomb chamber, and pieces of a sarcophagus have been found bearing her statuette at the corners. Her complete and final disappearance supports this idea, for even Pendlebury, who alleges that she lived with Tutankhamen, cannot produce any material from his reign that refers to her.

The Egyptians normally erased figures of disgraced persons wherever they appeared, but in the case of Nofretiti the only change of this kind is in the Maruaton, where it is confined to a name change. Nofretiti's figure on temple and tomb walls was left intact. In one of the Amarna letters written from Burnaburiash to Ikhnaton there is a reference to Maiati being at one time mistress of his house.[10] The parallel to the name of Meritaton is striking, and if she were mistress of the royal household it is difficult to see how she obtained this position during the lifetime of Nofretiti. All the positive evidence suggests death rather than disgrace, especially the fact that, except in the Maruaton where the circumstances are unusual, Nofretiti's name and figure are untouched.

# FOUR: The co-regency: the case against

After the notion that Ikhnaton succeeded to the throne as a child has been disposed of, it becomes less improbable that the so-called Atonist heresy was his work alone. Nevertheless, there are enough references to the Aton, coming from the years before Ikhnaton's reign, to make careful investigation of his primary responsibility for Aton worship necessary.

Throughout all history the possession of power to rule one's fellow men and control their destinies has been a lonely and difficult task, and various means of lightening the load have been tried. Democratic government in Britain may well have come about originally from a royal wish to lessen the burden of ruling. In imperial Rome the emperor frequently associated his chosen successor with himself in the administration, especially during the Antonine period, and the time of Diocletian and his successors. In the Middle Kingdom of Egypt this device was also used when the ruling pharaoh associated his son in power with him, and would not have been unknown to the Eighteenth Dynasty monarchs. The existence of such an arrangement between Amenhotep III and his son, so that they ruled jointly for some length of time, is supported by much evidence.

This matter has long been a bone of contention among Egyptologists, although until now the co-regency has neither been definitively affirmed nor denied. I believe, however, that the weight of evidence now renders proof possible, but I shall first outline the views of those opposing the idea of joint rule.

The late Sir Alan Gardiner had occasion to refer in passing to the co-regency in an article written in 1957.[1] Basing his argument on the Tell el Amarna letters, he stated that it was evident that Ikhnaton succeeded only on the death of his father and that he was a mere youth at the time of his succession. He quoted in proof of this a letter from the Hittite king Suppiluliuma,[2] and adduced the letter which Tushratta, king of Mitanni, wrote to Queen Tiy as indicating the same thing.[3] The relevant lines from the letter of Suppiluliuma are: 'When your father was living . . . Now thou my brother, hast ascended the throne of your father.' Gardiner also referred to the hieratic (the modified, cursive form of hieroglyphic writing) docket on the reverse of the first letter of Tushratta to Ikhnaton,[4] the first lines of which mention the fact that the king was in Thebes when the letter was received. The date of this document, however, is partially destroyed, the tablet being broken immediately before the signs indicating the numeral two.

These arguments are not convincing. The Suppiluliuma letter constitutes no argument either for or against the co-regency, except by inference, since I do not maintain that Ikhnaton possessed much power until the death of his father. The above material, and other examples from the same group of letters, certainly show that the monarchs of the time only began bringing their business to Ikhnaton after Amenhotep III had died,[5] but there is no question that Amenhotep III was the senior pharaoh and, since he was active at least until the year 38 of his reign, there is no reason to suppose that he abdicated his functions thereafter. Indeed, the Tell el Amarna letters speak for the fact that he was the ruler of Egypt until his death. During Amenhotep III's lifetime, there is no reason to suppose that his son and co-regent was anything more than an assistant, and that Ikhnaton only attained power in the eyes of foreign potentates on his father's death is no argument at all against a co-regency. With the contention that Ikhnaton succeeded as a mere youth we have dealt already. The letter of Tushratta of Mitanni to Queen Tiy may well mean that she was regent of the kingdom, but doesn't justify the assumption that the period of regency coincided with the minority of Ikhnaton, since regencies have been instituted for many other reasons.

The hieratic docket is also unreliable as evidence. The docket is broken at the beginning, and its date is a restoration. No less an Egyptologist than Adolph Erman read the surviving traces as 'year 12'.[6] It is most dangerous to make a reading of such great importance from a broken inscription, in the absence of anything but the most conclusive supporting evidence, and this Gardiner did not produce.

Gardiner continued in the same article to claim that the frequent juxtaposition of the two names was either filial piety on the part of Ikhnaton, or due to the fact that the praenomen of Amenhotep III contained the idea of 'truth', which was closely connected with Ikhnaton's religion, and so caused him to make the frequent association of the name of his dead father with his own. These are merely two bald statements, unsupported by any corroboration, and can be met by the evidence I shall discuss later.

The arguments against the co-regency presented by Wolfgang Helck,[7] a German scholar, are more complete but no more effective than those of Gardiner, since Helck has omitted from his discussion the most important pieces of evidence for the joint reign. The material which he attacks, although it is interesting and important corroborative testimony to the existence of the co-regency, does not constitute the heart of the case. Helck's arguments are as follows:

He first notes the wine-jar dockets[8] dated to years 28 and 30 of an un-named king which were found at Amarna by the Egypt Exploration Society expedition, and mentions the claim of some authorities that, since these pots were rather porous and wine could not long be preserved, the years 28 and 30 must be close to the time at which Amarna was being built. However, he at once attempts to demonstrate the weakness of this argument based on the permeability of jars or preservation period of wine by pointing out that when the Malqatta palace at Thebes was excavated some wine-jar dockets were unearthed from the rubbish dumps of the jubilee period of Amenhotep III which date from as early in the reign as the year 10. Unfortunately we have no evidence that the Malqatta rubbish dumps were used only for the period subsequent to the first jubilee. The jar dockets are unreliable evidence for quite other reasons. The occurrence of these year dates is unique,[9] and the jars may have been re-used from an earlier period. Further, we do not even know that the dockets come from the reign of Amenhotep, since Haremhab is known to have done a great deal of quarrying at Akhetaton—though on this point it must be conceded that such an advanced date of Haremhab's reign is otherwise unknown except for the inscription of Mes,[10] giving an account of a protracted litigation in which the date is generally considered unreliable. The dockets cannot stand by themselves but if we want the most probable explanation, it is that they come from the reign of Amenhotep III, the only reign certainly of that length in the period, and that years 28 and 30 would be approximate to the time of the building of Akhetaton.

More to the point is Helck's discussion of the temple of Soleb in Nubia,[11] which Amenhotep III built for his own divine essence. He notes that Ikhnaton here offers to Nebmaatre, lord of Nubia, and that Fairman says that the king is worshipping before the living Amenhotep III. Fairman also says, continues Helck, that in the same temple Amenhotep III offers before Nebmaatre the lord of Nubia. Helck now claims that this must be Amenhotep III offering before a statue of himself, and that Ikhnaton must therefore also be offering before a statue of his father, hence Amenhotep III is dead, and his son and successor is sacrificing to his memory. All this can be conceded, except the conclusion, without any danger to the case for the co-regency. The god in question is the divine essence of Nebmaatre, the lord of Nubia, and is certainly represented in the form of a statue. But, it does not follow because Ikhnaton offers before his father's divine statue that his father is dead. The living Amenhotep III sacrifices before his own divine statue, and if Ikhnaton were his junior co-regent we would expect that he would also sacrifice before the divine statue of his senior in rank, and so he does, no funerary aspects of the cult being present to suggest that Amenhotep III is other than alive.[12]

A somewhat similar problem arises in the case of the rock stele at Assuan[13] which shows Men, the chief sculptor of Amenhotep III, and Bek, the chief sculptor of Ikhnaton, each sacrificing before the king he served. Helck claims that, because the same epithet 'king of kings' is used of Amenhotep III as in the name of the southern Memnon colossus representing the king at Thebes,[14] the relief on the stele shows a statue of Amenhotep III as receiving the sacrifice of Men, and the whole depiction is a memorial. Yet surely it does not mean that either Amenhotep III or, for that matter, Ikhnaton is dead even if they are shown as statues. Nor does the use of 'king of kings' on both stele and colossus give any ground for believing that Amenhotep III was dead when represented on the stele. It would be much more reasonable to suppose that such an unusual double stele was commissioned to emphasize the contemporaneity of the two men in their jobs, especially since there is no hint of funerary material in the inscription.

Another stele,[15] this time of Amenhotep III and Tiy, found at Amarna has on it the late form of the Aton name which one would not expect if Amenhotep III ended his reign at the time scholars usually claim. Helck claims that this was a memorial erected by a private person, an official such as Huya who had served the old king and queen, but there is no evidence that the stele is a private memorial. A private Egyptian memorial that nowhere mentioned the name of the donor would be a complete anomaly.

Similarly, Helck[16] describes the lintel in the tomb of Huya at Amarna, which depicts both royal families, as simply a personal memorial of Huya. This is the single vital piece of evidence for the co-regency that Helck treats, but he supports his claim with no evidence at all. Throughout the Amarna necropolis royal influence is present to a much greater extent than is usual among tombs of the nobility, and virtually all of the major scenes depicted on every tomb are so dominated by the figures of Ikhnaton and his queen that it is the royal pair who are commemorated rather than their owners. In the scene in question there is nothing whatever to indicate that Amenhotep III is dead, and no one questions that everyone else depicted was alive at the time it was carved, yet Helck still maintains that the king was dead.

When we come to the presence of Amenhotep's name on the coffin of Ikhnaton's little daughter, Meketaton, Helck[17] explains this way as a mere stressing of family relationship. He gives a similar explanation of other doubly inscribed objects, an offering table[18] and broken granite bowl[19] which will be more fully discussed later, and says that the offering table, like the statues of Amenhotep III in the 'sunshade' of Tiy, is a memorial erected by Ikhnaton to his father.

Another tomb, with rather more bearing on the subject, is that of Heruef, also at Thebes. Helck[20] notes that the name of the seated royal pair before whom Ikhnaton offers is broken away, so that positive identification is impossible. Tiy is shown with Ikhnaton, and also with Amenhotep III elsewhere in the tomb, yet Helck hazards a number of other guesses. He first suggests a god and goddess, but since a goddess does not wear sandals, the woman seen here must be a queen. Other candidates put forward are Amenhotep III and his mother Mutemwiya; Amenhotep I and Aahmes Nefertari; and Menes and his wife, but he is finally forced to admit that Amenhotep III and Tiy are most probably the pair shown. Helck then goes on to claim this as evidence for the death of Amenhotep III, since his son is honouring him as a god. One co-regent, he argues, would be unlikely to worship another, and so it follows (as in Soleb) that this is a statue of Amenhotep III. Curiously, he thinks it insignificant that the presumably living queen Tiy is also honoured as divine, and presumably in statue form. That she, though alive, sits beside her dead husband he does not think strange because she does the same thing in the stele found at Amarna mentioned earlier.

Thus, by assuming the truth of two extremely shaky suppositions of his own, Helck assails the co-regency theory.

He has by no means tackled all the positive arguments for the co-regency, but he does also point out[21] that there is no double dating on the part of the two kings; no pictures exist of both together; Amarna-style art is known not to be used by the artists of Amenhotep III, nor is Amenhotep III himself ever shown in the Amarna-style; in the Malqatta palace inscriptions, the Aton and the aton temple are not mentioned; and Ikhnaton changed his own name. Only the first objection has any validity. There are no double dates from this period, but the surviving material is only a very small fraction of the original, and the absence of double dates does not prove none existed. The statement that there are no pictures of the two men together is true only if one accepts Helck's laboured explaining away of all occasions when they are so shown.[22] Again, Amenhotep III is never shown in the Amarna style only if one rejects, like Helck, the occasions on which he does appear in that style.[23] Hayes has shown that the name of Aton and his temple certainly do occur in the Malqatta palace and, indeed, the name of the palace complex was once compounded with Aton:[24] there is not enough left of the building to permit wall inscriptions to survive, which might have provided a great deal of data.

# FIVE: The co-regency: the case for

The case for a co-regency of Amenhotep III and Ikhnaton depends for the most part on evidence of excavated objects or still surviving inscriptions on the walls of tombs from all over Egypt and Nubia. The material is most easily discussed if grouped, and I shall deal in turn with inscribed objects, the material from tomb walls at Amarna and Thebes, the Gurob papyri, and finally the inscriptions from the temple of Soleb.

*Inscribed objects*

Near the Desert Altars at Amarna, the Egypt Exploration Society's expedition of 1931 under the direction of J. D. S. Pendlebury found in a small chapel some pieces of a pink granite bowl. It was inscribed round the rim with the beginnings of the

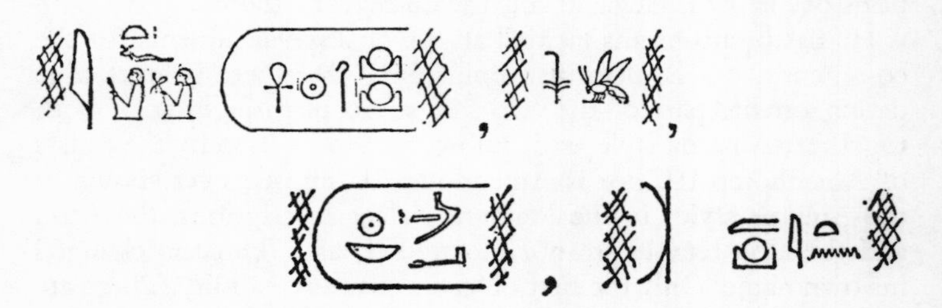

later Aton name plus (Neb-maat-re) and the words 'in Akhetaton'.[1] The names of both kings were originally present since the 'king of Upper and Lower Egypt phrase *nsw bity* cannot refer to the cartouche of Nebmaatre. This is one of the objects that Helck would have us regard as a memorial, evidence of the regard in which Ikhnaton held his father. If this bowl were the only object discovered which bore the two names side by side in this way, then this might be a logical conclusion, although the form of the Aton name which is used shows that it is rather a long time after the start of his supposed sole reign for Ikhnaton to have been thinking in terms of a memorial to his father. However, when we take into consideration the hostility of later rulers to Ikhnaton, we must be surprised by the number of objects which have survived not only this but later hazards and are found to be inscribed with the names of the king and his father. A mere expression of family feeling is inadequate to explain it, even if we had no evidence pointing in another direction. No material of other periods of ancient Egyptian history gives any hint that it was the custom of a king to associate the name of a dead predecessor with his own unless it was made quite clear that the other king named was actually dead. In the case of this granite bowl, small as it is, we find specific evidence which renders the memorial theory still more unlikely. If it had been made long after the death of Amenhotep III, one would have expected some such phrase as 'true of voice', i.e. deceased, but instead there is the phrase 'in Akhetaton' which would be entirely natural if the bowl, like several other objects to be discussed later, were a commemoration of a visit or prolonged stay by Amenhotep III and Tiy in that city.

In 1935 the same expedition led by Pendlebury also found in the sculptor's area near the palace a limestone offering table,[2] which would once have been held on the hands of a statue. On the underside, between the position of the hands, was the late Aton title followed by on the right, twice repeated, the praenomen of Amenhotep III (Nebmaatre), and on the left by the praenomen of Ikhnaton (Neferkheperure Uanre). The repetition of Amenhotep's praenomen seems significant, and also its place on the right, for the use of such a title as 'fanbearer on the right hand of the king' suggests that the Egyptians recognised a greater place of honour as being on the right. Then, again, an offering table is a cult object, and if Ikhnaton had intended it as a memorial for his father he could hardly have omitted to indicate that he was dead. It is much more probable that the table was prepared for dedication by Amenhotep III on a sojourn in Amarna, which would also be a logical explanation of the repetition of his name and of its being placed to the right in the most honoured position.

An earlier expedition of the Egypt Exploration Society in 1924 found at Amarna a small shrine-shaped stele[3] (see pl. IV) in the so-called Amarna style and showing Amenhotep III and Tiy seated under the rays of the Aton. The inscriptions give the name and titles of the Aton in the late form, followed by two cartouches of (Nebmaatre), and the name of Tiy. Like the bowl and offering table, it makes no mention of the death of Amenhotep III but depicts him as a corpulent man of advanced years sitting relaxed beside his wife. It is much more like the depictions of family life in the tombs of Akhetaton than any memorial stele, and it is particularly interesting that Amenhotep III is referred to here, as he is in the temple inscriptions at Soleb, by his praenomen only.

When the Tell el Amarna tablets were discovered several interesting objects were found with them. These comprised a clay seal bearing two impressions of the praenomen of Ikhnaton; five square alabaster plaques inlaid with the praenomen and nomen of Amenhotep—(Nebmaatre) (Amenhotep, ruler of Thebes)—in dark blue glazed faience; and a plaque of light blue glazed faience, which had originally been set into an alabaster tablet, and was inscribed in vertical columns: 'The beloved of Ptah, the king of the two lands, the good god (Nebmaatre) given life, the royal wife (Tiy), may she live', and across the bottom: 'the book of the sycamore and the olive'.[4] With the exception of the seal, which may have discharged a similar function, these objects were probably plates from the tops of box containers for tablets or papyri.

Only the clay seal is from the reign of Ikhnaton, but the comparative fragility of clay makes it possible that similar seals could have been destroyed while the Tell el Amarna tablets were still in the hands of the original finders. Nevertheless, it is still clear that many more of the tablets which can be assigned with certainty to a specific king belong to the reign of Amenhotep III than to that of Ikhnaton. It is also interesting that the series of letters from other monarchs to Ikhnaton apparently breaks off after about four or five years. Tushratta, the ruler of Mitanni, mentions in his latest letter that Ikhnaton has held his messengers in Egypt for four years. Burnaburiash, the king of Babylon, mentions in his penultimate letter that Ikhnaton's messengers have come to him three times—and a yearly embassy is likely. The king of Alashia (Cyprus) writes that he will himself send an embassy every year, but the contents of his second letter show that it was written less than a year after the first, and in his remaining five letters he desires more rapid communication with Egypt. There is no reason to suppose that the series of letters to Ikhnaton from vassal princes, which are much more difficult to deal with in the chronological sense, extend over a longer period.

Indeed what were these tablets doing in Akhetaton at all? For the most part they are apparently consecutive, and even although we may not have all the letters in such groups as those from Ribaddi or Tushratta of Mitanni, there is still a continuity of sense throughout the series. We find ourselves with a correspondence which comes largely from the later years of Amenhotep III or from the reign of Ikhnaton. The content of these documents will later be discussed in some detail, but we may usefully ask, now, if Akhetaton was under construction in the year 5 and actually occupied later than the year 6 (since even the later boundary stele of Ikhnaton refers to his still living at that time in what amounts to temporary shelter),[5] why so many already out-of-date documents were brought to the new city and carefully preserved. The answer must be that these were not old documents transferred to Akhetaton, but current correspondence received at the royal residence there, or while the king was in transit from one part of the country to another, and brought to Akhetaton's royal archives as a matter of course.[6] Most of the letters have no dockets, which may be taken as indicating that they were dealt with by routine procedure.

The letters addressed to Amenhotep, and mainly forming part of his current correspondence, are striking evidence of his having resided in the city, and the short period of time over which we find contemporary monarchs in correspondence with Ikhnaton would indicate that for much of his seventeen-year rule he shared power with his father. The argument gains added weight when we remember that Amenhotep III had royal estates near Akhetaton,[7] that buildings in the city were part of his household,[8] and that a man named Rames who occupied a tomb in the necropolis held office as his household steward.[9] If Amenhotep III was making Akhetaton his headquarters in this way, we should in turn expect evidence of his presence at Thebes to be sparse at this period, and, as far as we can tell from the material published from the New York Metropolitan Museum's excavation of the Malqatta palace at Thebes,[10] there is no evidence that the king resided in that locality except during jubilee periods. The jar sealings from the rubbish dumps there occur in large quantities in jubilee years, but are rather rare from the years before or between these celebrations.[11] It is perplexing that the royal letters preserved from Ikhnaton's reign appear to break off after some five years. If there were no co-regency this would mean that the latest letters from one monarch to another were written some time before the building of Akhetaton was finished and possibly even before its construction was commenced.

Turning again to inscribed objects, a fragment of a statuette[12] bearing the late Aton title and the names of Amenhotep III and Ikhnaton was found by the Egypt Exploration Society expedition to Amarna. More interesting from our viewpoint, however, was the first excavation of the royal tomb at Amarna which was undertaken before the turn of the century by Urbain Bouriant. He brought to light a fragment of the rose-granite coffin[13] of the princess Meketaton upon which was inscribed (Nebmaatre) and (Neferkheperure Uanre), the precedence of the praenomen of Amenhotep III over that of Ikhnaton again being noteworthy. Much more remarkable than this, however, is the very presence of the older king's name at all. As we have already seen, this second daughter of Ikhnaton and Nofretiti is mentioned on the tomb of Huya,[14] which was being carved in the year 12 of Ikhnaton's reign, and so must have died some time subsequently. If there had in fact been no co-regency, we should have the anomalous situation in Egyptian history (so far as we know) of a ruler placing the name of his father—dead twelve years—on the coffin of a daughter who may very well herself have been born after the old king died. It would be much more probable that such a doubly inscribed object would have been prepared during the joint reign of the two men.

The next object for consideration is the rock-cut stele of the overseers of works, the father and son, Men and Bek, at Assuan. This has been known since the early days of Egyptology[15] and, as we have seen, shows Men offering before Amenhotep III and Bek similarly offering before Ikhnaton, whose image has unfortunately been destroyed. We have already discarded Helck's tenuous argument that Men is making his offering before a statue of the dead Amenhotep III, and the wording of the inscription itself strongly indicates that both kings are living:

'The Horus, strong bull, arising in truth, the king of Upper and Lower Egypt, the lord of two lands (Nebmaatre) the son of Re of his body (Nebmaatre), the ruler of rulers, the lord of strength, the chosen one of Re, may he make the gift of life and be glad with his Ka, like Re forever and ever.' There follows an offering inscription by Men. The inscription by Bek reads: '(——) (——) given life forever, the living Aton, great of Heb-seds, lord of heaven, lord of earth, lord of all that the Aton encircles, lord of the house of Aton in Akhetaton, the King of Upper and Lower Egypt, living in truth (——) the son of Re, living in truth (——) great in his duration.' There follows an offering inscription by Bek. Noticeable again here is the omission of the nomen of Amenhotep III, and the repetition of the praenomen. This stele is unique in my experience, and it seems unlikely that such an expensive commemoration would be ordered simply to celebrate an event so comparatively common at this period as the holding of the same office by father and son in succession. As I have already mentioned, a more satisfactory explanation is that it was cut because both men held office simultaneously during the co-regency, the father serving Amenhotep and the son Ikhnaton.

Finally, we come to the most important object of this group, the funerary shrine[16] Ikhnaton had made for his mother, Queen Tiy. It was found in 1907 by the Theodore M. Davis expedition to the Valley of the Kings at Thebes in the tomb Davis called the tomb of Queen Tiy. The queen is now believed never to have been buried there, the bones in the coffin being ascribed to Smenkhkare, but the shrine was hers. It is typical Amarna work, and wherever the Aton is mentioned the late titulary is used: '(May Re who rules the two horizons, live, rejoicing on the horizon) (in his name of Re, the father who comes as the Aton).' There are five relevant inscriptions. The one on the upper traverse of the front of the shrine reads on the right: 'May the king of Upper and Lower Egypt (Nebmaatre) live, and the king's mother, the king's principal wife (Tiy) may (she) live,' and on the left: 'May the king of Upper and Lower Egypt who lives in truth, (——) live, that which he made for the king's mother, the king's principal wife (Tiy).' On the right jamb of the door we have: 'The king of Upper and Lower Egypt, living in truth, the lord of the two lands (Nebmaatre) and the king's principal wife, his beloved the royal mother of Uanre, the lady of two lands (Tiy), living forever,' and on the left: '—— the father (May Re live ——) (in his name of Re the father who comes as the Aton), given life forever and ever, the king of Upper and Lower Egypt, living in truth (Nebmaatre), and the king's mother (Tiy) living forever.' (In this last inscription the cartouche of Nebmaatre is written in red ink over a mutilated cartouche of Ikhnaton, and according to Georges Daressy, the first Egyptologist to study the shrine upon its discovery, this is the only non-original written material on the shrine.)[17] On the door itself the inscription reads: '—— (Nebmaatre) given life forever —— (—— hotep, ruler of Thebes), great in his duration —— (Tiy) living forever and ever.' (See pl. VI.)

There is no obscurity in these inscriptions, and any breaks can be restored easily and almost with certainty.

This shrine was intended for inclusion among the funerary equipment of the queen, though never actually so used. Generally speaking, an object such as this, which would require the labour of a skilled craftsman over a long period, would be likely to be prepared well in advance of need. Usually, whenever people were rich enough to afford a tomb and its equipment, and lived out their normal life-span, everything was prepared long before death. It can, therefore, be assumed as probable if not certain that this was presented to Tiy some time before her death.

The Aton name used on the shrine is the late form of the title[18] which appeared only after the year 9, so that its construction must have been begun after this date. In the door inscription the cartouche of the nomen of Amenhotep III originally appeared intact, but after the shrine was finished the first half—the name of the god Amen—was erased, which means that the initiation of the aggressive promotion of the Aton cult must be placed later in the reign than had once been thought possible. Furthermore, the cartouches and figures of Ikhnaton were then obliterated at a later date, and in one place the cartouche of Nebmaatre was inscribed in red ink over the erased cartouches of Neferkheperure Uanre. This last defacement shows that the shrine must have been readily accessible to those who hated Ikhnaton, and it would not have been so if it had been concealed in the tomb of the powerful queen Tiy.[19] The queen is known to have visited Akhetaton, in company at least with her little daughter, in or about the year 12, and this was most probably the occasion of the presentation. There are no later inscriptions mentioning Tiy that can be dated, but, as she had a chief steward in Akhetaton who is shown on the walls of his tomb hiring servants for her establishment,[20] we can presume that she intended a prolonged stay. There is no indication that she died immediately after this date, indeed Tutankhamen had time to grow so fond of her that he had a lock of her hair in his own tomb. Hence she would seem to have survived the visit some years, and the shrine must surely have been presented to her while she was still alive.

We can, therefore, be certain that Ikhnaton was alive when he commissioned the shrine and presented it, and reasonably sure that Queen Tiy was alive when it was presented to her. This makes it incredible that Amenhotep III could have been dead more than nine years when the shrine was produced, for he is referred to in the same manner as Ikhnaton and Tiy, and there is no indication whatever of his death in these inscriptions. Had he been so long dead, the words 'May the king (Nebmaatre) live' would have been replaced by the usual term 'true of voice' (meaning deceased) after his name, and his name would not be placed always to the right of Ikhnaton's indicating that he was still regarded as the senior of the two men. All this evidence is conclusive that the shrine was produced during the period of joint rule.

A curious feature, perhaps due to the shrine being one of the rare objects wherein the name and titles of Amenhotep III are treated by Amarna craftsmen, is that the two epithets most frequently used of Ikhnaton are here unquestionably applied to his father, i.e. 'living in truth', and 'great in his duration'.

### *Material from the tomb walls at Amarna*

The most important tomb in the necropolis of Akhetaton, from the point of view of proving the co-regency, is that of Huya, the chief steward of the household of Queen Tiy.[21] One of its inscriptions records, as we have seen, an event in the year 12, showing that the carving of the tomb is to be dated close to this period. Huya's tomb, with its three rooms and two halls, is no exception to the others in the cemetery and gives the same prominence to royal activities. Its reliefs deal in particular with an important celebration of some sort which is dated to the year 12,[22] and a visit paid to Akhetaton by Amenhotep III, Queen Tiy, and their daughter, Beketaton.[23] The usual scenes of the rewarding of Huya[24] by Ikhnaton and the sun hymn[25] are, however, also portrayed. The owner of the tomb plays the same subordinate role in all these scenes that he would have done in real life. (See pp. 205–215.)

Looking first at the royal visit to the city, we see the royal family at dinner.[26] On the left are Ikhnaton, Nofretiti and two of their daughters: on the right are Tiy and Beketaton, and serving in the lower centre of the scene is Huya. In another relief, Ikhnaton and Nofretiti entertain[27] Tiy and Beketaton in what appears to be a light supper, Huya again serving. The visitors were obviously taken on a tour of the city, and another relief shows Ikhnaton taking Tiy and Beketaton round the temple of Aton and showing them the 'sunshade' of Tiy.[28] We even have the equivalent of the holiday photograph, for a statue of Beketaton is seen in a sculptor's studio[29] with the sculptor Auta shown finishing off his work. Now we come to the very controversial lintel.[30] The two royal families here appear together, with Amenhotep, Tiy and Beketaton on the right, and Ikhnaton, Nofretiti and four of their daughters on the left. Both groups are shown in the Amarna style under the rays of the Aton, as is usual in these tomb reliefs, and everyone is agreed that all those depicted are alive, Amenhotep III excepted. Yet, the fact that Tiy and Beketaton have their hands raised is no indication that their husband and father is dead, as Davies thought,[31] and the inscriptions do not suggest he is dead either. To the right the text reads:[32] 'The king of Upper and Lower Egypt (Nebmaatre) given life, the king's principal wife (Tiy) may she live,' and the inscription on the other side is: 'The king of Upper and Lower Egypt (Neferkheperure Uanre) the king's principal wife (Nefernefruaton Nofretiti)' followed by the usual formulae naming the children.

The situation is this, Huya's tomb was executed in or near the year 12, certainly after the year 9 since the late Aton titulary was used throughout, and if Amenhotep III is dead he has been so for approximately twelve years. Nevertheless, he is present here in a family group without any mention of his death in the inscription. A further feature, confirming beyond reasonable doubt that he was alive, is the portrayal on several occasions in the tomb of Beketaton with her mother, and once a statue of Beketaton, for which it is reasonable to assume that she posed, is shown in a relief of a sculptor's studio. This little daughter of Amenhotep III and Tiy also appears in the complete relief of the two families, and is here, as elsewhere, shown as being uniformly the same size. If Egyptian relief work has any historical value whatever, as I am sure it has, then this fact indubitably means that the occasions depicted were all roughly contemporaneous. Realism is a mark of the so-called Amarna style, where we never encounter the usual habit of Egyptian artist of making everyone but the king of inferior size. The artists even make a gradation in size among Ikhnaton's daughters,[33] and in the case of Beketaton, too, we have the sidelock of childhood[34] depicted wherever she is shown.

We have already calculated that Tiy must have been approximately sixteen[35] at the start of the reign, and so, after forty years, would be about fifty-six. If there was no co-regency, then the 'two families' relief shows her some twelve years after the end of her husband's reign, when she was sixty-eight. However, Beketaton is shown with the sidelock which indicates her age as probably less than fourteen, which would mean that the child must have been born at the most two years before the death of Amenhotep III when the queen was fifty-four or more. These figures seem outside probable limits. It is also likely, moreover, that Beketaton was at this time a good deal younger than fourteen, and that Tiy had been more than sixteen at her marriage. Queen Tiy was in many ways a remarkable woman, but it is doubtful if she was physically so remarkable as to bear a child when she was well over fifty-four. If, on the other hand, we assume that it is the living Amenhotep III pictured with his family on the tomb wall, we have no need to go to the ridiculous length of postulating a child born to a woman of such advanced age to explain the situation. In this case Tiy would have been between forty and forty-five when Beketaton was born, old to have a child but not a medical curiosity.

To recapitulate: the lintel shows Amenhotep III in a typical Amarna pose, there is no mention of his being dead, and his little daughter is shown the same size as in the rest of the reliefs. His omission from the other reliefs was probably dictated by the same lack of space which may have prevented two daughters of Ikhnaton and Nofretiti from being shown elsewhere than in the 'two families' scene, or perhaps by the fact that these reliefs portrayed specific occasions on which Amenhotep III was not present. Besides, Huya was the steward of the house of Queen Tiy, and it would be natural for him to be chiefly concerned with her activities.

Looking back for a moment at the relief showing Ikhnaton taking Tiy on a tour of the temple, it can be seen that this further supports the co-regency. He points out to her the 'sunshade' of Tiy,[36] presumably a shrine dedicated in her honour, and the court of this building is lined on two sides with statues of her, her husband, and himself. These are inscribed without any hint that any of the three is dead, and since we know that Tiy and Ikhnaton were alive at the time, the statues themselves have no funerary significance, so that it follows that Amenhotep III was also alive. The absence of statues of Nofretiti may be because the 'sunshade' was a personal shrine, and Nofretiti would have her own elsewhere, but it may be the first sign of Nofretiti's disappearance from history.

The name Nebmaatre is included again in the inscriptions on the jambs of the north door of the tomb.[37] These are arranged in five columns. The first reads: 'Live the father (——) (——) given life forever and ever, the king of Upper and Lower Egypt, living in truth, the lord of the two lands (Neferkheperure Uanre) the son of Re, living in truth the lord of diadems (Ikhnaton) great in his duration, the king's principal wife (Nefernefruaton Nofretiti) may she live forever and ever', and the second: 'Live the father (——) (——) given life forever and ever, the king of Upper and Lower Egypt, living in truth, the lord of the two lands (Neferkheperure Uanre) given life, the king of Upper and Lower Egypt, the lord of two lands (Nebmaatre), the king's principal wife, the king's mother (Tiy) living forever and ever.' Columns three and four are like the first, and column five is the same as the second. Both kings are introduced in the same way, with no indication that one is dead and the other living, and this is strong confirmation of the co-regency theory. It is also worth noting that in this case the name of Ikhnaton occupies the premier position.

All the material so far studied belongs to the later period, since references to the Aton use the titulary which appeared only after the year 9. Earlier double inscriptions may be lacking because Akhetaton was not really ready for occupation until year 8, or perhaps because many of these objects were made specially to commemorate the visit of the senior royal family to Amarna. The highest date for which there is evidence of a co-regency is the year 12, and the ceremony recorded as of this date in the tomb of Huya is close to the point at which Amenhotep vanishes from contemporary record, and may have some connection with his disappearance.

Besides the tomb of Huya,[38] this ceremony is also recorded in that of Meryre II,[39] but the aspect depicted in each is different. In Huya's version Ikhnaton and Nofretiti are being carried on a palanquin to the place where a large durbar is about to take place, and are accompanied by their daughters Mekataton and Meritaton. The inscription reads: 'Regnal year 12, the second month of winter, day eight. Live the father (——) (——) given life forever and ever. Appearance of the king of Upper and Lower Egypt (——) and the king's principal wife (——) living forever and ever upon the great sedan chair of gold to receive the "inw" of Syria, Kush, the west, the east, and every foreign country joined together at one time. The islands in the midst of the "Great Green" bring "inw" to the king upon the great throne of Akhetaton in a reception of homage from every foreign land to give them the breath of life.'

In the tomb of Meryre II the inscription reads: 'Regnal year 12 . . . , of the king of Upper and Lower Egypt [living] in truth the lord of two lands (Neferkheperure Uanre) the son of Re, living in truth, the lord of diadems (Ikhnaton) great in his duration. The king's [principal] wife his beloved (——) living forever. Appearance upon the throne of his father the Aton living in truth while the chiefs of every foreign country present . . . offerings in his hand.' In this second scene, however, the royal party is shown as arrived at the kiosk shown empty in the former, and the king and queen are depicted enthroned in it with six princesses behind them.[40] Envoys to the durbar are shown as coming from all parts of the world known to the Egyptians, bringing presents which are called *inw*. This same word is used to indicate forced tribute elsewhere, but it is merely a participle of the verb to bring, and this is an entirely peaceful scene. The king, with his wife and daughters around him, sits receiving gifts, not only from foreigners but from representatives of his own people. Interspersed with the scenes of presentation are others of athletic competitions and games.

The importance of the ceremony is illustrated by its being carved on the walls of two separate tombs, and the absence of military trappings clearly demonstrates that this is no reception of tribute after a campaign or war. Bound slaves do appear, but these were a regular article of commerce, and there are no long columns of prisoners here, such as we find after successful warfare. It is not connected either with a Heb-sed festival, since the king does not wear the bull's tail[41] which was the mark of being in festival, and is also shown in company with his family which was not the practice at such times.

What then can the event celebrated be? The term 'appear on the throne' is used in the tomb of Meryre II, and the similar term 'appear upon the great sedan chair of gold', is used in the tomb of Huya. Sometimes 'appear on the throne' was used by a ruler to mean 'be crowned',[42] and it is possible that this lavishly depicted festival is part of the celebrations opening the sole rule of Ikhnaton. The appearance of Amenhotep III on the lintel only of Huya's tomb might also then be explained by his death having occurred between the time at which it was carved and the carving of the rest of the tomb. It is also curious that no similar scenes of presentation occur until the year 12 of Ikhnaton, and it may be that no such durbar could be held unless a ruler were either senior pharaoh or ruling alone. There is not sufficient evidence to be decisive on this point, but the death of Amenhotep III certainly seems to fall close to this date, and makes such an explanation for the pageantry of the tombs very persuasive.

*Material from the tomb walls at Thebes*

The principal support for the theory of a co-regency to be found at Thebes is again to be found in two tombs, those of Ramose[43] and Heruef.[44] Both were officials of Amenhotep III, but their tombs also contain reliefs[45] and inscriptions[46] of Ikhnaton. In the tomb of Ramose the name of Nebmaatre is mentioned in the following context: 'May he [Amon Re] cause (Nebmaatre) to endure, may he grant his life united with eternity, his years joined in hundred thousands.'[45] Another relief shows Ikhnaton, seen with Nofretiti at the window of appearances of a palace, and under the rayed disc of the Aton.[46] Although the style is solidly in the Amarna tradition the king is named as Amenhotep IV and this, together with the use of the early titulary of the Aton, dates the relief as earlier than the year 9 of Ikhnaton, but the style is too advanced for it to be very much earlier.

Ramose was vizier of the southern half of Egypt under Amenhotep III, for whose first jubilee he donated four jars of ale, and one of the dockets on these reads: 'Year 30 ale for the first "Heb-sed" of His Majesty (life prosperity health) which the vizier Ramose made.'[47] He joined with his northern colleague, Amenhotep the son of Hapu, in carrying out the official ceremonies on this occasion, as we see in the reliefs of the temple at Soleb.[48] Ramose fails to appear, however, in any reliefs or inscriptions of the period after the first jubilee, and was not present when the funerary temple of Vizier Amenhotep was decicated.[49] We find also that, although the relief of his own funeral procession is present, the rest of his tomb is incomplete. Death presumably overtook him suddenly, but he was not disgraced and removed from office because his figure is left unscathed in the carvings. Among those represented as attending his obsequies was the fourth prophet of Amen, whose name must be restored as Simut,[50] and who was promoted to being second prophet of the god in the year 35 of Amenhotep III. From this we can deduce that work on the tomb of Ramose must have been complete before this last-named date, and the presence in it of reliefs of Ikhnaton would be difficult to explain except by a co-regency.

In the tomb of Heruef, to which Helck referred in his arguments against the theory, there is material dated to both the first and third jubilees of Amenhotep III, in years 30 and 36,[51] so that this official was certainly active in the intervening period. However, the scene of the third jubilee is incomplete, so that whenever the scenes dated to year 30 were carved, those of year 36 must mark the close of his career. That it ended in disgrace we can see by the destruction of his figure wherever it appeared, and the attempted obliteration of his name. The scene sequence is particularly interesting in this tomb. In the entrance Ikhnaton and his mother worship; on the right Re Harakhte and Maat, and on the left the sun god of Edfu, Atum and Hathor. Tiy is called the mother of the god and the great royal wife. Inside the entrance on the south side, Ikhnaton is seen offering to Re Harakhte on the left, and on the right is a relief in which a king, over whom the protecting vulture hovers and behind whom is the blessing of Re, pours a libation on offerings before another king facing him. The king receiving the sacrifice wears a skirt and sandals, and the bull's tail apron of the Heb-sed festival over a leopard skin: a queen stands behind him on his right. The names have been hacked out, but Fakry, an Egyptian archaeologist working on the tomb, found a fragment on its floor bearing the cartouche of Amenhotep III and Queen Tiy.[52] This makes it certain that Ikhnaton is here pictured sacrificing before his mother and father. All these scenes occur on the façade or just inside the tomb entrance, but those dealing with the first and third jubilees of Amenhotep III are inside the first court.

To appreciate the significance of this, we must consider how an Egyptian tomb was made.[53] It was not a matter of first cutting the complete tomb from the rock, then smoothing the walls, and finally carving the reliefs. All stages were apparently carried out simultaneously. As soon as the façade had been hewn the artists started work on the decoration, and so on throughout. In some tombs the rooms inside were no more than half cut out of the rock before the artists began decorating the ceilings and available wall space. As we have seen, the interior of Heruef's tomb has scenes dating to years 30 and 36 of Amenhotep III, and details of the figures of the bottom register are incomplete in both. Presumably these are the last scenes on which the artists were working before Heruef's fall from power, but in this case how do we explain the presence of Ikhnaton depicted as a ruling monarch on the façade and in the entrance hall? His depiction in these earlier carved scenes can only be taken as conclusive evidence that Ikhnaton was co-regent with his father long before the latter's death. (See p. 220.)

*The Gurob Papyri*

Four in number, two of these papyri were found by Petrie in his excavation at Kahun and Gurob, and were subsequently published by Griffith,[54] and the others were purchased from a dealer for the Berlin Museum by Dr. Borchardt in 1901. All four were ultimately published by Sir Alan Gardiner.[55] They form part of the business records of a cowherd called Mesy, and are mainly concerned with the hiring of the services of female slaves. I shall give here only such details of the transactions as are relevant to our purpose.

Each of the papyri is dated, the dates running from year 27 of Amenhotep III to year 4 of Ikhnaton, and, since Amenhotep III reigned thirty-eight to thirty-nine years, this would mean that the documents cover a period of sixteen years if there was no joint reign. Most interesting of the four is Berlin Papyrus 9784, which I shall here call A.[56] It records three of Mesy's transactions, two with a man called Nebmehy, who is referred to in $A^1$ as a herdsman, whose occupation is not listed in $A^2$, although the nature of the transaction (the exchange of a cow for three acres of field) indicates that he is still a herdsman, and who, among the witnesses in $A^3$, is referred to as a soldier. The same scribe, Tet, was employed on all three occasions, and the entries are dated: in the case of $A^1$ 'year 27, 3rd month of summer, day 20' in the reign of Amenhotep III; in $A^2$ 'year 2, —— month of winter, day 27' from the reign of Ikhnaton; and in $A^3$ 'year 3' of Ikhnaton. In $A^1$, recording a transaction involving the services of two female slaves Kherit and Henout, the first sentence of the body of the document reads: 'The day that Nebmehy——came before the cowherd Mesy,' and in $A^2$ the first sentence reads: 'On this day came again Nebmehy before the herdsman Mesy.' In $A^3$ the transaction once again concerns the female slave Henout.

The Egyptian is quite clear and the notion of repetitive action cannot be contested, the use of the term 'again' indicating that $A^1$ and $A^2$ were inscribed with only a short interval between. Other details confirm the quick sequence of events: all three transactions are recorded by a single scribe on the same piece of papyrus and, of the witnesses, the herdsman Nen witnessed all three, another herdsman Aper witnessed the first and third, and Pen, whose occupation is not given, also witnessed the first and third.

If there was no co-regency these are amazing coincidences, and it seems impossible that fourteen years should have elapsed between the first and second transactions, and fifteen between the first and third. Fourteen years is a long time in the life of a business or business man in our day; it was, relatively speaking, a much longer time under the Eighteenth Dynasty. We should surely accept that the year 27 of Amenhotep III and year 2 of Ikhnaton were so close together that a scribe writing down one transaction in the former year would naturally use the word 'again' when he came to record the transaction which took place in the latter. It followed that Amenhotep III associated his son as co-ruler sometime between the years 25 and 27, and this would accord well with the year 12 date in the tomb of Huya at Amarna, which gives some indication that the senior pharaoh died in that year. If the accession date of Ikhnaton occurred around the year 27 of Amenhotep III, the twelve years of the co-regency being added, then the reign would endure the thirty-nine years plus which is what other sources suggest.

The rest of the Gurob Papyri do not bear so definitely on this problem, although some points from them are relevant. Gurob Papyrus II 1 and Gurob Papyrus II 2, which I shall here refer to as B and C, date from the 33rd year of Amenhotep III, and are transactions of Mesy again dealing with his two female slaves, Kherit and Henout.[57] The other party to the transaction in both cases is a women called Pekey dwelling in the town, and who is also referred to in A[3]. The interval here would be approximately ten years if the co-regency is not accepted. The Berlin Papyrus 9785, the fourth member of the group, is dated to the year 4 of Ikhnaton, but has no relevance for us.[58]

Undoubtedly, the parallels in A are the most striking, but the material gleaned from B and C is definitely helpful. It is difficult to imagine any explanation other than the co-regency which would solve the problems these papyri present.

### *The Temple of Soleb*

The final evidence for the co-regency comes from the temple of Soleb, built by Amenhotep III to commemorate his first jubilee, approximately nine years before the end of his reign. Opponents of the co-regency would have us believe that the façade of this temple was left undecorated from the time of the first jubilee until the reign of Ikhnaton, and that after this lapse of time Ikhnaton finished the decoration. This is evidently absurd, and it must be that the scenes showing Ikhnaton sacrificing to the divine essence of Amenhotep III were carved during the joint reign of the two kings. Unfortunately, the temple of Soleb has never been fully or satisfactorily published. The plates of Lepsius who sketched the temple remains in the middle of the last century still give the best copies of its inscriptions readily available, since new material now in preparation has not yet appeared. However, one relief of the façade is shown in Lepsius.[59] It is carved in four registers, the two middle ones showing scenes of Ikhnaton offering before his father, and the uppermost and lowest consisting of hieroglyphs only. Lepsius' drawing shows no difference between the two figures other than dress. Amenhotep III wears a head-dress upon which the sun's disc appears between horns. His son wears the war crown. Amenhotep III wears the

Keni waistcoat (an upper garment of obscure significance probably connected with the 'Heb-sed' festival, not usually shown on statues),[60] while his son's upper body is bare. Amenhotep III holds a 'was' sceptre, and his son holds an offering jar. Both kings wear a kilt, that of Ikhnaton being more widely flared at the base than that of his father, and also the bull tail indicating that a 'Heb-sed' festival is being represented. There is no reason to claim that either figure is a statue, rather the scene appears to depict a part of the ritual celebration of a jubilee.

The top register of the scene shows a row of large cartouches. The two preserved intact belong to Ikhnaton; part of an obliterated cartouche appears to the right of this over the figure of Amenhotep below it. This was certainly the name of Amenhotep III, and makes it clear that Amenhotep III still occupied the more senior position on the right.

This concludes the evidence supporting the co-regency. The core of the case consists of the shrine which Ikhnaton made for Tiy; the representations of Beketaton in the tomb of Huya at Amarna; the presence of depictions of Ikhnaton on the first finished parts of the tomb of Heruef; and the contents of the Gurob Papyri. Each one of these pieces of evidence is very formidable and taken together they seem to me to form a conclusive case. The remaining material has considerable corroborative value, and even taken by itself without the use of any of the four above-mentioned conclusive pieces of evidence would present a strong argument.

From this point, therefore, I shall take the co-regency as a matter of fact, not theory, and it follows that the Ikhnaton legend must have little historical validity and can be discarded as a working hypothesis.

# SIX: The co-regency: final remarks

Before we leave the subject of the co-regency, it should be mentioned that several scholars[1] in recent times have held that a co-regency did exist, but that Ikhnaton was the more important of the two rulers. It has even been suggested that Amenhotep III abdicated his functions and lived on as a sort of Duke of Windsor. Little evidence exists which can be interpreted as favouring the theory, and it is positively contradicted by Amenhotep III's building activity and his jubilees dated in his thirty-sixth and later regnal years, and by the Tell el Amarna correspondence which makes it clear that those who wrote to the Egyptian court from abroad only addressed their letters to Ikhnaton after the death of his father. Besides, the king of Egypt was a god in his own right, and the son of a god: in such circumstances it is difficult to imagine how an 'abdication' could be accomplished. Gods on earth, if their presence is inconvenient, generally attain their apotheosis and enter heaven rather than go into retirement.

Nevertheless, Professor Fairman[2] has reopened this question. During the Liverpool University Expedition to Athribis in April of 1938, the director of the excavation, A. Rowe, deduced from a broken block found there that Amenhotep III had erected a building at this place, supporting this by quoting an inscription by one of the king's officials dealing with some construction activity there. This conclusion was eminently sensible.

Fairman's view of this block is very different, and seems scarcely reasonable. For him the remarkable feature of this block is the association of the names of Amenhotep III and Amenhotep IV (Ikhnaton), with Amenhotep IV in the position of precedence. Fairman concludes from this that even before his change of name in the fifth year of his reign, the younger pharaoh was the dominant partner in the co-regency and his father little more than a figurehead. (See illus. p. 86.)

Such a theory renders a very careful examination of the stone necessary. Unfortunately, its importance was not apparent to its discoverers, for when they uncovered it on the last day of the expedition they merely copied it, turned it once again face down, and left it where it was. There remains no way to check the copy, which may be correct, but since the vital point in question is the presence of one sign, it may also be wrong. How easily such

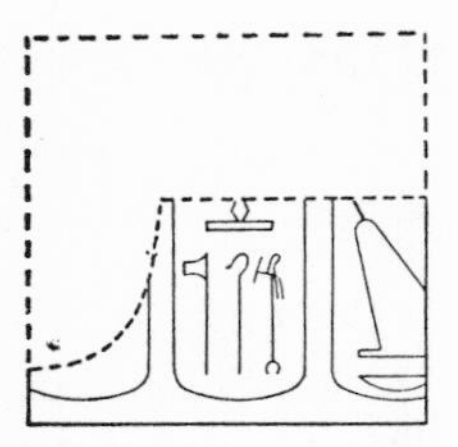

an error can occur is shown by the fact that although on the block the 'wast' sign is written , in Fairman's restoration of the text of the block the sign appears as . A trifling error indeed, but if the same *kind* of error had been made by the original copyist the whole meaning of the inscription could well have been changed. It must be remembered that it was the expedition's last day and everyone would undoubtedly have been working in haste. Further, no record exists of the condition of the stone and its inscription, so that we do not know whether the hieroglyphs were clear and easily legible, or whether they were so worn and broken as to be legible only with difficulty. All these are factors to be kept in mind when considering Fairman's conclusion.

We can at least be sure that the block was inscribed with three royal names, the second and third being restored to read: '(Amenhotep the Divine King of Wast)' and '(Nebmaatre)', the praenomen of Amenhotep III. The problem lies in the second cartouche, which Fairman declares cannot be that of Amenhotep III, since it is his son who is *always* referred to as the Divine King of Wast, he himself being known simply as King of Wast. This statement is inaccurate. Long before Fairman's article was published, I drew his attention to an example in Gautier's *Livre des Rois* of the writing of the elder king with the title 'Divine King of Wast', and it was this example in particular which led me to regard this broken block as merely tantalising, its condition being too fragmentary to have any value as a basis for historical conclusions. Although it is generally true that Amenhotep III is referred to as 'King of Wast' and his son as 'Divine King of Wast', it is improper to reason even in the presence of one attested example of Amenhotep III having been designated 'Divine King of Wast' that this, no longer available, badly broken block of stone, of which less than half remains, *must* have composed part of the names of both Amenhotep III and Amenhotep IV restored as: '(Neferkheperure Uanre) (Amenhotep Divine King of Wast), (Nebmaatre), (Amenhotep, King of Wast)'. A small point, but not insignificant when added to the rest, is that the official whose inscription refers to construction activity at Athribis was Amenhotep, the son of Hapu, a man particularly connected in his capacity as vizier of northern Egypt with the court of Amenhotep III.

Finally, and perhaps most important, even admitting the accuracy of the copy and the restorations (which I by no means do), it needs to be made clear that Fairman's conclusions as to the relative importance of the two kings are not at all a necessary outcome of his reasoning.

Fairman's belief that the block originally came from a temple wall may well be justified, but this is all that can be said. We have no means of deducing its position on the wall, and although it may, as Fairman contends, be part of an inscription of historical significance, it may have been merely a section from a frieze or top register decorated so:

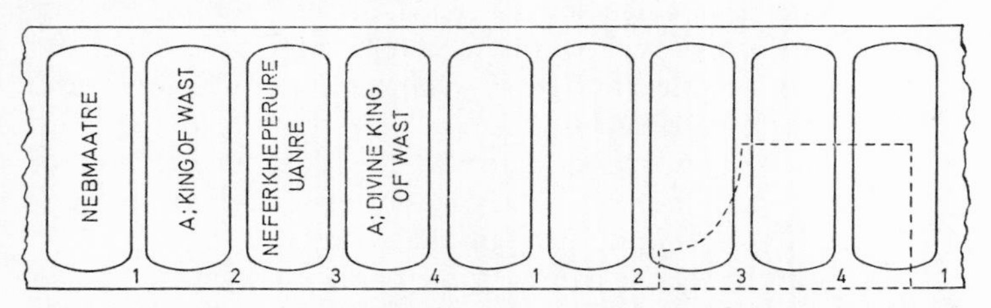


—the provenance of the block is shown by the dotted lines. It is impossible to say whether this or any other speculative reconstruction is more likely than Fairman's hypothesis, but I would emphasise the danger of erecting towering flights of theory upon such scanty, ambiguous, and incomplete evidence. Fairman's reasoning is especially strange in view of his certainly justified castigation[3] of Professor K. Seele of Chicago for similar reconstructions on entirely inadequate evidence.

# SEVEN: Ikhnaton and Smenkhkare

The existence of a co-regency between Ikhnaton and Smenkhkare has never seriously been doubted, although the evidence is much less conclusive and voluminous than that for the co-regency between Amenhotep III and Ikhnaton. The same objections could be made as in the previous case, but they have never been advanced. It could be argued here, too, that Smenkhkare could have had double representations of Ikhnaton and himself, as well as doubly inscribed objects, made for very obscure reasons of his own. It is equally unlikely that he did.

In 1891 Petrie discovered at Amarna some fragments of a private stele.[1] On the reverse is a human figure in fine relief work, and on the obverse a very hastily incised scene containing cartouches of Ikhnaton and Smenkhkare. The latter is named as (Ankhkheperure, beloved of Uanre) and (Nefernefruaton, beloved of Ikhnaton), and it is interesting to note the differences between the forms used here and those in a graffito from the Theban tomb of a man named Pere—(Ankhkheperure, beloved of Neferkheperure) and (Nefernefruaton, beloved of Uanre),[2] and in the tomb of Meryre II[3] at Akhetaton—(Ankhkheperure) (Smenkhkare Djeserkheperu). Since the form in the graffito comes from Thebes and is dated to the third regnal year of Smenkhkare, and the other two come from Akhetaton, it is likely that the Akhetaton forms are the earlier.

The appearance of the names of the two kings side by side on the stele, and the evident change of Smenkhkare's name to a form compounded with the name of Ikhnaton, argue powerfully in favour of a co-regency. The graffito carries us further, for it not only provides the highest known year date for Smenkhkare's reign, but was written for the blind Pawah, 'the "wab" priest, the scribe of divine offerings of Amen in the mansion of (Ankhkheperure)', by his brother. The existence of an Amen prayer by an official in the service of Smenkhkare indicates that the persecution of the cult which Ikhnaton had initiated was over by this third year of his co-regent. This is confirmed by the depiction of a scribe of the divine offerings in what may well have been a mortuary temple of Smenkhkare.

In discussing the tomb of Meryre II at Akhetaton,[3] the existence of a scene showing Smenkhkare and Meritaton under the rays of the Aton in a typical Amarna posture has already been mentioned. The carving had been barely begun, and the crudity of the style represents a complete break with the rest of the tomb designs which are dated by an inscription to the year 12 of Ikhnaton and comprise scenes of this king and his family. This sudden departure might justify the belief that this particular scene was a monument of the succeeding reign, but other evidence is conclusive that it belongs to the period of the co-regency. (See pp. 218–19.)

A box was found in the tomb of Tutankhamen inscribed as follows: 'The king of Upper and Lower Egypt, living in truth the lord of two lands (Neferkheperure Uanre) the son of Re living in truth, lord of diadems (Ikhnaton) great in his duration, the king of Upper and Lower Egypt, the lord of two lands (Ankhkheperure, the beloved of Neferkheperure) the son of Re, lord of diadems (Nefernefruaton, beloved of Uanre) and the king's principal wife (Meritaton) may she live eternally.'[4]

Two interesting items which support the co-regency were discovered by the Deutsches Orient Gesellschaft expedition[5] to Akhetaton. The first is the stele now in the Berlin Museum which shows two kings in the Amarna fashion: one wears the double crown, has his arm round the other, who wears the war crown, is touching his chin with his other hand. Both monarchs are nude. The cartouches of the Aton appear at the top centre, and the king with the double crown and the king with the war crown respectively have three and two cartouches over their heads. All the cartouches are obliterated but identification is possible because the features of both kings, though not identical, resemble the usual portrayals of Ikhnaton: the king with the double crown is Ikhnaton and the other Smenkhkare. We can be sure that Amenhotep III is not involved here because the portraits we have of him in the Amarna style allow no room for confusion, either in age, build, or feature. The other German find shows a similar scene in what appears to be an unfinished sculptor's trial piece.[6] A seated king, dressed in cloak, cap and uraeus, has another king standing before him, wearing a shirt and the war crown with the uraeus, and pouring wine into his cup. The facial and bodily resemblance is again striking, though this may be merely an honorific extension by the sculptors of the senior king's

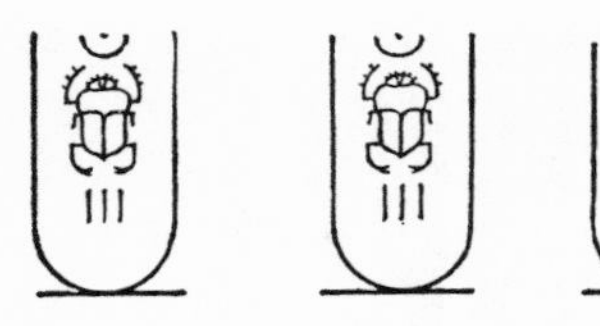

peculiar physique to his co-regent. Although no names were ever present on this slab, it seems beyond reasonable doubt that here again we have Smenkhkare and Ikhnaton. (Pl. VIII.)

The final objects which seem definitely attributable to a postulated co-regency between Smenkhkare and Ikhnaton are some blocks in the Amarna style[7] which were discovered in 1854 near a prostrate figure of Ramesses II at Memphis. One mentions the Aton temple at Memphis, another shows a king walking behind a very much larger king of whose figure only the legs remain, and a third preserves the lower part of three cartouches (see above).

The style of the blocks means that only one restoration of these cartouches is feasible, for we can rule out Ikhnaton whose cartouches would not both end with 'kheperu'. They must have read (Ankhkheperure) (Smenkhkare Djeserkheperu) and (Meritaton). A good deal more material exists which might, by a stretch of imagination, be ascribed to the co-regency, but I will not stretch my imagination so far as to discuss objects which do not show the two kings together or have not at least the traces of an inscription.

It remains only to ascertain when the co-regency began and its length. The first can be estimated from the edifice known as the Coronation Hall[8] which Ikhnaton built at Akhetaton in his fourteenth or fifteenth regnal year either to celebrate Smenkhkare's elevation as co-regent or his marriage with Meritaton, the royal heiress. This means that any earlier date than the late part of year 14 of Ikhnaton for Smenkhkare's accession would conflict with the use of this hall. The graffito from the tomb of Pere being dated in the first third of Smenkhkare's third regnal year—the highest year date known—then makes it probable that his rule lasted two and a fraction years.

# EIGHT: The reign of Ikhnaton: a reconstruction

The reign of Ikhnaton now takes shape as being two-thirds spent in a co-regency with Amenhotep III, after whose death Queen Tiy was apparently regent for her son. Then followed a short period of sole rule by Ikhnaton, and the last part of the reign was passed in a co-regency with his son-in-law.

The co-regency with Amenhotep III, from the evidence of the late Aton names used on the doubly inscribed objects, lasted at least nine years. The Gurob Papyri suggest approximately twelve years as the shortest period that will fit the chronology. This second figure agrees with my interpretation of the durbar depicted in the tombs of Huya and Meryre II at Amarna, as either the celebration of the start of Ikhnaton's sole rule, or the funeral and deification of Amenhotep III. The docket on the Amarna letter which Gardiner would read 2, actually must be read 12, and the presence of Ikhnaton in Thebes might well be in connection with the obsequies of Amenhotep III. The period when Tiy apparently held power could only be that immediately succeeding the death of her husband. Its duration is uncertain, but anything more than an outside limit of six months would make the period of Ikhnaton's sole rule very short indeed. We do not know how much longer Smenkhkare reigned after the graffito in the tomb of Pere was written, nor at what period in year 17 Ikhnaton's reign ended, but late in the year 14 seems the most likely time at which the co-regency with Smenkhkare began. Thus Ikhnaton ruled alone two years, if the above figures are approximately accurate, and two and a half years if the figures are both erroneous to the largest extent possible in the existing circumstances.

Certainly the persecution of the Amen cult and the erasing of the names of other gods as well, which extended in a few cases even to the erasure of the plural noun 'gods', could not have taken place while Amenhotep III was alive, since until his death he was building Luxor, a large temple to Amen. Besides, the shrine Ikhnaton presented to Tiy, which was certainly produced after the year 9 on his order by his own workmen, originally contained the Amen name of Amenhotep III. Tiy, in her steles to the Osiris Amenhotep III, used her husband's Amen name so that this policy was not a feature of her regency. By his third year Smenkhkare had a temple in Thebes, in which a scribe of the divine offerings of Amen officiated. Thus, the only period left at which the fanatical Atonism of the reign could have broken out was the period of Ikhnaton's sole rule, the two years between the latter part of years twelve and fourteen.

The fact is, then, that out of a reign of seventeen years, Ikhnaton ruled only between two and two and a half years by himself. The most obvious conclusion is that Ikhnaton was incompetent to rule. This was recognised by Amenhotep III, and by Tiy and the court officials after the death of the old king, and it resulted in the earliest possible opportunity being taken to put another ruler on the throne with Ikhnaton. This theory is corroborated by the fact that it was during the sole rule of Ikhnaton that such an outbreak of fanatical religious frenzy occurred, wherein workmen were travelling around Egypt chiselling gods' names out of inscriptions. The pictures of Ikhnaton, if they correspond in any way to his actual condition, certainly point in the same direction, for such a badly deformed body might indicate the presence of some mental abnormality as well.

It is scarcely reasonable to assume that Amenhotep III elevated his son to the co-regency knowing that he was completely incompetent to rule, hence if Ikhnaton was actually mentally deranged, he probably became so after his appointment as co-regent, his condition deteriorating to a point at which he could no longer be allowed to rule. It is possible that his father was aware of this, and let Akhetaton be built as a place where Ikhnaton might be kept out of trouble, and left him there hoping that his state of health might improve. It may also be that the Egyptians suffered a mad king as long as they were able, but finally for the safety of their state they had to remove him.

With all of this information in mind, it is possible now to attempt an explanation for the co-regency. We have already seen the extraordinary influence of Queen Tiy, and that she must have possessed quite a command over her husband's affections in order to achieve the position she did. Her origins were well known, indeed Amenhotep III published them far and wide, and there is no possibility whatever that she was the royal heiress, so that, in Egyptian eyes, her children would have no right to the throne. However, because of the affection which he held for his wife, Amenhotep III quite naturally wished that the son of their marriage might succeed him. To this end he elevated Ikhnaton to a position of power long before there was any question of his own health failing. He recognised that, despite his own wishes, the claims of Tiy's children were invalid by custom, and that if he died before Ikhnaton had grasped the reigns of power very firmly, some other prince might be accepted instead of the son whom he wished to succeed him.

Another piece of evidence indirectly supports the same idea. When the kings of the Nineteenth Dynasty prepared a king list they had the reign of Amenhotep III directly succeeded by that of Haremhab. It has been represented that this was the doing of the Amen priesthood, but, as we shall see, this explanation is improbable. Perhaps the reason for this elimination is that the Nineteenth Dynasty kings did not consider any of the Amarna period rulers legitimate kings of Egypt. That Tutankhamen was a close relative of Amenhotep III and Tiy is certain. We have seen that he had a lock of hair of the queen buried in a nest of little anthropoid coffins in the tomb with him,[1] and when he is depicted in the Amarna style his features resemble those of Ikhnaton who was certainly their son. However, physical likeness may or may not be indicative, since the peculiar traits of Ikhnaton were extended to include the members of his court. Tutankhamen calls Amenhotep III his father on a restoration inscription on one of the lions found at Soleb,[2] but this may be a mere form of address, and, in accordance with what seems to be the custom at this period, he never specifically names his parents. Though it is sure that Amenhotep III and Tiy are among his forbears, we have no means of knowing whether they were his parents or grandparents, it has even been suggested that he was the son of Amenhotep III and Sitamen, but it does seem that he would have been too young to have been a son of Amenhotep III at all. In view of the Tell el Amarna letters both Tutankhamen and Smenkhkare could be sons of Ikhnaton. Their successor, Eye, may well have had no direct title to the throne at all, only enough of a shadow of a claim to keep armed revolt at bay for a while.

These arguments are vital to any reasonable explanation of the omissions we find in the Nineteenth Dynasty king list, since the usual theories will not fit all the facts. Ikhnaton could have been eliminated from the list on the grounds of his sacrilege and insanity; Smenkhkare had no independent reign; and Eye's claim to the throne, if indeed it was not based solely on force or bribery, was very slight, but on none of these grounds can the omission of Tutankhamen be justified. Tutankhamen was a perfectly legitimate pharaoh who came to terms with orthodoxy and picked up the pieces after the Amarna débâcle. It is true that his death probably occurred before he was twenty, yet the people who spoke through him did their best to rule in the fashion to which Egypt had been accustomed. He was buried in the normal fashion for a king and, though the necropolis officials knew the location of his tomb, it was never desecrated. It is evident from this that his contemporaries recognised his legitimacy, and yet his name is omitted from the Nineteenth Dynasty king list.

The one thing that Ikhnaton, Smenkhkare and Tutankhamen probably have in common is their descent from Queen Tiy. If the Nineteenth Dynasty rulers did not recognise her as a true queen, and chose to regard her issue as non-legitimate rulers, they would naturally leave them out of their king list. The claim to legitimacy of Haremhab, if this reasoning is sound, is also unknown. However, in the absence of any severe upset and more positive evidence of revolt than is contained in the restoration steles of Tutankhamen and Haremhab, we must assume that every ruler of Egypt in this period had some claim on the throne by descent with the possible exception of Eye, who may have been regarded by the Nineteenth Dynasty as a usurper, pure and simple.

These suggestions are all hypothetical and not really capable of much evidential support in the state of our knowledge. It may be that further research will permit more definite conclusions to be drawn in these matters.

# NINE: Smenkhkare

Smenkhkare has aroused much scholarly controversy, and a thorough re-examination of his reign is desirable. His co-regency with Ikhnaton has already been discussed, but his exact relationship with his senior partner is of interest.

We have seen that the name of Smenkhkare was changed sometime after he became co-regent from (Ankhkheperure) (Smenkhkare Djeserkheperu)[1] to (Ankheperure, beloved of Neferkheperure) (Nefernefruaton, beloved of Uanre),[2] a name compounded with that of Ikhnaton. The name in the second cartouche is, however, even more peculiar since it is the first part of the name borne by Nofretiti when she was queen. This circumstance in itself is sufficient to raise certain questions about what was happening in Akhetaton.

The intriguing relief already mentioned as having been found at Akhetaton,[3] and now in Berlin, portrays the two kings seated nude: the one wearing the double crown has his left arm around the other, and is touching his fellow monarch under the chin with his free hand. It is useful to recall here the piece of statuary found by the German expedition to Amarna, called the kissing king, wherein a king, certainly Ikhnaton, is shown kissing a young person.[4] It has been said that the young person concerned is not one of Ikhnaton's daughters, since these little girls are invariably shown wearing the sidelock marking their youth, but is perhaps Smenkhkare. These two works of art, taken together with the change in Smenkhkare's name and the grossly effeminate physical distortions of the statues and reliefs of Ikhnaton with their swollen belly and enlarged thighs, are more than tentative evidence of a homosexual relationship between Ikhnaton and Smenkhkare.[5] This idea cannot be pushed too far, since I do not wish to produce the same sort of thing as the claptrap diagnoses, derived from 3500-year-old statuary and reliefs with grossly exaggerated characteristics, made by various medical practitioners who should know better. (Pl. VIII.)

It is their intimacy which also could suggest as an alternative possibility a father and son relationship between the two men, an idea also supported by the Tell el Amarna letters, but whether this could account for all the peculiarities we have mentioned is open to question. In this connection, however, it should be remembered that very frequently Ikhnaton and Nofretiti were shown nude and with the figures of both similarly distorted.

We do not know precisely how the Egyptians regarded homosexuality. In the story of Horus and Set, it is apparent that the successful seduction of one god by the other gave the seducer power over the seduced. Whether this was the kind of thinking then common, we cannot speculate, but it seems probable that Smenkhkare was either Ikhnaton's son or involved in a homosexual relationship with him.

The graffito in the Tomb of Pere at Thebes shows that Smenkhkare had a temple in the city, and since its author was a member of the Amen priesthood attached to this temple, it is obvious that Smenkhkare had come to terms with the Theban cult. Smenkhkare may himself have visited Thebes in this connection and established residence there, and the form of his name which is used shows that this would have been done during the time he was co-regent. The date of the graffito being the year 3 of his reign, the highest date extant, and it being most likely that he was made co-regent in the latter part of the fourteenth or early part of the fifteenth year of Ikhnaton's reign, it is most probable that Smenkhkare never ruled independently.

That he never did so is confirmed by a wine jar docket discovered by the Egypt Exploration Society's expedition to Amarna in 1932-3. It comes from the seventeenth year of an unnamed king,[6] but this year date has been crossed out and the year one written over it. This would indicate that the year 17 of one reign was succeeded by the year one of another reign. There is no higher date than year 17 in existence for Ikhnaton's rule, nor is there any other king who ruled in the Amarna period whose rule lasted approximately seventeen years. Therefore, the earlier of the reigns concerned here must be that of Ikhnaton. This would mean that Ikhnaton's last year was succeeded by the year one of a new ruler, who was not his co-regent, for in that case the year date would be higher than one. The ruler who succeeded Ikhnaton, then, was Tutankhamen. Smenkhkare, who was co-regent of Ikhnaton for more than two years, must have either predeceased him, been murdered at his death, or been one victim of a successful plot to murder both rulers.

We should, however, pause a moment here to look at an article published by Professor Keith Seele[7] of Chicago in which he claims that Ikhnaton actually ruled twenty-one years. He quotes two ostraca, neither of which he has seen: 'Some Egyptologists, including the Egypt Exploration Society's excavators of Amarna, allow him (Ikhnaton) but seventeen years. However, documents found by them bore, in one case, regnal year 18 and in another year 21. Both of these were discarded by the members of the expedition, owing to their preconceived notions of the chronology of Akenaton's reign. They must be reconsidered and accepted in consideration of such evidence as I am attempting to present in this paper.' Fairman wrote of the first of these ostraca[8]: 'Bennett gives year 18 in the ostracon; the ostracon was not kept but according to a rough facsimile this reading is certainly wrong.' In a conversation with me Fairman amplified his remarks, saying that the ostracon in question did not contain a date of any kind, and that Bennett had simply been mistaken in his translation. As regards the second ostracon Gunn wrote:[9] 'In the absence of other evidence as to the reign extending beyond year 17, no one will want to read the dating . . . as "year 21".' Professor Fairman also discussed this ostracon with me in some detail. This one was not discarded, and is now in the British Museum as item No. 55640. When Seele first delivered this paper Fairman sent for the ostracon and asked Professor Černy's opinion. He declared without hesitation that the date was year 11 and not year 21, but although Fairman then wrote to inform Seele, the article was published without this objection being noted. On publication Fairman again checked the ostracon himself, and asked Černy to look at it again, as well as approaching Mr. Edwards of the British Museum for yet another independent opinion. All read the ostracon as year 11. Fairman wrote again to Seele but there was no reply. I have not myself seen the original, but I am satisfied from the facsimile that the date in question is year 11. Dr. Faulkner also has seen the facsimile, and agrees that the date is certainly year 11. Besides this, the ostracon itself gives further information as to how the date should be read. It continues 'wine of the estate of Nefernefruaton', etc., and that there should be an isolated reference to Nofretiti in an ostracon of a hypothetical year 21 seems highly improbable. These ostraca are the only support for Seele's theory of a twenty-one-year reign for Ikhnaton, and they are certainly not good enough.

There are also supporters for Smenkhkare's having had an independent reign after Ikhnaton's death. In discussing this supposed sole rule Gunter Roeder[4] used as evidence the wall relief of the king with Meritaton in the tomb of Meryre II. If this is from the sole rule of Smenkhkare then the situation is rather peculiar indeed, for though the tomb is one of the latest in the Amarna necropolis, most of the work in it can be dated around the year 12. Still taking Ikhnaton's rule as lasting seventeen years, this relief would then be more than four years later than the rest and perhaps six years. This is possible, but we have already seen that in the graffito from the tomb of Pere (which is dated in the third year of Smenkhkare) the new king's name is compounded with that of Ikhnaton, something which seems strange if he has embarked on his sole rule. Smenkhkare was buried at Thebes, and so must at the time of his death have been exercising power from that place, yet in Meryre II's tomb he is depicted in Amarna rewarding the tomb owner. This would imply that Smenkhkare ruled some time after the graffito was written and that he returned to Amarna for a period before finally going to Thebes. When the docket 'year 17' surcharged 'year 1' is considered this course of action seems improbable.

We have earlier referred to Smenkhkare's change of name, and it helps to elucidate the question of a joint reign. The form (Ankhkheperure) (Smenkhkare Djeserkheperu) is on the Meryre II tomb relief and also—the only place outside Akhetaton where the name Smenkhkare is found—in the probable restoration of the cartouches of the Memphis block, but we also have the variant forms (Ankhkheperure beloved of Uanre) (Nefernefruaton beloved of Ikhnaton) on the fragmentary stele and (Ankhkeperure beloved of Neferkheperure) (Nefernefruaton beloved of Uanre) in the graffito from the tomb of Pere written in Smenkhkare's third regnal year and on the box discovered in the tomb of Tutankhamen.

A piece of gold was found in the coffin with the body thought to be that of Smenkhkare which bears the epithet beloved of Uanre,[10] and this, as well as the age of the corpse at death, was the chief reason for the belief that the body was that of Smenkhkare.[11] The name used at the burial was therefore one of the two allied forms quoted above, and it would be reasonable to assume that the Smenkhkare Djeserkheperu name was the one that he used before he became co-regent and in the earliest period of the co-regency. It is extremely unlikely that he would have used both names interchangeably, or that he would have used a name compounded with that of the unpopular Ikhnaton, had he ruled alone.

The remainder of the pictorial material which Roeder uses to illustrate his hypothesis regarding the sole rule of Smenkhkare is without exception uninscribed, and I do not regard it as useful evidence. However, not only does Roeder categorically declare that some of these examples are Smenkhkare, but he hazards such speculations as that Smenkhkare is shown here in the grip of a wasting illness, or there prematurely aged by disease.[12] The very scanty evidence we have indicates only that Smenkhkare was associated with Ikhnaton in the year 14 to 15, reigned with him two and a fraction years, and died in Thebes either before or at the same time as Ikhnaton.

We can now go on to an analysis of the further evidence which exists to suggest that Smenkhkare either predeceased Ikhnaton, or died practically simultaneously with him.

It has been established from an examination of the mummy of Tutankhamen that he was no more than twenty when he died.[13] The highest year date recorded for his reign is year 9,[14] which indicates that he was eleven at the most at his accession. From this it is apparent that power was in other hands during the early years of the reign and probably throughout. Certainly both Haremhab and Eye held considerable power, and others whose names and titles have not survived were probably also important. The policy of the reign seems to continue the trend established in the co-regency of Smenkhkare, that is, the return to the *status quo* before Ikhnaton. Smenkhkare ended his reign in Thebes, but Tutankhamen began his reign in Amarna, and either lived there or made it his headquarters, without returning to Thebes or changing his name, for some time after his rule began. Still, evidence exists even from this early part of the reign that continuing efforts were made to close the breach between the royal house and the Theban powers. Erman[15] published a relief wherein the king named 'The lord of two lands (Nebkheperure), the lord of diadems, (Tutankhaton) given life forever' is shown offering before Amenre and Mut 'Amen the king of the gods' and Mut 'the lady of heaven the mistress of the gods'. This relief was found in Amarna, but if Smenkhkare had reigned alone, surely the court would have been located near the king. Since he ruled from Thebes, Tutankhamen would have succeeded him there. The fact that Tutankhamen succeeded in Amarna indicates that the major part of the court was there, and not with Smenkhkare in Thebes. The only conditions which could give rise to that situation were that Ikhnaton was still living at Amarna and that the major portion of the court was there with him.

The other indication that Smenkhkare did not outlive Ikhnaton was the manner of his burial.[16] He was buried in an unfinished tomb, which in any case was not of royal quality, with funerary equipment largely not made for him. This suggests a hasty job, for the burial of a pharaoh normally entailed certain ritual ceremonies omitted in this case, and the conclusion is that it was necessary for the Egyptians to get rid of Smenkhkare's corpse in a great hurry. I myself suspect that Smenkhkare's death was not in the course of nature but rather a matter of politics, his disappearance at approximately the same time as Ikhnaton adding weight to the supposition. Perhaps the death of one of the co-regents was the signal for the death of the other, or a successful plot to assassinate both was accomplished.

Smenkhkare appears only once in what might be the crown of Upper or Lower Egypt, or the double crown, and that is on the block found at Memphis where he follows behind a much larger king.[17] The absence of these crowns prevails not only where Smenkhkare is definitely depicted, but also in the uninscribed material which Roeder alleges to show Smenkhkare. This is a small point, but a much more frequent use of the crown of Upper or Lower Egypt, or the double crown would be expected had Smenkhkare really reigned alone.

Roeder finds 'very obscure' the ostracon discovered by the Egypt Exploration Fund expedition which reads 'year one, wine of the house of Smenkhkare deceased',[18] and says 'that Smenkhkare in year one was called deceased is difficult to explain, even if one thinks his reign to be little more than one calendar year in length'.[19] This difficulty could be speedily resolved if Roeder had recognized that, although the estate referred to was that of Smenkhkare it was a mortuary estate and the year one was that of Tutankhamen. It is worth noting that the name (Smenkhkare) is used here once more and the name (Nefernefru-aton beloved of Uanre) is dropped. Both Ikhnaton and Smenkh-kare are shown by this ostracon to be deceased, and once again the latter is called by his original name. As we have already seen, the gold foil fragment from his burial calls him beloved of Uanre, and the retention of this name during his funeral rites is one piece of evidence which could indicate that these occurred during the reign of Ikhnaton and that Smenkhkare therefore died first.

Roeder contends that Smenkhkare's trip to Thebes was a 'personal move which concerned himself only and not the court.'[20] This statement seems to need considerable qualification. Smenkh-kare married the oldest daughter of Ikhnaton and at the same time, or shortly thereafter, was made co-regent. Whether he was appointed by Ikhnaton, or by some one else in control of affairs, it seems sure that Smenkhkare was not a free agent. His trip to Thebes seems a part of the policy of deliberate reconciliation with Thebes on the part of some individual.

We have already reviewed material which on further analysis also clarifies the career of Smenkhkare. We can date his marriage fairly accurately since his future bride still appears in the tomb chamber of her sister Meketaton with the sidelock indicative of childhood,[21] and the date of her sister's death is fixed as subse-quent to year 12 by Meketaton's appearance in the tomb of Meryre II.[22] The wedding must have taken place after this date but before Smenkhkare became co-regent, or at least no later, and his marriage or accession must coincide with the building of his Coronation Hall which dates to year 14 or 15 of Ikhnaton.[23] The sequence of events appears somewhat precipiate. Meritaton was little more than a child at her marriage, and since Smenkhkare was approximately twenty-three at his death, he could have been no more than about twenty on his appointment as co-regent.

It had perhaps become politically essential that he should marry the royal heiress and be raised to the co-regency, and this is confirmed by the fact that his installation coincides with a change of policy towards Amen or the Theban party. We can deduce that the Amen persecution did not begin before the year 12 because the god's name originally appeared on the shrine, certainly commissioned less than three years before, which Ikhnaton probably presented to his mother on her visit to Akhetaton about the year 12: it would also have been unlikely to have begun during the co-regency with Amenhotep III. We can also deduce from the reference to Amen in the graffito of Pere dated to Smenkhkare's third year, which cannot be dated earlier than the late part of year 16 or 17 of Ikhnaton, that the persecution was by then past. This is consistent with Smenkhkare having joined Ikhnaton on the throne in 14 or 15 and initiated a policy of conciliation. Whether the change was accomplished with the co-operation of Ikhnaton we cannot know, but it is a fact that the largest part of the court remained in Akhetaton for some time after Tutankhamen's accession. Smenkhkare's visit to Thebes would seem not to have been of his own volition, and it is doubtful whether he was acting on behalf of Ikhnaton. I myself feel there is ample evidence of some power behind the throne, and that this was so becomes more obvious when, after the end of the joint reign of Ikhnaton and Smenkhkare, a child between nine and eleven years old—Tutankhamen—succeeded.

# TEN: The burial of Smenkhkare?

The so-called tomb of Queen Tiy and its contents, discovered in 1907 in the Valley of the Kings by the T. M. Davis expedition, have been a source of controversy among Egyptologists ever since. The matter has been discussed at great length but even now no conclusion can be drawn with certainty.[1] George Daressy, a French scholar attached to the Egyptian Department of Antiquities, was the first to study the objects after their discovery. Some twenty years later—about 1930—Reginald Engelbach,[2] an Englishman then holding a position at the Cairo Museum, re-studied the items preserved there, and in the very recent past four scholars have written on this burial—Sir Alan Gardiner,[3] Gunther Roeder,[4] H. W. Fairman,[5] Professor of Egyptology at the University of Liverpool, and C. Aldred[6] of the Edinburgh Museum. It is interesting to compare the results of their labours.

Daressy and Aldred think the body is that of Ikhnaton; Engelbach, Roeder and Fairman maintain that the body is that of Smenkhkare; and Gardiner is uncertain of its identity. It seems reasonably certain to me, however, that the remains are those of Smenkhkare, not only because of a piece of gold leaf was found in the coffin bearing the epithet 'beloved of Uanre'—a title which in my opinion appears only in the name of Smenkhkare and nowhere else—but also because the head of the coffin bore the royal uraeus, and in its hands were held the royal sceptres,[7] hence indicating a royal burial. Indeed, the fact of the matter is that Smenkhkare is the only king of the period who could fit the circumstances. Seals of Tutankhamen were found in the tomb[8] so the burial must be of his reign or earlier, and the tomb of Tutankhamen is known. Ikhnaton at the time of his death was in his mid-thirties at least. Thus, only Smenkhkare of the kings of the period remains. This is a most peculiar royal interment, however, for the tomb appears to have been a dump for old mortuary furniture. The inscriptions on the coffin were first changed and later mutilated. The shrine which Ikhnaton had presented to Queen Tiy also found a home in this tomb, as well as four magic bricks inscribed with the name of Ikhnaton, and bearing a most peculiar text inscribed on them in which this Atonist king was called an Osiris.[9] The tomb itself was a small unfinished piece of work.

In the Egyptian religion it was desirable that the successor of a monarch perform the rites at the burial of his deceased predecessor, as Horus for Osiris, and by that symbolic act he became the god and thus helped to establish his title to rule Egypt.[10] It is evident that these rites were not performed for Smenkhkare. Instead of the usual nest of coffins inside a sarcophagus, only one coffin was used. The walls of the tomb were completely uninscribed and the furniture was literally thrown into the place, so hastily was the job done. As well, water had seeped into the tomb, and the coffin and body were also badly damaged by a rock fall from the tomb roof.[11]

The first problem is whether or not this was an original burial in the form in which it was found. Smenkhkare and Ikhnaton died at approximately the same time. The burial of Smenkhkare at Thebes certainly indicates that it was here his death occurred, for had he died at Amarna it would be expected that he should be buried there. Seals with the name Nebkheperure, praenomen of Tutankhamen, were found in the tomb,[12] but since the tomb had been entered and resealed at least once, and probably more often, these seals need not be part of the debris from the original entombment. The discovery of a pit near this tomb, containing a piece of linen dated from the year 6 of Tutankhamen, may well have no connection with it whatever, or refer to a later opening of it than the original burial.[13] As Tutankhamen was not hostile either to the Aton cult or to Ikhnaton himself, and since objects bearing the names of both were found in his tomb,[14] in all probability the damage to the names and figure of Ikhnaton in this tomb was effected after the end of Tutankhamen's reign. The fact that canopic coffins, and perhaps a sepulchral shrine, originally made for Smenkhkare were eventually used for Tutankhamen indicated that those who buried him did not have access to his funerary equipment when it was needed.[15] It is implicitly extremely improbable that the coffinettes containing Smenkhkare's internal organs would have been snatched from his tomb and reused for Tutankhamen, as Fairman[16] suggests. The burial contained material bearing the names of Tiy and Amenhotep III and also Ikhnaton,[17] all of which would have been of some age by this date. All things considered, the funerary equipment appears to be such as could be discovered in storerooms and pressed into emergency use, the inference being that Smenkhkare's burial was accomplished in extreme haste and that those who buried him, unable to get all his funerary equipment which may well have been kept at Amarna, were compelled to entomb him with whatever was at hand.

Some support exists for this view. Since the tomb of Tutankhamen preserves material inscribed with the names of Ikhnaton and Smenkhkare, it is clear that there was no officially expressed hostility in his lifetime to the memory of the two men. Hence, if the burial of Smenkhkare had been transferred from Amarna to Thebes during the reign of Tutankhamen, the funerary equipment prepared for Smenkhkare would have been used. On the other hand, if the burial had been accomplished on the spot in Thebes even hastily, it is doubtful whether it would have been violated by Tutankhamen even to put Smenkhkare's proper equipment into use. Debris from the tombs of Ramesses I, II, III, IX and Sety I was afterwards deposited on top of this tomb area,[18] so the probability is that it was not entered subsequent to the reign of Ramesses I. This fact makes nonsense out of the contention that the burial was mutilated during the Nineteenth Dynasty. Hence the destruction of the name and figure of Ikhnaton must have happened after the reign of Tutankhamen, and before the site was covered with debris, that is, during the reigns of Eye or Haremhab. The kind of material buried with Smenkhkare is not such as would have been restored by the priests of the necropolis some long time after the actual burial if the tomb had been robbed by private parties. In short, the whole burial seems to be contemporary with his death and consistent with the idea that for some reason it was necessary to bury the king so quickly that makeshift funerary equipment had to be found; his own coffin, a funerary shrine of Queen Tiy, four funerary bricks of Ikhnaton which had been made for that king in the early part of his reign when he would not have objected to being called an Osiris, the canopic chest of an unnamed person, and smaller objects bearing Queen Tiy's and Amenhotep III's names. It is noteworthy that, although the tomb was entered and the name and figure of Ikhnaton destroyed, no serious official attempt was made to destroy Smenkhkare's burial except for the mutilation of the gold bands on the mummy and the coffin inscriptions, which may well have occurred incidentally to the removal of the names of Ikhnaton. To sum up, it seems clear that Smenkhkare died at Thebes and was hastily buried, largely without his own funerary equipment, but that the burial was made at a time roughly contemporary with his death and that the equipment found with him was that put in the tomb at the time of the burial. Tomb robbers could have entered the tomb without effecting much damage, however, and certainly at some time before it became inaccessible objects bearing the figure and names of Ikhnaton were attacked by those who hated his memory. The tomb was opened and resealed during the reign of Tutankhamen and probably also later, though the original publication most unfortunately does not make clear the date of these later openings.

It has been contended by Aldred[19] that the bones attributed to Smenkhkare are actually those of Ikhnaton, whose physical condition was so peculiar that his skeleton—even though he was much older—would be in the condition of a man of twenty-five or less. Aldred adds that, if he was so much of a glandular freak as this, he would have been unable to beget children, so another father would have to be found for Nofretiti's children.[20] There is no need to pursue this excursion into fantasy, for anyone contending that this was Ikhnaton's body must first explain its presence in Thebes, in a miserable uninscribed little tomb, when there is no suggestion that Tutankhamen hated his father-in-law. Since material of Tutankhamen occurs among the debris, it is evident that the burial was in the tomb from the time of his reign, and had not been transferred to this small crypt from somewhere else by Ikhnaton's enemies. Aldred's further assertion that Tiy also was buried in this tomb and later removed because Ikhnaton was unworthy to lie with her is equally fantastic,[21] for the long-lived Tiy would assuredly have had a properly inscribed tomb all ready prepared for her burial.

# ELEVEN: Tutankhamen and Eye

From evidence already discussed we can conclude that Tutankhamen was a member of the royal house of the Eighteenth Dynasty. This is also indicated by two of his inscriptions, restoring monuments of Amenhotep III and Thutmose IV, in which he calls the first his 'father' and claims the second also as an ancestor. Whether he was a son of Ikhnaton cannot be determined, and although this may be the most likely solution, the age of his body at death—about twenty years, would not completely preclude his being a son of Amenhotep III, if (as I think certain) Smenkhkare did not have an independent reign.

It was the discovery of Tutankhamen's virtually unrobbed tomb shortly after the end of the First World War which aroused an unprecedented thrill of interest in Egyptology throughout the world, an interest that has regrettably lapsed over the years. The expedition was jointly led by Howard Carter and Lord Carnarvon. Unfortunately, despite the world-wide publicity given to the finds they have never been properly published and to this day Carter's almost journalistic account remains the sole significant source. The present condition of the objects found is at the moment unknown: some of the smaller pieces are even said to have vanished and it has been suggested that the solid gold coffin of Tutankhamen be melted down to realise its intrinsic value.

The treasures of the burial were legion. From the data they provided much of the life of the time might well have been reconstructed. There was a great deal of gold work, and the coffin itself, besides its value as precious metal, was an extremely beautiful work of art, and the gold and enamel funeral mask covering the head of the king's mummy was a masterpiece. Everything needed for setting up house in the next world was here, including quantities of furniture of all kinds, among which were some magnificent throne chairs.

Little beyond what has already been told is known of the reign of Tutankhamen, but it is important to note that he (or his sponsors) was no fanatical Atonist. A stele from Akhetaton now in the Berlin Museum shows him, though named as Tutankhaton, worshipping Amen, and we also have an ingenious little ring of his on which either of his two names, depending as they do on a change of one sign only, can be read: a 'mn' sign for

Tutankha*men* and ⌓ 't' sign for Tutankha*ton* are placed side by side.[1] Nevertheless, for one reason or another, about the middle of his reign Tutankhamen dropped his Aton name altogether and returned his court to Thebes.

During the latter part of his reign a good deal of building was apparently carried out, not only in the Theban area but in Nubia and Memphis. Later his name was deleted on these structures in favour of Haremhab's, his successor after the brief intervening reign of Eye, or else the buildings were demolished. Why this happened we have no idea, but it was not due to personal animus against the dead king for his tomb was protected and his burial left undisturbed. Eye, who called himself (Kheperkheperure, the doer of right) (The god's fàther, Eye, the divine king of Wast), undoubtedly succeeded after Tutankhamen's wife Ankhsenamen's short period of sole rule.[2] He is evidently the same person as the owner of the large tomb in the Akhetaton necropolis, wherein the great Aton hymn is inscribed. The tomb also tells us that his wife's name was Tiy, but a ring bearing his cartouche joined with that of Ankhsenamen,[3] the wife of Tutankhamen, shows that he married her, too, after her husband's death. On grounds to be discussed later we may assume that this was a forced marriage.

The highest date of Eye's reign of which we have record is the fourth regnal year[4] on a stele, and Haremhab's succession probably followed soon after. On this stele the name of the god Wepwawet is written over the disc of the Aton and the name of that god, so we may conclude that the Aton cult continued to have some patronage during Eye's reign.

We have just seen that Haremhab removed Tutankhamen's name from monuments and substituted his own, but left his predecessor's burial intact. In contrast, his treatment of Eye was savage. He refused him burial, took for himself the tomb his predecessor had been preparing in Thebes (thus denying him all hope of an afterlife), erased his name wherever it appeared, and appropriated for his own use the mortuary temple which Eye had been building for his own funerary cult. All points to the throne having changed hands by force in this case, but the sketchy outline I have given underlines how little we know of the reigns of either Tutankhamen or Eye.

# PART THREE

# The origin, nature and distribution of the Aton cult

*The royal family worship the Aton*

# ONE: The background

Until recently most scholars were very reluctant to admit that the Aton cult had any real historical background before the reign of Ikhnaton. An article of Marianne and Jean Doresse[1] in 1941–2 was the first discussion in detail of the history of the cult, and even today there is no study of the surviving traces of the Aton cult after the Amarna period, or of the extent of its distribution throughout Egypt during that period.

At one time it was thought to have links with western Asia and particularly with the Mitannian sun cult, but there was no definite supporting evidence from either inside or outside Egypt, except rather improbable theories about the Asiatic ancestry of Queen Tiy or Nofretiti. Queen Tiy's father is alleged to have been a western Asiatic[2] on no evidence whatever, and Nofretiti has been thought to be the Mitannian princess sent by Tushratta to Amenhotep III shortly before the latter's death.[3] Mitannian, Babylonian and other princesses were taken in marriage by the king of Egypt, but such alliances would probably be political, the ladies having little influence with their husband.

Moreover, neither the nature nor the literature of the cult shows signs of foreign elements. It is true that the word 'Adon' in Hebrew meant 'lord' but such a comparison is of very little value since Hebrew appears as a literary language long after this period, and even parallels between the Aton hymns and Hebrew religious literature may well be the result of Egyptian influence on the Hebrews whose familiarity with the older culture[4] is known.

It is enough to say here that the word Aton has an eminently respectable Egyptian history going back at least to the Middle Kingdom,[5] and to mention that the title of the Amarna high priest 'greatest of seers' is borne also by the high priests of Re at Heliopolis and at Southern On, whether the latter be identified with Hermonthis or Thebes.[6] It is interesting, also, that the name of the Aton in its early form in Ikhnaton's reign is compounded with that of Re Harakhte. The Aton temple as preserved at Amarna and in pictorial form in the necropolis there is similar in appearance and structure to the sun temples of older times,[7] and the sun hymns of the Aton are very similar to older sun hymns.[8] The house of the benben (shrine) of the Aton temples in Amarna and Thebes is parallel to similar structures in sun temples. The Mnevis bull was held sacred at Amarna as it was in Heliopolis.[9] It is also worth mention that the fanaticism of the Aton cult was not directed against the solar gods. Worship of the Aton was closely connected with, if not an offshoot from, that of Re.

From the earliest to the latest times there was a particular link between the monarch and the Re cult, the kings almost invariably compounding their praenomen with Re, and the cult figuring to a large extent in the royal burial rites. In the Fifth Dynasty it became pre-eminent throughout Egypt, a pre-eminence to some extent lost by the start of the Middle Kingdom, but still leaving the cult a very powerful church. The Amen cult, perhaps wishing to take advantage of this established reputation, made a syncretic identification between Amen and Re, and Amen is very frequently called Amen-Re. Which cult derived the most benefit from this association is not clear. The Amen priesthood may have regarded the connection as necessary, because of the particular attachment of the king to the Re cult, which manifested itself especially in the Atonist fanaticism under Ikhnaton, but it may well have been a factor in royal policy since the beginning of the dynasty, either because of the close connection of the Re cult with the burial ritual, or as a means of fostering the interests of the king in Lower Egypt where it was the most important church.

It is possible to trace the god Aton back to the Middle Kingdom. References exist from the early Eighteenth Dynasty, but as yet no monuments have been discovered which are connected directly or indirectly with the Aton church apparatus before the reign of Amenhotep III. It is arguable that if the Aton cult were the private religion of the monarch, as it appears to have been at the time of Ikhnaton, references to it would not need to be very numerous. In addition, both Amenhotep II and Thutmose IV had close connections with Lower Egypt, Amenhotep II having been born there[10] and Thutmose IV recording on the 'Dream Stele' a prophecy received while he was living in Lower Egypt that he would be king.[11]

It is certainly conceivable, if not probable, that the kings might have played one cult against another, but this idea can be overworked since all the kings concerned constructed portions of

Karnak, and Amenhotep III probably constructed more buildings in honour of Amen than any previous king.

On balance, it would seem that the fanaticism of Ikhnaton resulted more from a disordered brain than policy. The Egyptian king was always considered a god and an incarnation of god, but it is worth considering whether Ikhnaton might not have taken this idea literally where other more stable monarchs took it figuratively. In other words, he identified himself with the Aton whose high priest he became at the beginning of his reign,[12] considering himself Egypt's paramount god, and attempted to destroy the worship of all the gods except those connected with Aton (that is himself).[13] If all the data were available it might prove that too much emphasis has been given to his destruction of the name of Amen. He made an effort to destroy the names of other gods than the Theban Triad, Amen, Mut and Khonsu, and these may only have received the most attention because Thebes was a most important centre, because a relatively large number of Amen buildings have survived from this period, and because the Amen cult was probably, except for that of Re, the most powerful in Egypt. We have also seen that Ikhnaton did not destroy the names of the gods over a long period of time, such a policy only being put into practice over a two-year period, from the death of Amenhotep III until the elevation of Smenkh-kare as co-regent.

To see the end of the Amarna period as the triumph of the Amen cult is a mistake, for the Amarna period was a complete disaster not only for the Amen cult but for Thebes. Never again did the city enjoy the position which it had held until the reign of Ikhnaton. Where Tutankhamen (for the latter part of his reign) and Eye made their headquarters is not definitely known. Haremhab, the so-called violent proponent of Amen, probably spent much of his time in Lower Egypt, and the Nineteenth Dynasty which succeeded him seemed to regard Thebes as no more than a religious centre. From this I venture to argue that the role of the Amen cult in this situation may have been over-emphasised. The Amarna revolt was neither against the power of the Amen priesthood nor against Thebes, and its end was no triumph for either.

# TWO: The inscriptional evidence

Surviving references to the Aton are not common from the Middle Kingdom, *circa* 2000 to 1750 B.C., however, the passage from the beginning of the story of Sinuhe makes it almost sure that reference is made to a god and not to the physical sun. The Twelfth Dynasty manuscript reads: 'As for King (Sehetepibre) he went up to heaven, being joined with Aton, the body of the god being united with him who made him.'[1]

In the Middle Kingdom version of the tale of a prince in exile the word Aton possesses no god determinative but, as far as I am concerned, the sense of the sentence is absolutely convincing, especially as there is no other god name present to which the participial form 'who made' could refer. It is obvious that the Egyptians themselves believed that this reference was to a god since in the later Ramesside versions of the story the scribes used the divine determinative, and two of the later versions enclose the name of the Aton in a cartouche.[2]

References to the divinity of the Aton occur in texts throughout the Eighteenth Dynasty, the phrase 'that which the Aton encircles' being used repeatedly. Sometimes the hieroglyph indicating that the preceding word is the name of a god—the divine determinative—appears and sometimes it does not, but its use shows that it is the god which is spoken of rather than the sun's disc.

In a stele found in front of the eighth pylon of the Karnak temple at Thebes which dates from the time of Ahmose, the first king of the Eighteenth Dynasty, there is a reference: 'He has ruled what the Aton encircled',[3] in which the divine determinative is not used. Later in the same inscription, however, this passage occurs: 'He [the king] is seen like Re when he rises, like the shining Aton, like the appearing of Khepry in the eyes, his rays are in faces like Atum in the west of the heavens.'[4] The reference in this passage must surely be to a god, despite the absence of the divine determinative, since it occurs in a section sandwiched in between the names of other solar gods, all of which do have the divine determinative. It seems to me that either all of these names must refer to the physical sun, and this is precluded by most of these names being followed by the divine determinative, or they must all be the names of gods, which is supported by the occurrence of this short passage within a much longer section comparing the king with divinities.

A similar expression to that which occurs in the quoted section of Sinuhe appears in the biographical inscription of Ineni in his tomb. Although this man lived on into the joint reign of Thutmose III and Hatshepsut, there is a reference to the death of Amenhotep I: 'Having gone forth to heaven he joined the Aton,'[5] which would be illogical if the physical disc of the sun were meant. A parallel expression referring to the death of Thutmose II reads: 'Having gone forth to heaven he has joined with the gods,'[6] and adds weight to the previous argument.

There are also references to the Aton from the reign of Thutmose I. In the rock-cut stele from the second regnal year of this king carved near the third cataract of the Nile, is the following passage: 'He appears as chief of the two lands to rule that which the Aton has encircled.'[7]

Here nothing is left to the imagination, for the name of the Aton is provided with a divine determinative, and the reference occurs in a section where the names of other gods are mentioned.

In an inscription from the time of Hatshepsut a speech is put into the mouth of Thutmose I in which, among other things, he thanks Amen for the accession of Hatshepsut. It is on the northern façade of the eighth pylon in the Karnak temple, and begins: 'The Horus (strong bull, beloved of Maat) sharp of horns, going forth as the Aton.'[8] The word Aton has not the divine determinative, but any other translation would seem quite inappropriate.

In the Punt expedition inscription of this reign from Deir el Bahri occurs another example of the use of the word Aton to signify the deity: 'Hail to thee sovereign of Ta Meri [Egypt], Female Re who shines like the Aton,'[9] and in the same inscription a speech of Amen contains the reference: 'He [Amen] has given to her [Hatshepsut] what the Aton encircles and what Geb and Nut enclose.'[10] Here again, though the word Aton is not followed by the divine determinative, it is joined with the names of other gods in a parallel expression. Significant also is the later remark, again from a speech of Amen: 'While heaven exists you [Hatshepsut] shall exist before me [Amen]. Your lifetime shall be like the Aton in its [heaven],'[11] which would seem, in view of the other examples, to be a stock expression referring to the deity.

Again from the reign of Hatshepsut, from the private tomb of a man called Ahmose, Sethe has restored a passage in a funerary text, referring to the death of the owner of the tomb, which is exactly parallel to another in the grave of one Sennofry: 'Going forth from upon earth to see the Aton.'[12] Also, though the word Aton does not possess the divine determinative, it would be strange to think of the physical sun in such a context.

Another private inscription of a provincial governor of Thinis from this reign reads: 'You shall see Re in the course of every day. Thy face shall see the Aton when he rises. and one shall put for you an offering loaf in On.'[13] The word Re has the divine determinative, the word Aton has not, yet any interpretation which accepted only the word Re as referring to a god would seem unjustified. The reference to On (Heliopolis) seems to make the parallel certain.

From the reign of Thutmose III an inscription from Semna reads: 'They [various gods] shall cause your [King Thutmose III] stability to be like the stability of the heavens, your lifetime like the Aton in it.'[14] This appears to be a definite personification of Aton, again without a divine determinative. An inscription to similar effect from Karnak reads: 'Thy monuments shall be established like the heaven, thy lifetime like the Aton in them.'[15]

In a stele from Sinai of his twenty-fifth year, Thutmose III adds a reference which can scarcely be taken otherwise than showing the divinity of Aton: epithets applied to the king are: 'King of kings, ruler of rulers, Aton of all lands, the son of Re (Thutmose beautiful of forms).'[16] A personification seems required in this context, and the translation of the term as 'the sun disc' without any idea of divinity would seem wrong.

In the tomb of Amenemhab, an officer of Thutmose III, the king's death is mentioned as follows: 'He [the king] went up to heaven, joined with the Aton, the body of the god [king] united with him who made him.'[17] This reference, identical to Sinuhe and parallel to the use in Ineni, leaves no doubt that the Aton was felt

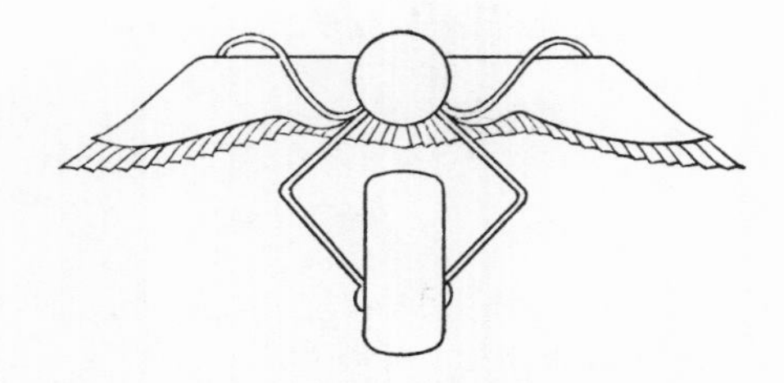

to be a god. On a broken granite statue of Minnacht, an official of this reign, the phrase: 'He may go in and out of his mansion to see the Aton of the day.'[18]

in which the word Aton possesses the divine determinative, leaves no doubt that a divinity is named.

In the reign of Amenhotep II such phrases as 'that which the Aton encircles' and 'that which the Aton illumines' are not infrequent. The divine determinative is usually lacking, but there is one example, in the duplicate of the Amada stele of Amenhotep II from Elephantine, that does possess a divine determinative, though the Amada copy itself does not: 'One with him [Amen] to rule that which the Aton has encircled.'[19]

This example, like the one from the reign of Thutmose I, shows that in these stereotyped phrases the word Aton refers not to the physical sun but to the god.

On the stele of the scribe of the treasury, Minhotep, there is the following passage: 'May they give bread, water, breath, the sight of Aton, the adoration of Re when he rises.'[20]

Other material from the reign of Amenhotep II is very interesting. Selim Hassan, an Egyptian scholar, has published[21] a small stele found in the mud brick temple at Gizeh near Cairo as a companion piece to the 'sphinx' stele of Amenhotep II. It is topped with a representation of the winged solar disc in the form of Horus of Behdet with a pair of human hands and arms holding a cartouche. The latter appeared to contain the Thoth sign,[22] and thus the object is probably a memorial set up by Amenhotep II for his father Thutmose III, or Thutmose IV for his father Amenhotep II, depending on how it is read. There seems little doubt that this figure, drawn above, is an ancestor of the Aton emblem, and it is worth noting that, although the Atonists had erased divine names throughout the stele, they left untouched the figure of the disc.

The references in the body of the stele are largely to Horus, but in line eight of the text the following passage occurs: 'All the gods are in possession of [lit. under] love of him whom [Amen] has promoted himself as chieftain of what his eye encircles and what the Aton illumines every day.'[23] Also important evidence are the stamped bricks found near the Sphinx in a surrounding wall by Ahmed Bey Kamal.[24] The stamp is in the form of two cartouches, one containing the name of king Amenhotep II in the form (Aakheperure) and the other being inscribed with first the sun sign and then 'splendour, (*tḥn*) wine of the western river' ( ). This is an unprecedented piece of material. The presence of a cartouche around a king's name or around the word '*ḥḳꜣ* sovereign' is well known, but the presence of a cartouche around the above words is strange. In Ikhnaton's reign, however, the name of the Aton is almost invariably written within a cartouche. It is also certain that in the reign of Amenhotep III the phrase, the sun sign plus the word '*tḥn*' means 'the splendour of Aton', whether the word Aton is written out or whether only the sun disc is shown.[25] The presence of the cartouche around an epithet, plentifully familiar from the reign of Amenhotep III as referring to the Aton, strongly suggests that here, too, the word should be read Aton. Moreover, Hays mentions a wine jar docket from the Malqatta palace of Amenhotep III inscribed: 'Wine of the house of Nebmaatre is the splendour (*tḥn*) of Aton.'[26]

From the reign of Thutmose IV an increasing amount of Aton material would be expected, but not many relevant pieces of evidence are extant. However, one extremely important document does survive, a scarab with the inscription: 'The princes of Naharin bearing their gifts behold (Menkheperure) (Thutmose IV) as he comes forth from the palace. They hear his voice like that of the son of Nut, his bow in his hand, like the son of Isis. If he arouses himself to fight with the Aton before him he destroys the mountains, trampling down the foreign lands, treading unto Naharin and unto Karoy in order to bring the inhabitants of foreign lands like subjects to the rule of the Aton forever.'[27]

There are also other indications that the reign of Thutmose IV was important in the history of the Aton cult. Like Amenhotep III, he had an establishment in Akhetaton,[28] which was, unlike the properties belonging to Amenhotep III in that city, within the Aton temple itself. Thutmose IV is mentioned on a badly broken portion of the earlier recension of the Amarna boundary stele.[29] Such things as the fact that the shawabtis of Thutmose IV bore no magical texts[29] and that the art of his reign on some occasions seems to foreshadow the Amarna style may perhaps also bear weight though this kind of evidence cannot be trusted very far.

From a private stele found by Petrie at Sedment near Lahun, dated to the reign of Thutmose IV or early in the reign of Amenhotep III, comes the following: 'You see the Aton in [its] daily course. Your face sees Amen when he rises.'[30] Here the word Aton possesses the divine determinative, but the word Amen does not, though in this passage both Aton and Amen are certainly conceived as solar deities.

On a kneeling statue of a viceroy of Kush, Amenhotep, of this reign we find 'Adoring Re when he rises seeing the Aton in the course of every day.'[31] This passage from the tomb of Tnuna, an official who lived from the reign of Thutmose III until that of Thutmose IV, is also interesting: 'The prince, the count, the unique companion, greatly beloved, the two eyes of the king of Upper Egypt, the two ears of the king of Lower Egypt, the one who is in the mind of the good god, who enters in unto his lord the holy one in the palace, who sees the Aton on his *horizon* from time to time.'[32] The word '*ꜣḫt*' horizon, which is used here connected with the word Aton, is the earliest juxtaposition of these two words so commonly used in the same expression during the Amarna period, for example in the official name of the God.

The material from the reign of Amenhotep III is copious and important. Probably the most significant object is a block now in the Berlin museum which was built into a pylon of Haremhab at Karnak,[33] on which a king is depicted offering to the Aton. The Aton on this occasion is shown as a falcon-headed man over whose head is the sun's disc. The name of the god is 'Horus of the horizon who rejoices on the horizon in his name of Shu who is in the Aton'. The name of the king now apparent in the cartouche is (Neferkheperure Uanre) but Borchardt observed that this cartouche has been altered and underneath was the name of Amenhotep III, presumably the praenomen (Nebmaatre). The importance of this, when it was the only evidence indicating that a temple dedicated to the Aton existed in Thebes during the reign of Amenhotep III, was paramount, but much more material has since come to light.

This includes a passage from a rock stele of Amenhotep III on the road from Philae to Assuan, near Mahatta: 'You shall have the kingship of Re in heaven, thy lifetime [shall be] like the Aton in it.'[34] Other passages mentioning the Aton occur in the dedication inscription of Amenhotep III of the Montu temple at Karnak: 'Whom Amen has placed upon his throne to rule what the Aton encircles, the throne of Set, the office of Atum, the kingship of Re Khepri,'[35] and 'Divine king, the likeness of Re who illumines the two lands like [the one of] the two horizons, the lord of rays in the face like the Aton, everyone rejoices for him.'[36] In this latter quotation there is a divine determinative after '[the one of] the two horizons', and 'Re' but not after 'the Aton'. An architrave from the temple of Luxor is inscribed: 'The son of Amen born of heaven to rule what the Aton encircles,'[37] and later in the same inscription is a cartouche of the king in the form: '(Nebmaatre, the splendour of Aton).'[38]

On a commemorative scarab Amenhotep III calls the royal barge the splendour of Aton, the word Aton being written out fully,[39] and the inscription from the great scarab at Karnak includes the words: 'While you are lord of what the Aton illumines.'[40] One of the jackal statues from the mortuary temple there bears the words: 'The good god, image of Re, the splendid of face, who appears like the Aton,'[41] and one of the Sekhmet statues also from Karnak has the name of the god as: 'Sekhmet the Aton.'[42] Stock phrases, such as 'that which the Aton encircles' or 'illumines', occur not infrequently in the inscriptions of this reign, and naturally not all of them have been noted here.

The private inscriptions of the courtiers of Amenhotep III also make frequent reference to the Aton. On a statue of Amenhotep the son of Hapu, is the following: 'May you see Horus beautiful of face, Thoth with Maat upon his hands. May you see the Aton when he shines upon the mountains. May his rays lighten your cavern, his form be upon your breast.'[43] The inclusion of the name of Aton with these other god names would make the translation 'sun disc' incorrect. A passage from another inscribed statue of the same man reads: 'O Egypt, every eye has seen the Aton, which has come northward or southward to Thebes to pray to the lord of the gods,'[44] which is of great interest, since the Aton seems here to be equated to the lord of the gods. A fragment from still another of this man's statues has inscribed on it: 'Who sees the living Aton' or 'Who sees the Aton—the eye.'[45]

The tomb of the overseer of the double granary, Khaemhat, has a most important Atonist inscription in it as follows: 'O thou Aton, lord of rays who rises on the horizon of Re Atum mayst thou shine in the face of' (the deceased's names and titles).[46] A statuette of the standard bearer Kamesu, now in the British Museum, also has an interesting twice-repeated inscription: 'The standard bearer of the regiment of (Nebmaatre is the splendour of Aton).'[47] on the first occasion the word Aton is written out and in the second only the sun's disc is written.

On a graffito of a Nubian official the following extremely important inscription appears: 'The second prophet of Amen the servant of Aton son of Pa-Re Parennefer.'[48]

Here also there can be no doubt that a god is meant, and in this case, too, the name Aton has the divine determinative while the name Amen lacks it.

In the stele of the overseers of works Hery and Shuty mention of the Aton is not infrequent, 'Greetings O Aton of the day,'[49] is one example.

The incomplete tomb of a man called Nefersekheru, an 'overseer of the house of the estate of Nebmaatre is the splendour of the Aton', of which only the façade remains is also very important, in view of the title of this official.[50] Tomb number 46 at Thebes of a man called Ramose whose function was 'overseer of the house in the mansion of the Aton' dates from this reign or earlier.[51] It should not be overlooked that both these men also bore titles as officials of the Amen cult: Nefersekheru was overseer of the cattle of Amen,[52] and overseer of the double granary of Amen, and Ramose was the chief priest of Amen in Menset.[51] Legrain, a French scholar of the beginning of the century, notes[53] the coffin of a man called Hatay from Gurnah which he says by the text and the style of the piece was definitely early Eighteenth Dynasty: its owner was a 'scribe of the overseer of the double granary of the mansion of the Aton', but on his coffin, however, he does not invoke the Aton, but rather the usual funerary gods and spirits.

Bouriant, another French Egyptologist, noted[54] that the Museum of Boulaq possessed three or four funerary steles of various persons who qualified as priests of the Aton, and claimed them as pre-Amarna, a dating confirmed by their style and the frequent presence of the name of Osiris. These steles came from Sakkara, and Bouriant concluded that there existed a temple of the Aton in Memphis before the reign of Ikhnaton.

There is a scarab of Amenhotep III on which is inscribed: '(Nebmaatre) appearing like the Aton.'[55]

Legrain described some canopic jar fragments[56] which were put on sale in Luxor, and were apparently the spoils of illicit excavation in the Valley of the Queens. The use in the Atonist inscriptions of the epithet 'Tehen Aton', which does not occur later than the reign of Amenhotep III, means they date to his period or earlier, and their owners were all 'royal concubines.[56]' Examples 17 and 26 to 29 are of a (royal hairdresser=concubine) of 'Tehen Aton the great,'; examples 19 and 23 refer to 'the house [or estate] of Tehen Aton,' and 24 to the 'house [or estate] of Aton'; and example 21 mentions the 'city of Tehen Aton'.

The work of W. C. Hayes of the Metropolitan Museum of New York at the Malqatta palace at Thebes of Amenhotep III has added to the knowledge of the period considerably. It seems that supplies for the first Sed festival of Amenhotep III were drawn from 'the estate of (Nebmaatre) life, prosperity and health is the splendour of Aton' (this name occurs twenty-five times),[57] 'the estate of (Amenhotep) life prosperity and health is the splendour of Aton' (this name occurs once),[57] and 'the estate of the splendour of Aton' (this name occurs fifteen times).[57] Hayes believes, in all probability correctly, that the first of these names was that of Malqatta palace area, which was changed in the later period to 'the house of rejoicing.'[58] Lacau has published three stela of officials of this area, as Hayes notes, 'A guardian of Tehen Aton', 'a guardian of the storeroom of donations of Tehen Aton', and 'a scribe of Tehen Aton'. They are apparently not the same as those described by Bouriant,[59] and referred to earlier, since these stela evidently come from Thebes. This palace name of Amenhotep III makes it evident that the officials of Tehen Aton were connected with a palace complex and not with an Aton temple, except in the case of Ramose of tomb 46 at Gurna, where the use of the word '*ḥwt* mansion' makes it clear that he was an actual temple official. In view of the co-regency the presence of the name of Tehen Aton applied to a palace complex certainly makes it very highly probable that an Aton temple was involved in this case also.

It might also be noted that in the Nubian temple of Kawa, which we shall discuss again later, the only thing that the excavators could find in the way of foundation deposit was a large scarab of Amenhotep III. This place was known as Pergematon as late as the time of the Nubian kings. No blocks survive, however, from the reign of Ikhnaton and the earliest structure on the site of which traces remain is from the time of Tutankhamen.[60]

The Book of the Dead also makes reference to the Aton in the Eighteenth Dynasty papyri. The following passages come from the papyrus of Nebseni: 'O thou who is in his egg who shines as his Aton who rises on his horizon of gold of Re',[61] 'my hair is that of Nut, my face is that of the Aton, my eyes are those of Hathor, my ears are those of Wepwawet, etc.',[62] and, 'He sees the Aton, he rejoices in the presence of the great God, he is Shu who is in eternity.'[63] In all these the word 'Aton' has the divine determinative. I have taken my example from Nebseni because this papyrus is pre-Amarna,[64] but in the later papyri of the Book of the Dead more frequent mentions of the Aton occur.

# THREE: Interpretation of the inscriptions

Does the evidence of the preceding chapter prove that Aton worship had a history as least as long as the Eighteenth Dynasty? To my mind it does.

It is also logical that the cult should have such a history, for no religious innovator begins his development *ex nihilo*. Christ built on the foundation of Judaism, and Mohammed drew from both Christianity and Judaism. Yet, it is constantly said of Ikhnaton that he transformed the religion of his country single-handed into what was much like a monotheism, and created the Aton cult by his own efforts. Such thinking only indicates the prejudgments of the scholars concerned, and it seemed to me that what had occurred was less original, and that it should be possible to trace the Aton cult back from reign to reign for some time before Ikhnaton.

It is evident that the word Aton, like the word Re, meant various things, and had a secular as well as a divine use. It is not suggested that every example of the use of the word should be taken as a god name, and I have gathered here by no means all the examples, leaving out both definite references to the disc of the sun, and those which seem very ambiguous in their reference, as well as repetitions of stock formulae. Also omitted are such tombs as those of Heruef and the vizier Ramose in which both Amenhotep III and Ikhnaton appear.

One of the problems which immediately stands out in a study of the quotations I have given in the text, is the use of the divine determinative. Five of the examples above noted from the inscriptions of kings or private persons show the word Aton with the divine determinative, a single hieroglyph of a god or a divine symbol, indicating that the previous word is to be read as the name of a God. The three examples from the Book of the Dead are determined in the same fashion. In the example from Sinuhe the divine determinative is not used in the Middle Kingdom text, but all the Rammeside texts in which the passage is extant show it, and two of them also show the cartouche. The Egyptians were never consistent, and it was used or not, like most other determinatives, at the whim of the scribe. After the Nineteenth Dynasty, however, the use of such determinatives multiplied, and signs which were void of meaning appeared in words frequently, and certain letters, 𓏏 't' and 𓏲 or 𓅱 'w' especially, were inserted in numerous places where they were not pronounced. The divine determinative also was sprinkled freely where it had no real significance. This practice had, however, not really started in the Eighteenth Dynasty, and at that time, the divine determinative was often left out where it should have been used. The names of Amen Re, Ptah, Osiris and so on, are frequently left undetermined, so that at least for this period, the absence of the divine determinative is no indication that a god is not mentioned. If it is present, however, it seems that a reference to a god is definitely intended, and this is especially true of the period previous to the Amarna schism.

The Middle Kingdom example of the use of the word Aton in the text of Sinuhe is exactly paralleled by two inscriptions of the Eighteenth Dynasty, and a third example substitutes the word 'gods' for 'Aton'. The phrase concerned is certainly a routine convention in texts mentioning the death of a king, for it would not otherwise reappear in the same context in the relatively small number of texts preserved over a four-hundred-year period, and the substitution, where one would expect a word of equivalent meaning, shows that the phrase was a recognized idiom used on such occasions and is in itself strong ground for the conclusion that the Aton was itself a god. This is confirmed when the Ramesside scribes responsible for recopying the text of Sinuhe in a more up-to-date 'spelling' chose to insert in the two cases where the MS is intact a divine determinative after the word Aton, and in two other cases, one fully preserved and the other broken away after the beginning of the word, added also a cartouche.

Other examples name the Aton in a parallel sequence to the names of other gods, and the cumulative effect is unmistakable.

The reference from the reign of Ahmose names Re, Aton, Khepry, and Atum in parallel epithets of the king, and further epithets in the same section of the inscription compare the king to other gods. The reference from the Punt expedition of Hatshepsut calls her a 'female Re who shines like the Aton', another reference from the same reign declares that Amen gives to the Queen 'what the Aton encircles and what Geb and Nut enclose'. A private text of a Thinite nomarch of this reign notes: 'You shall see Re . . . thy face shall see the Aton . . . and one shall put for you an offering loaf in On.' Epithets of Thutmose IV put the Aton in parallel before the 'son of Re' expression 'king of kings, ruler of rulers, Aton of all lands, son of Re, etc. (Thutmose beautiful of forms)'. A private funerary inscription of the reign of Amenhotep II has the expression 'the sight of Aton, the adoration of Re when he rises'. From the period close to the accession of Amenhotep III comes the phrase from the Sedment stele: 'You see the Aton . . . your face sees Amen. . . .' In an inscription of Amenhotep III appears 'to rule, what the Aton encircles, the throne of Geb, the office of Atum, the Kingship of Khepri.' In the comparison of members of the body with the gods text from the Book of the Dead of Nebseni the words occur 'my hair . . . Nut, my face . . . the Aton, my eyes . . . Hathor, my ears . . . Wepwawet'.

It seems to me that any translation which, in these series of parallel phrases, translates the rest of the divine names as gods and singles out the Aton for rendering as 'the disc', ignores the repeatedly revealed fondness of Egyptians for such parallelism in their hieroglyphic texts. Yet other examples use the name of the Aton in stock expressions in which the name of another god is sometimes found, for example the four-times-used, 'Your lifetime shall be like the Aton in it'; and 'who sees the Aton in his horizon from time to time' which recalls similar expressions wherein the name of Horus appears. And on one occasion, in the tomb of Khaemhat, a prayer is addressed to the Aton.

The evidence forces the conclusion that the Aton was considered a divinity from the beginning of the New Kingdom, and perhaps earlier.

It is apparent from the early Aton inscriptions of Ikhnaton that the god Re Harakhte[1] was very closely bound up with his version of Atonism, but the connection of the two gods can be traced back into the reign of Amenhotep III. The block on which the name of Amenhotep III originally appeared, showing a king offering to a deity in the form of a falcon-headed man, bore the name 'Horus of the horizon who rejoices on the horizon in his name of Shu who is in the Aton', almost identical to that used under Ikhnaton. This is an isolated example of such close association of Re Harakte and the Aton in the pre-Amarna period, but association of the Aton with the other solar gods is frequent, though what kind of a relationship existed among the solar cults, or whether all the solar divinities were part of one large church centred at Heliopolis cannot be discerned.

The nature of Egyptian religion is something western scholars can appreciate only with the most extreme difficulty, if at all. This can best be illustrated by an analogy. Let us suppose that at some time long after this age has become history, and with the advance of time, this western culture and all that which appertains to it has passed so far into the past that of its written records only the smallest fragments remain. If at such a time it should become the task of historical scholars to reconstruct, for example, Roman Catholicism, the most ritualistic form of Christian religion, totally from the external remains, and such fragments of written material as the chance of the centuries has spared, having lost all knowledge of, or feeling for, the inward nature of the belief, would it not be that these people might produce an intellectual reconstruction fearfully similar to our ideas of Egyptian religion? It is with this thought in mind that I do not attempt to deal with the beliefs of this religious system, recognising the limits of the material.

# FOUR: The priests and the king

Many of the remarks which M. and Mme Doresse make with regard to the political history of the Aton cult seem difficult to justify. For them the high priests of Amen were the moving spirits in all the intrigues of Egyptian internal history from the death of Amenhotep I to the accession of Amenhotep III. The high priests, they believe, deposed Thutmose I in favour of Queen Hatshepsut and Thutmose II, and Thutmose II in favour of Thutmose III, and this caused the successors of Thutmose III to make overtures to the Theban sun clergy and the Heliopolitan priesthood. They then list a number of approaches to Heliopolis and Lower Egypt on the part of Amenhotep II and Thutmose IV.[1]

Entirely apart from any bearing this may have on pre-Amarna Atonism, I should like to point out that the statement as to the deposition of Thutmose I and Thutmose II is highly conjectural, and the attribution of such acts to intrigues of the high priest of Amen is not based on evidence.

Numerous pieces of inscriptional evidence connect both Amenhotep II and Thutmose IV with Lower Egypt and the Re cult, including scarabs which say '(Aakheperure) is born at Memphis', and '(Aakheperure) the son of Re appears on the throne of Re', and Amenhotep II's placing of the epithet 'the Divine ruler of On' in his second cartouche. The Doresses call attention to these as well as to the two steles of Amenhotep II near Gizeh invoking solar divinities and the Dream Stele of Thutmose IV which also invokes the solar gods.[2] However, only the smaller Gizeh stele of Amenhotep II and the scarab above noted of Thutmose IV are connected with the Aton cult as such. It is an open question whether it was Amenhotep II's attachment to Lower Egypt that strengthened the Aton cult, or whether it was Amenhotep II's attachment to the Aton cult that made him pay more attention to Lower Egypt. I feel sure that Amenhotep II was involved with the Aton cult, but the question is only obscured by introducing the factor of either his involvement in Lower Egypt or that of Thutmose IV. The apparent connection may be merely the result of the haphazard preservation of evidence from these particular reigns, and the fact must be faced that Amenhotep III had no very strong apparent Lower Egyptian connections, and probably built more Amenist structures than any other king, yet it was under his reign that the Aton really began to flourish, and not in any apparent enmity to Amen.

The Doresses are on even less reliable ground in attempting to draw conclusions from the title of Theban officials of this period.[3] The High Priest of Amen was not vizier under Thutmose IV, but we cannot know whether this indicates a dispute between the royal house and the priesthood because the vizierate is still an obscure subject, and we do not even know for sure how many viziers there were at this period. Again, although the titular control of all the priests of Egypt was usually held by the High Priest of Amen, and the title was at this period given to Haremhab,[4] a layman of military experience, we do not know whether it was merely honorary. Supposing the award to have carried with it active power, we should still have no ground for assuming a quarrel between the royal house and the Amen hierarchy, for relations between the king and the Amen cult seem very good throughout the long reign of Amenhotep III. The document upon which the idea of a quarrel is chiefly based is a very badly broken passage of the early version of Ikhnaton's[5] boundary stele of Akhetaton in which the king refers to the untrustworthiness of priests, and connects Thutmose IV with this view. It is certainly tempting to take this meaning from the passage, but a great deal of the context is missing.

Anen, the brother of Queen Tiy, was high priest at Southern On, but it would be going too far to follow the Doresses in seeing him as also high priest at Heliopolis,[6] especially in view of his office as second prophet of Amen. They are also unjustified in claiming that Amenhotep III shared his father's dislike of the Amen priesthood.[7] It seems to me strange that, if Amenhotep III disliked the Amen priesthood, he should have taken so many steps to strengthen it. The addition of Luxor alone to the Amen cult establishment must have given it a tremendous extension. As well, I can scarcely believe that any Egyptian institution could be a real threat to the king once he was firmly established on his throne. It is apparent that Ikhnaton, who does not seem to have been by any means Egypt's strongest ruler, upset many of the land's traditional ideas. Surely a pharaoh such as Amenhotep III firmly established on the throne for almost two score years would be in full control of the elements of power in Egypt. It is impossible to agree with M. and Mme Doresse that Amenhotep III's building of his palace complex on the west bank of the river was an attempt to get away from the influence of Karnak, nor is it acceptable that the period in office of Ptahmose, as first prophet of Amen, Vizier and overseer of works, was only a passing reaction.[8]

A man named Ramose held cult offices in both the Amen and Aton churches in this early period, suggesting that there was then little bad feeling. The evidence of Egyptian records shows them as a remarkably tolerant nation, and we can see this also in the fact that people connected with Amenhotep III's palace—the estate of Tehen Aton—also bore offices in the Amen establishment. For example, Nefersekheru was 'overseer of the house of the estate of Nebmaatre is the splendour of Aton', and also, 'overseer of the cattle of Amen' and 'overseer of the double granary of Amen'. At least as probable as the views advanced by M. and Mme Doresse is the theory that the hostility shown to many other religious establishments in Egypt by the Aton cult of Ikhnaton was a function of his own personality. Certainly there are no overt signs of hostility to the Amen cult in the preceding reigns, but rather, especially under Amenhotep III, much evidence of good relations.

# FIVE: The distribution of the Aton cult

In view of the publications of those who have excavated Akhet-aton over the last seventy years, I do not feel there is anything which may usefully be said on the manifestation of the Aton cult there, but I feel it desirable to review its distribution throughout the rest of Egypt.

Amenhotep III frequently used the name 'Tehen Aton'. Though the expression can be translated 'the sun shines' there seems little doubt that the many places to which it refers and objects on which it is written demand a translation 'the Aton shines' or 'is splendid'. The barge of the king was called 'Tehen Aton', the Malqatta palace area was called 'the estate of Neb-maatre is the splendour of the Aton' (Tehen Aton). The term 'the city of Tehen Aton' is also used. One of the divisions of the army was called 'Nebmaatre is the splendour of the Aton' (Tehen Aton). Though these terms do not specifically refer to a religious structure, it is not unreasonable to suppose that there existed a temple of Aton connected with this general estate. The term 'the house [or estate] of Aton' (Per Aton) occurs on the canopic jars bought by Legrain; and Ramose of Tomb 46 at Gurna is an official of a *ḥwt* (mansion) of the Aton.[1] These names probably indicate three different Atonist structures at Thebes, dating from the reign of Amenhotep III. The term Tehen Aton at any rate is closely connected with Amenhotep III, and Ramose is thought to have lived in his reign. In addition the term Tehen Aton is not used by Ikhnaton. The canopic jar, which mentions the 'estate of Aton', was found among others referring to Tehen Aton.

In Nubia at the modern Kawa, the earliest building of which portions survive was constructed by Tutankhamen, and seems to have started out as an Aton temple, although it ended by being dedicated to Amen. The inscriptional material includes a reference to Gempaaton, an earlier form of the place-name Pergematon by which the area is known in the time of the Twenty-fifth Dynasty, which hence suggests an original Atonist foundation on the site. The excavators of the site, searching for a foundation deposit for the temple, could find only a large scarab of Amenhotep III in the place where such a deposit would normally be located.[2] The cautious opinion of the archaeologist will perhaps permit of a little enlargement since normally the hunt for such foundation deposits is thorough. What a scarab, which would have some value, would be doing in such a location other than as a foundation deposit is difficult to say. Chance is too easy an explanation. Such a name as Gempaaton demands a more positive Atonist connection. There is, however, no trace of Ikhnaton's work on the site, and the only definite sign of the enterprise of Amenhotep III is the above-mentioned scarab. There is certainly an Atonist foundation of Ikhnaton at Sesebi.[3] The evidence at Kawa is scanty, but there is some ground for the opinion that the founder of a certainly existing Atonist structure before the reign of Tutankhamen, was Amenhotep III.

Breasted[4] and Bouriant both refer to stela from Sakkara, referring to priests of an Aton temple, which by their style were clearly pre-Amarna. It has not been possible to locate them, but they would not have been invented by these scholars, and may be taken as indicating that during the reign of Amenhotep III at least an Aton temple existed at Memphis or Heliopolis or both.

Scanty though these remains are, one would not expect (in view of the later reaction) more than the most tenuous traces, and there is enough to show the presence of a network of temples to the Aton throughout Egypt, apparently begun at least as early as the reign of Amenhotep III. This raises the question of motive. In Egypt gods were generally attached pretty closely to their cult centres. Amen for example, was at one time a local god of Thebes, and always remained very closely associated with that place as did Re with Heliopolis, and it is possible that both were never really anything other than transplanted local deities. Perhaps the kings intended to construct in the Aton worship a cult which would exist on a national basis, since there is no traceable geographical centre. This process may be analagous to the establishment of the worship of Serapis by the Ptolemies.

During the reign of Ikhnaton very many Atonist structures were built. As far as Akhetaton itself was concerned, construction of the city was not begun before the year 4, and apparently it was not extensively inhabited before the year 8, since the recension of the boundary stele of year 6 still uses a word indicative of a temporary dwelling when Ikhnaton speaks of his domicile in the city. We do not know why it was founded, and it may reasonably be doubted whether Ikhnaton left Thebes because of priestly opposition. It might conceivably have been constructed as a cult centre, or perhaps the senior pharaoh felt that it would be better for all concerned if his son left Thebes, since the violent fanaticism of the Aton belief seems to centre around the person of Ikhnaton. Whatever the reason for the foundation of Akhet-aton, it is evident that Aton temples continued to be built on various sites throughout the country.

In the Theban area a great mass of material from Aton structures has been found which were particularly connected with Ikhnaton. In the tomb of the vizier Ramose the Aton is referred to in this fashion: 'The living Aton, the great one who is in Hebsed [festival] lord of heaven and earth in the midst of Gempaaton in the house of Aton.'[5] Another official, Parennefer, the owner of Tomb 188 at Thebes, has a scene from the Per Aton shown in his tomb in which Ikhnaton and Nofretiti appear,[6]

Although the name 'per Aton' (house or estate of Aton) has been noted before, the 'Gempaaton' is a structure the name of which first appears in connection with Ikhnaton. It might perhaps refer to a smaller shrine in the house or estate of Aton noted above, or to a major new foundation. In a stele of Ikhnaton found at Gebel Silsileh he called himself the high priest of Re Harakhte[7] and stated his intention of making the 'benben of Re Harakhte' at Ipet Sewet. This reference indicates another Atonist structure in the Karnak area.

For many years the excavations at Karnak under Chevrier[8] have produced a multitude of blocks from an Aton temple in Thebes, which are now in the possession of the Egyptian authorities. They differ from the blocks used in temple construction before and after this period in that they are much smaller. The Atonists obviously believed in rapid construction, since the smaller size would make for easier handling even though the walls might be more unstable. The thousands of blocks located make it clear that one or more major structures were involved, but since a definitive study—even were this possible—has not yet been published, neither the name nor number of buildings, or parts of buildings, present is known.

Fakhry thought his discovery of Aton blocks in Luxor meant there was an Aton shrine there.[9] The name on these is 'the mansion of the benben in Gempaaton',[10] and it may well have been a different structure from the one with which the benben of Re Harakhte at Ipet Sewet was connected, and yet the structure Gempaaton was located in all probability in Karnak. The question of whether the blocks concerned were transported to Luxor from Karnak for re-use or whether there actually existed an Aton shrine at Luxor must remain open.

Certainly, however, at least one Aton structure existed at Southern On, whether this place be located at Thebes or Hermonthis. Its name is quite different from those mentioned above, and it is called 'the horizon of Aton in southern On'.[11]

In Lower Egypt there were Aton temples connected with Ikhnaton at Heliopolis and Memphis. The one at Heliopolis was called 'the wall of Re in On',[12] the reference being preceded by the early form of the Aton name and followed by the name of Meritaton. The Aton temple in Memphis was known as 'the mansion [*ḥwt*] of the Aton,'[13] and building at the site was carried on late in the reign of the king since a relief of Smenkhkare as co-regent has been found there. Petrie mentions a scribe of the overseer of the field of Per Aton.[14]

An early traveller mentions Atonist statuary at Appolinopolis Parva, not far from Thebes,[15] and since it does not seem likely that statuary would be transported for re-use, its presence indicates an Aton shrine in this locality. The large number of Aton blocks at Hermopolis, however, could well have been transported as building material from Amarna, since no name of an Aton shrine here is known.

Blocks at Assiout excavated by Gabra do,[16] however, bear the name 'The one who is in festival, the lord of all that which the Aton encircles . . . in the midst of the "*rwd ʿnḫw* ?" of the Aton' which would indicate that an Aton shrine existed on this site.

The Atonist foundation at Sesebi in Nubia noted above was also a temple.

We thus have evidence of the existence of a network of these temples, probably covering almost the whole of Egypt and

Nubia, and perhaps extending into western Asia. Many more may have existed for most of the possible Delta sites have not been excavated, and large numbers in Upper Egypt and Nubia are still virtually untouched. The evident hatred of certain later monarchs for the name of Ikhnaton would certainly have contributed to the disappearance of monuments from this reign, and the large number of areas which show even till this day evidence of building is remarkable.

Ikhnaton having ruled for twelve of the seventeen years of his reign as co-regent with his father, it is more than probable that much of this Aton building took place during this period. Such a construction programme would be inconceivable unless the senior pharaoh approved, and impossible to accomplish in the five years during which Ikhnaton was the senior ruler. The fact that the city of Akhetaton was itself almost completed while both kings were reigning is additional confirmation of the point.

There was nothing haphazard about these projects, which rather suggest a coherent policy, although we have not sufficient information to understand it in detail. It may well be that the Egyptian rulers were attempting to unify their possessions by introducing a worship which was not tied to a specific locality as was that of all the great Egyptian gods. How far this policy was successful is obscure, but that it was so for a short time is probable. It does not correspond with the facts to say that Atonism possessed no more than a limited court following, for the scanty traces of the post-Amarna history of Atonism do not show that the cult collapsed immediately upon the death of its chief proponent. There must have been a considerable party of which the young pharaoh was the titular head, and if this were not true there would seem no reason for the dislike later rulers felt for him.

The attempted integration of diverse territorial possessions by imposing a common religion, if that was what happened, is by no means uncommon and has often been successful.

In Imperial Rome the Caesar cult was pushed out by Christianity, which was then in turn used by later Roman rulers as a unifying principle. In more recent times the Spaniards and the

Carolingians consolidated their conquests by Christianity, Islam pursued a similar course. In Egypt itself the Serapis cult, though almost a creation of Ptolemy, flourished for some centuries, and it is tempting speculation whether the example of the Aton cult was in his mind to inspire its introduction.

Whatever lay behind, it seems that the fanaticism of Ikhnaton and the consequent division of views weakened the Aton form of worship, so that after his death the cult declined and shortly thereafter, in the absence of royal patronage, became unimportant if it did not disappear.

# SIX: The Aton after Amarna

Material dealing with the Aton cult after the end of the reign of Ikhnaton is very scanty, but it does exist. Bouriant noted,[1] though without adducing evidence, that both Eye and Tutankhamen added to the Aton temple in Thebes, but a full report of this Theban material is as yet not published.

Nevertheless, the fact that Tutankhamen did not change his name from Tukankhaton until quite some time after his accession indicates that he, or more likely his advisers, were still interested in the new cult. The royal residence was not removed from Akhetaton to Thebes until the reign had well started, and in the tomb of Tutankhamen a number of objects inscribed in the Atonist fashion were found. However, except for Bouriant's statement, no evidence of Aton buildings of this reign exists, unless the remark that the Kawa temple of Tutankhamen was first planned as an Aton structure, and only later changed to an Amen temple, be literally correct. In the inscriptions of this temple the phrase 'rule what the Aton encircles'[2] occurs, and a noble who calls himself 'a child of the court, the overseer of the southern countries, fan bearer on the king's right', Khay, uses the epithet 'the chosen one of the Aton' on a stele.[3]

There are, however, a number of surviving inscribed objects of Tutankhamen's reign which include the Aton name. In a stele from the hypostyle hall of Karnak the word is used twice[4], and though in both passages the context is broken, its presence indicates that the cult has not been proscribed. Yet this inscription largely refers to Amen. The names of both gods also appear in the Festival of Opet inscription from Luxor in the stock expression 'May thou [Amen] make his [Tutankhamen's] lifetime, like the lifetime of heaven, may he appear like the Aton in it.'[5] Again in an inscription from a box in Cairo, the circuit of the Aton is mentioned, and later sections of the same inscription read: 'The good god, the image of Re, the eldest son of the Aton in heaven',[6] and: 'May the good god live, the image of Re, the efficient son of the Aton in heaven',[7] yet there is also a reference to the name of Amen. Objects from the tomb of the king include a draught board inscribed 'May the good god live, the son of Amen, born of the Aton in heaven'[8] and also a sceptre bearing the words: 'Splendid of face like the Aton when he shines',[9] referring to the king. And finally, from the Memphite tomb of Haremhab, later the king, a label on one of the figures reads 'the standard bearer of the troop "love of the Aton" Minkhay'[10].

These are very scanty traces; on the other hand very little material has survived from the reign except from Tutankhamen's tomb. The inscriptions from the box and draught board refer to the divinity beyond all question, and it seems almost certain that the label from the tomb of Haremhab does likewise, but the other references are ambiguous.

There is a small stele in Leyden of Haremhab, which is entirely in the Amarna style and shows him as a general, wearing one of those collars which appeared in the rewarding scenes at Akhetaton[11]. The inscription is Atonist in form, using epithets commonly attached to the Aton, and although it does not use the actual word, still the piece has value as evidence: 'Harakhte the great god, lord of heaven, lord of earth who goes forth from the horizon . . . praise to the Re, lord of Maat, the great god, ruler of Heliopolis.' Perhaps in this context the sun sign plus the uraeus is to be read Aton rather than Re. Another interesting reference is from the tomb of Neferhotep, dated to year 3 of Haremhab: 'The man who is pleasing to Amen', among other things 'he is Re, his body is the Aton, he exists unto eternity'.[12]

Other miscellaneous items include the dual reading cartouche ring of Tutankhamen found by Petrie; a peculiar stele of Pareemheb, a Heliopolitan priest, which was originally a normal Amarna product showing Ikhnaton and a daughter but was usurped for the reigning king, Haremhab, though the sun disc with hands—symbol of the Aton—is left untouched[13]; and the frequent writing, in the Ramesside manuscripts of the Book of the Dead of the word of Aton with the divine determinative and, on occasion, a cartouche. It is also worth noting that Kawa in Nubia was known as late as the reign of the Nubian king Aspelta in the sixth century BC as Pergematon.

Yet it is noticeable that after Ikhnaton the Atonists were no longer fanatical. In almost all of the quoted examples the name of Amen appears as well as that of Aton, and it is obvious that at least by the reign of Haremhab the cult apparatus of the Aton has disappeared. There seems, however, to have been no attempt to destroy the emblem of the god, although there was undoubted enmity on the part of some against Ikhnaton. By the reign of Haremhab the buildings which were erected to the Aton had become handy sources of stone for filling between wall spaces or other such purposes. Whatever officially fostered pro-Aton party had existed between the reigns of Amenhotep II and Tutankhamen had largely died out by the time of Haremhab's death.

It should be stressed, however, that the decline of the Aton cult did not result in the triumph of Amen, since even though Atonism disappeared as a popular religion—though probably not as an article of worship—Amenism never recovered the pre-eminent position it had enjoyed during the first three-quarters of the Eighteenth Dynasty. The kings from Haremhab onward had their main royal residence in Lower Egypt, Thebes ceasing to be the major administrative headquarters of the government, and becoming only a religious centre.

What the disappearance of Atonism from the records signifies is as much of a mystery as its original appearance. If my idea that it was an attempt to construct an empire-wide religion from above has any merit, then its disappearance was a consequence of the failure of a policy of religious nationalism. Since it seems, from what traces remain, that the cult was constructed for personal or political purposes by the rulers rather than evoked as a response to some particular religious need, its disappearance for all practical purposes was not surprising.

# PART FOUR
# Foreign policy in the Amarna age

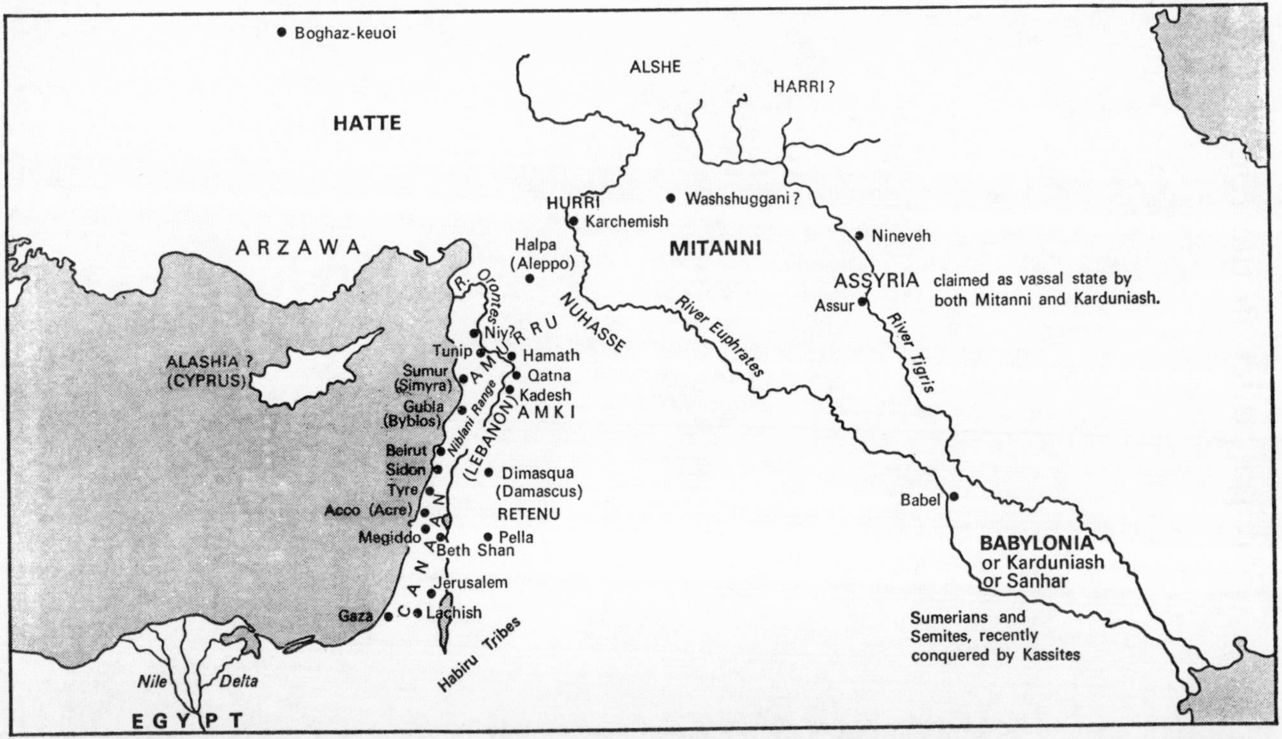

*Western Asia in the Amarna Age*

# ONE: The historical setting

The period of Egyptian history of which the Amarna interlude is a part is called the Empire, since at this time control had been extended beyond Egypt proper into the nearer part of Western Asia. This was a long and gradual process. Approximately three hundred years before our period begins, the Egyptians had suffered extremely heavily through an invasion by a people coming from Western Asia who had completely conquered the land. These people, whom the Egyptians called Hyksos, were a mixture of racial groups, although certainly some of them were Semitic-speaking tribes, as the use of such a name as Yakhub (Jacob) for one of their kings shows. After more than a hundred years of subjection the expulsion of the conquerors began, and the Eighteenth Dynasty opens with the launching by pharaoh Ahmose[1] of the first really successful counter-attack.

To ensure that no similar foreign conquest should ever again take place, Egypt's rulers determined as a matter of policy to dominate the nearer part of Asia, and in all probability every king of the period conducted, or had conducted in his name, military expeditions in this area.

Thutmose I, for example, led his troops as far as the Euphrates. To secure a safe passage to such a great distance, he must have been able to pacify a very large amount of Palestine and Syria. No such expeditions are recorded of his immediate successors Thutmose II and Hatshepsut, but Thutmose III (probably the most well known Egyptian conqueror) who reigned for almost twenty-two years as a subordinate co-ruler with Hatshepsut, during his subsequent sole reign made repeated expeditions into the Palestine and Syria area, reaching the Euphrates several times. His campaigns were directed against the people of northern Syria and the Hittites, and his interest in the area is likely to have developed during the period when he was subordinate to his mother-in-law, but there would probably have been activity in Syria during the brief reign of his father, Thutmose II, which is unrecorded in the scanty surviving sources.

By the end of his reign Thutmose III had achieved some kind of a stable sphere of influence over pretty well the whole of Palestine, Syria, and the Lebanon, so that modern scholars have described the area of the Egyptian hegemony in Palestine-Syria as the Egyptian Empire. Yet Egyptian control of its dominated territory was probably not quite what we have in mind when we speak of the Roman Empire or the British Empire. Few, if any, permanent garrisons seem to have been maintained in the conquered territory, not enough to enable all parts of the country to be dominated at all times, nor were governors and a staff of royal administrators appointed over specific regions. Instead, the local monarchs were maintained in control of their own petty kingdoms, as long as their loyalty could be assured, the Egyptians only interfering in local affairs so far as was necessary to collect tribute, protect caravan routes, and investigate any suspicious activities by the despatch of travelling administrators and advisers, who would also be available on request to any subject ruler in difficulties.

This is a much more unstable arrangement than our usual concept of 'empire', and consequently admirably designed to produce a constant series of rebellions and uprisings. Contemporary records suggest exactly that, for not only were one or more of the Syrian kinglets constantly intriguing against Egypt, but enmities developed among them, as the Tell el Amarna letters illustrate. Counter measures to ensure greater loyalty included removal of the heirs to these petty kingdoms for education in Egypt, and a good deal of success may have been achieved by such indoctrination, but the main factor in maintaining order would be the knowledge that the pharaoh and his army would descend in fury on any prince, or combination of princes, who exerted any serious threat to Egyptian security.

By the end of the reign of Thutmose III this method of control had become the rule. His many campaigns indicate that he stationed permanently few, if any, troops in western Asia at any great distance from the Egyptian border. His successor, Amenhotep II, was also forced to campaign there, as did Amenhotep II's son, Thutmose IV. Every time a new king succeeded there was a great temptation for any disaffected Syrian princeling to take his chance for independence by staging a rebellion before the new ruler was properly established. In both the reigns of Amenhotep II and Thutmose IV military activity in Syria-Palestine occurred near the start of the reign.

With the accession of Amenhotep III, after the short reign of Thutmose IV, the prelude to the Amarna period began, and it is interesting to glance at the situation in the Near East as it was during the early part of his reign. There is some resemblance to the nineteenth century of our own era, in that it was a highly cultivated period of numerous great powers in diplomatic relations with one another, each contending for advantage. The analogy can easily be pressed too far, but a mental picture of the map of Europe in the 1800s gives a useful insight into the political situation in Western Asia *c.* 1400 B.C.

To the east was Babylonia, known to Egyptians as Karduniash. The Sumerian and Semite peoples of southern Mesopotamia had long since become fused, but had shortly before this time been themselves conquered by the Kassites, probably a branch of the Indo-European peoples who had come into Babylonia at the period of the general migration which was manifest in Egypt as the Hyksos invasion. Unlike the Egyptians, the native peoples had not risen up against their conquerors, perhaps because Mesopotamia was much more vulnerable to attack or because they were more used to foreign rule. During the long reign of Amenhotep III, there were four successive rulers of Karduniash—Karaindash, Kurigalzu, Kadashman Enlil, and Burnaburiash. The order in which they ruled may be calculated with the aid of the Tell el Amarna letters, as I shall later explain. So, we have a sequence of friendly relations between Egypt and Karduniash from the time of Amenhotep III's father, Thutmose IV, until the end of the Amarna period. These relations were cemented, at least during the reign of Amenhotep III, with gold subsidies from Egypt.

To the north and slightly west of the kingdom of Karduniash was the kingdom of Mitanni. It had not the long history of Babylonia, but held a very nominal suzerainty over Assryia though its main centres were to the west of Assyrian lands, between them and the Syrian plain. At the beginning of Amenhotep III's reign Mitanni was a considerable power and a close ally of Egypt, but by the reign's end was beginning to decline under the menace to the north-west of the Hittites and to the east the rising strength of Assyria. In the tenth year of his reign

Amenhotep III married the daughter of its king, Sutarna who had ruled since at least the time of his own accession, but later it was a king called Tushratta who wrote both to Amenhotep and Ikhnaton. Between the reigns of these two Mitannian kings, there was a brief period of rule by another king, and a period of anarchy consequent upon his assassination.

To the north and west of Mitanni in Asia Minor was the kingdom of Hatte, familiar to us as the land of the Hittites. There was contact of some kind between the Egyptians and these people, but its exact nature needs more than passing mention. For most of the reign of Amenhotep III its king was Suppiluliuma, a very powerful and able man.

The king of the Hittites and the king of Mitanni shared the interest of Egypt's pharaoh in north Syria, which formed a triangle of no-man's-land, a disputed area between their various boundaries.

Besides these powerful nations, there are others which are mentioned in the various sources, but whose strength cannot be accurately assessed. Alashia was possibly on Cyprus, although its exact situation and centre of government have not yet been located; Arzawa was another kingdom in Asia Minor, the neighbour of Hatte; and Assyria, claimed as a vassal state by both Karduniash and Mitanni, had a king who addressed his letters to the ruler of Egypt as to a brother monarch.

The picture is of an age not so much unlike nineteenth-century Europe, wherein the rivalry among a group of great powers for the control of various commercial or territorial advantages was the determining factor of international relations.

The scattered sources which enable us to build up this picture comprise the Tell el Amarna letters (correspondence abstracted from the official files of the pharaonic government); the Annals of Suppiluliuma and Mursilis I, the kings of Hatte, together with certain other Hittite documents; and material discovered by archaeologists in Egypt, Palestine and Syria. The Egyptian and Hittite written documents are at the moment the more important for our purposes, especially the Tell el Amarna letters. However, the archaeology of Palestine and Syria may well be of much more importance in the study of this period when more data has been published and evaluated.

It is in connection with Egypt's position in Western Asia that the influence of the Ikhnaton legend has been most profound. The belief that Egyptian rule in this area collapsed during and after the Amarna period has been universal among Egyptologists and Syrian scholars. I have for some time believed that the sources do not support this view.

# TWO: The Tell el Amarna letters

The idea that Iknaton, through innate pacifism and devotion to his religion, allowed his empire in Asia to collapse derives directly from an interpretation of the Tell el Amarna letters. It is easy enough when reading them to find the material on which this view is based, but even a cursory examination shows that grounds exist, perhaps far better grounds, for an entirely different interpretation.

The story of their discovery has more than one version. The most appealing tells of an old peasant woman who had a little farm near the place where Ikhnaton's royal city had once stood. One day as she was digging among the ruins, she chanced to discover a large number of clay tablets covered with cuneiform signs. Well aware that she had found something of possible value, since the interest of foreigners in relics of ancient Egypt was common knowledge among the people of Egypt, she tried to sell them, only to find that the scholars and dealers alike regarded them as forgeries. After this setback the woman decided that the pieces of clay were indeed worthless, and began to pound them up for use as fertilizer on her farm. Only after a great many had perished in this way did the world of scholarship become convinced of the genuineness of the tablets and try to obtain them. This story, to be sure, is more to the credit of the old lady's intelligence than the reputation of the savants.

Flinders Petrie, probably the most outstanding archaeologist ever to work in Egypt, told another story. According to him the tablets were found by peasants who were digging in the ruins of Amarna, hunting for mud bricks and other building materials to use in their own homes. When the peasants, recognizing their value, tried to sell the tablets, the scholarly world was sceptical and the Egyptian Department of Antiquities (for whose activities Petrie had not a great deal of respect) as usual said nothing. As in the previous story, the finders began to feel that perhaps the little oblong blocks of clay had no substantial value, and so they threw them into sacks and peddled them to dealers in antiquities and probably passers-by in the streets of Luxor, near Thebes. In this way, says Petrie, many were lost. Both tales are amusing in their way, but really they illustrate how much uncertainty there is about what actually did happen at the time that the tablets were first found.

Later Petrie himself persuaded the finder or finders of the documents to guide him to the place where they had been discovered—only, let us be sure, after the Egyptians had satisfied themselves that all the tablets had been removed. There Petrie found some bricks stamped with the words: 'The place of the records of the palace of the king', thus removing any doubt that the letters were indeed part of the royal archives.

Either story of the discovery, however, gives the impression that the majority of the tablets were destroyed between the time of their first location and the time when the remainder came into the hands of museums and private collectors. This is rather a doubtful point, and it would seem uncertain whether Egyptian peasants would ever have kept any count of the number of tablets they discovered. About 350 letters, or fragments of letters now exist, together with a number of small fragments of tablets and some material other than letters, such as word lists and literary texts. This would represent a total of 350 to 375 original whole tablets. Doubtless some tablets were destroyed by rough treatment, but it is questionable whether such a large number of texts perished so completely that fragments from them are not still in the collection. There is support for this theory in the continuity of idea to be traced in the series of letters from various people, which would certainly not exist if we had only a fraction of the original find.

Before we look at their contents, let us consider a moment the setting in which the letters were found and which may help clarify their real significance. As we have already seen, the letters were discovered on the site of the royal residence of Ikhnaton at Akhetaton, in the equivalent of the Royal Archives Office. Together with the tablets were six faience plates from the tops of wooden boxes and a clay seal. Only the seal bore the name of Ikhnaton, the plaques were stamped with the names of Amenhotep III.

Presumably the tablets were once packed in these boxes and placed on shelves round the room, and although after many centuries the shelves collapsed and the boxes fell to the ground and burst, the very durable clay tablets survived without a great deal of damage.

The city of Akhetaton, it must be remembered, was not one of those ancient sites destroyed by enemy action or burned to the ground. It was a city which, after being abandoned by its inhabitants, became a ghost town. Even this abandonment was not a hurried process, since archaeologists have found that the population made preparations for their departure and closed up their houses, as though they were uncertain whether they might not be coming back one day.

The royal sculptor Thutmose closed up his studio and left many of his casts and models behind, including the world-famous bust of an Egyptian queen, the peer of any individual work of art, ancient or modern. Unfortunately, we cannot tell just how much equipment was left behind since the city has been thoroughly ransacked over the centuries by people in search of building material, but we may be sure that everyone had ample opportunity to take away any property for current use, or needed, for example, to carry on his business. The Egyptian court itself did not leave Akhetaton until the middle of the reign of Tutankhamen, that is, some four or more years after the death of Ikhnaton.

The inescapable conclusion is that the crown officials did not simply forget the royal archives. When the Tell el Amarna letters were left behind in the old records office on the departure of the court, it was because they were no longer current or pertinent.

Turning to the contents, these documents can be divided into two general groups: the first consists of correspondence with reigning monarchs of the day, and the second of letters concerning the affairs of various subject princes. Only two Egyptian kings are mentioned by name, Amenhotep III and Ikhnaton, and this agrees with there being only the names of these two kings on the box plates and seals found with the tablets. Yet the city was not abandoned until approximately one half of the reign of Tutankhamen had passed. This would surely mean that when the documents were left behind, there was more involved than just closing the office door and taking the boat to Thebes. It is evident from this that the royal officials made an inspection, sorting the letters before they decided which were worthless.

If this had not been so we should have to accuse the modern finders of the documents of very selective destruction of the tablets, since they would have managed to destroy all the late ones.

There are also other indications that the letters were sorted. Each of them is in effect a report to the Egyptian crown of events either in a foreign court or in its own dominions, and hardly one could be left without an answer. Yet, where are they? Only ten of some 350 documents surviving are written from the Egyptian court, and it seems reasonable to suppose that these replies from the king or the foreign office were largely abstracted from the letters to be left behind and taken away when the court left Amarna. Indeed, this is proved by the fact that on two of the letters sent by a foreign king to a king of Egypt there is an appended gloss which uses the word 'copy' in reference to the surviving letters. One such gloss reads: 'year thirty-five, month four, of winter . . . ' they were in the 'southern mountain -------- house -------- copy (of the letter) -------- the messenger brought ---------'[1] From this it is apparent that the Egyptians were in the habit of keeping copies of correspondence, and certainly the letters from the Egyptian king to the princes also must have been copied.

Finally, the names of quite a number of Egyptian officials are mentioned who were on various missions for the king in Syria, whereas not one dispatch from any Egyptian official survives among these tablets. Reports by these royal officials must have been sent to the court, since various client princes refer to letters written by Egyptian officials to the king, and whatever action the king took in a given case would be based largely upon their reports. It seems incredible that their letters dealing with the situation in Western Asia should have been simply thrown away after being read and not filed, and equally so that they should have been kept anywhere but in the royal records office.

Coincidence could account for the absence of any one of these three varieties of correspondence, but coincidence will not stretch far enough to cover the virtual absence of all three of these types, so important in any archive.

The Tell el Amarna letters, therefore, were documents which the Egyptians themselves did not think worth carrying away;

they were left behind as the residue of an archive from which all information of current value had been extracted. This means that they cannot be taken at their face value as evidence for or against anything whatever. They must be very carefully and sceptically analysed, something neglected by the creators of the Ikhnaton legend when they paid too much attention to the complaints of various Syrian princelings and ignored largely the interchange of letters between the various monarchs of the day and the letters which certainly emanated from the Egyptian court.

# THREE: The date of the letters

It is most important to date the Tell el Amarna letters as precisely as possible. We have already seen that they come from the reigns of Amenhotep III and Ikhnaton, but it would be useful to ascertain more definitely the period within these reigns over which they were written. Amenhotep III ruled more than thirty-nine years, for approximately twelve of which he had his son as co-regent, and Ikhnaton had a further five years of rule after his father's death—a total for both kings of forty-three to forty-four years.

The building of Akhetaton, where the documents were found, was begun in the fourth or fifth year of the co-regency, and was abandoned by the fourth or fifth year of Ikhnaton's successor, Tutankhamen. Thus, it was probably occupied for less than fifteen years in all, since it is unlikely that the king and his court took up permanent residence there before the seventh year of the co-regency at the earliest.

The letters contain numerous references to the death of Amenhotep III and the accession of Ikhnaton,[1] but none to the death of Ikhnaton or the enthronement of any successor to him. There is also no surviving letter which can *certainly* be dated to a reign later than Ikhnaton's.[2] On the other hand, there is a letter from Tushratta, the king of Mitanni, mentioning that Ikhnaton has held in Egypt for four years the messengers Tushratta sent on the occasion of the death of Amenhotep III.[3] This tends to show that the collection runs almost to the end of Ikhnaton's reign, since the death of his father probably came after twelve years of their joint rule, and he himself ruled only five years thereafter. Letters of Burnaburiash of Babylon, though not specifically dated, point to a similar lapse of time.[4] In short, as far as royal letters to Ikhnaton are concerned, they range from the beginning of his sole reign until almost the end of his co-regency with Smenkhkare.

Among the letters from the subject princes to the Egyptian court there is only one which might be of later date than the end of the reign of Ikhnaton and even in that one there is no reference to the death of Ikhnaton or the succession of Tut-ankhamen, but since the letter is written to the Amorite prince Aziru by two of his officers this is perhaps not remarkable.

There is, then, a period of approximately five years before the city was deserted which is almost unrepresented in the letters. In this connection it should be re-emphasised that, although box plates and seals were found bearing the names of Amenhotep III and Ikhnaton, there was none naming either Smenkhkare or Tutankhamen, although this would have been expected if the collection contained material related to these reigns. From this it seems evident that any correspondence later than the end of the reign of Ikhnaton was considered to be current business, and was removed from Akhetaton. Thus it would seem that the year 17 of Ikhnaton, the last year of his reign, would be a reasonable date for the latest of the letters.

By this time the city would have been occupied for eight or nine years, so that, if the records office contained material from years before full occupation had begun, this could be explained by its having been brought, or copied, for the use of officials at the new office, or else by some of the letters having been actually received at Akhetaton during visits by the king, or both kings, while building was in progress. One would expect to find no material earlier than the twenty-ninth regnal year of Amenhotep III, which corresponds approximately to the year four or five of Ikhnaton.

We have seen earlier that in the tenth year of Amenhotep III a comemorative scarab was issued on the occasion of the marriage of the king with the daughter of Sutarna of Mitanni.[5] The first letter in the series from Mitanni is from Tushratta, the son of Sutarna, whose reign was separated from his father's by a period of anarchy and another short reign.[6] By this time Tushratta himself had a daughter of marriageable age, and her forthcoming union with the king of Egypt is the topic of most of the letters between Amenhotep III and himself.[7]

Between Amenhotep III and the kings of Babylon or Karduniash, correspondence is preserved from two reigns, those of Kadashman Enlil[8] and Burnaburiash,[9] but the long-lived Egyptian actually seems to have been the contemporary of four Babylonian rulers: Karaindash, Kurigalzu, Kadashman Enlil, and Burnaburiash.[10] Karaindash is placed first because Amenhotep III mentions in a letter that Kadashman Enlil had remarked to him that messengers were going back and forth between their two countries in the time of their fathers, that is, in the time of Thutmose IV[11] and of Karaindash, whom we know fairly certainly from other sources to have been the father of Kadashman Enlil.[12] Burnaburiash is placed last since he wrote to both Amenhotep III and Ikhnaton, and because he refers in his letters to events in the reign of his father, Kurigalzu. It seems unreasonable to put the reign of Kurigalzu between Kadashman Enlil and Burnaburiash, since the latter mentions an alliance between Egypt and Babylon when his father was king,[13] and yet no letters survive from Kurigalzu's reign, presumably because it ended before the time of the Amarna letters. Kadashman Enlil also says that Amenhotep III married his sister, who had been given to him by Kadashman Enlil's father.[14] From all this we may conclude that much of the reign of Amenhotep III was over by the date of the Amarna collection, which encompasses only the last ten years of his rule and the succeeding five years of Ikhnaton's reign—a total of a little over fifteen years.

Since most of the letters are not addressed by name to any particular pharaoh, confusion has arisen as to which letters were actually addressed to Amenhotep III and which to Ikhnaton. However, exhaustive analysis of the personal names appearing in the letters has enabled most of them to be placed in the relevant reign (a full discussion of this matter can be found in the Appendix). Here a few examples are sufficient to show the kind of research carried out on this particular point.

In his second letter to Ikhnaton, the Babylonian king, Burnaburiash, complains that one of his caravans has been robbed at Hinnatuni, a place in Palestine, by subjects of the Egyptian king. He names one of the culprits as Shutatna, the son of Sharatum, prince of Acco.[15] As Shutatna is a contemporary of Ikhnaton,[16] it might be assumed that Sharatum would be a contemporary of Amenhotep III. Looking elsewhere in the correspondence, we find there are also letters to the Egyptian court from a Zurata and Zatatna of Acco,[17] and the resemblance of the names of father and son is too close to admit of any doubt of their being the same. Since Burnaburiash's second letter to Ikhnaton was obviously written comparatively soon after the latter's accession, Zatatna may have succeeded his father, Zurata, as prince of Acco during the reign of Amenhotep III, but Zurata himself is surely a contemporary of Amenhotep III. Any mention, then, of this man as living dates a letter to the reign of Amenhotep III. Thus, another letter in the correspondence which was written by Zurata to an un-named king of Egypt will, in all probability, have been written to Amenhotep III.

Another excellent example of this kind of detective work occurs in the series of letters written by Biridiya of Megiddo to an un-named pharaoh. On one occasion he writes that he and his brother, Jasdata, perhaps acting in concert with Zurata, succeeded in capturing Labaia, a city king who had been outlawed by Egypt for his depredations. They had been instructed to deliver him alive to the Egyptian court, and Zurata took him home with him to his city of Acco, ostensibly with the intention of putting him on board a ship bound for Egypt. Instead, he took a bribe and freed his prisoner. Biridiya and his brother, as soon as they had found out what had happened, set out to recapture Labaia, but before they could overtake him he had been killed[18] by the people of a city called Gina.[19] It seems that the death of Labaia and his misdeeds while alive must also be dated to the reign of Amenhotep III (because of the reference to Zurata), so that the letters of Biridiya and Jasdata, too, most likely belong to this reign, as do the letters of Labaia himself.

Even more interesting is the long series of more than fifty letters written to the Egyptian court by Ribaddi, prince of Gubla—the Roman Byblos, and modern Jebeil in the Lebanon. It would be informative if these could be divided between the two reigns, since Ribaddi refers to the activities of a number of other people. Fortunately, letter 116 in the Knudtzon edition of the Amarna letters refers almost certainly to the accession of a new king in Egypt,[20] and Ribaddi goes on in the same letter to say that Aziru, the king of Amurru, has captured the city of Sumur, which had until this time been held by Ribaddi as part of his own territory. This provides a convenient dividing point for the two reigns in the events of Western Asian history: Amenhotep III reigned until Aziru's capture of Sumur, and from then on Ikhnaton was probably Egypt's reigning king.

By a similar process the vast majority of the significant letters can be tentatively assigned to one reign or the other. Of a total of 347 documents, 138 can be assigned to the reign of Amenhotep III, 78 to that of Ikhnaton, and 5 seem to have been written so close to the change of reign that any more precise attribution is impossible—one may even be later in date than the end of Ikhnaton's reign, but this is in several ways a special case. The remaining 131 letters include fragments and many short notes, and other material where no personal names or particular events mentioned in other places are found.

# FOUR: The situation in Western Asia: the royal letters

For the purpose of political analysis the letters are best divided into two separate groups: correspondence between Egypt's rulers and their fellow monarchs of Western Asia, and letters between Egypt and her subject princes. Independent rulers who wrote to Amenhotep III and Ikhnaton were—Kadashman Enlil[1] and Burnaburiash[2] of Babylon or Karduniash; Tushratta[3] of Mitanni; Assur Uballit[4] of Assyria; Suppiluliuma[5] of Hatte; Tarhundaraba,[6] king of Arzawa; and the king of Alashia[7] perhaps Cyprus.

As we have seen, people writing about this period have generally assumed that, while Ikhnaton devoted all his time and energy to worshipping the Aton in Akhetaton, his empire was crumbling through neglect. However, in his final letter written towards the end of Ikhnaton's reign, Burnaburiash objects to the Egyptian king sending an escort of five chariots to fetch the Babylonian princess who is being given to him in marriage. This is not the protest of a father anxious for his daughter's safety on a long and dangerous route through hostile territory; the ground of his objection is simply that five chariots constitute insufficient pomp and circumstance for the transport of a future queen of Egypt.[8] It is evident that he considers the country safe enough for a small expedition to cross from Egypt to Babylon, and also for the letters themselves to be sent from one court to the other. Nowhere, either in the letters of Burnaburiash or those of other kings, is there any mention of marauding tribes, such as those Khabiru or SA·GAZ peoples to whom various princes subject to Egypt, notably Abdi Hiba, the ruler of Jerusalem, refer. (The use of capitals in the name SA·GAZ is simply an indication that this is a phonetic rendering of two signs whose interpretation is at present impossible.)

If it be objected that the real danger to Egypt's power in Western Asia lay in north Syria, and that though the route from Egypt to Babylon was still safe for messengers during the latter part of the reign of Ikhnaton, in the north there was ample cause for belief that the Egyptian hegemony was collapsing, there are two conclusive reasons for rejecting such a hypothesis.

During the reign of Ikhnaton three kings were writing to Egypt: Tushratta of Mitanni, Assur Uballit of Assyria, and

Suppiluliuma of Hatte. All ruled inland countries, and a messenger from any of them had to travel a very long way overland from his own capital in order to reach the borders of Egypt. Nevertheless, in all their letters there is no reference to rebellion or hostile conditions *en route*. Only two letters each survive from Suppiluliuma of Hatte and Assur Uballit of Assyria, but the series from Tushratta of Mitanni seems to be reasonably complete from the beginning of Ikhnaton's reign until the time the correspondence ended.

The second reason for the rejection of such a hypothesis will be further discussed in the section dealing with the correspondence from the vassal kings, but it should be pointed out here that most of the letters which deal with the alleged collapse of the Egyptian empire during the Amarna period come from the reign of Amenhotep III.

If the picture of general collapse is not justified, then what is the situation portrayed in the correspondence of the Asian kings?

As we have seen, Babylonian correspondence with Egypt was carried on over a long period of time. Both Kadashman Enlil and Burnaburiash mention that Amenhotep III was in communication with their fathers,[9] and as we have already seen Amenhotep had married a sister of Kadashman Enlil,[10] given to him by Karaindash. Relations were sometimes strained, as when Kadashman Enlil accused Amenhotep III of breaking his father's (i.e. Thutmose IV) word,[11] but they were continuous and also frequent, for in letter 10 Burnaburiash mentions that Ikhnaton's messengers have come to his court three times.[12] The next letter—the last preserved in the series—is that in which Burnaburiash indignantly refuses to send a daughter of his to Egypt as a bride because he considers the escort of five chariots sent by the royal bridegroom to be humiliatingly small.

The Tell el Amarna correspondence between Egypt and Babylon opens with Amenhotep III and Kadashman Enlil in the midst of their long and somewhat acrimonious negotiations over this marriage, which apparently arose from a request of the Egyptian king.[13] Apart from the wedding and a complaint that the Babylonian messenger had been detained six years, the chief topic in the letters is Kadashman Enlil's desire for gold,[14] and

Amenhotep III was apparently sending him thirty units each year,[15] too regular an allowance to be regarded as merely a present. The fact that a similar policy was pursued by Amenhotep III in dealing with Tushratta of Mitanni has a great deal of significance.

At the death of Amenhotep III the ruler of Babylon was Burnaburiash, and his first two letters to Ikhnaton are the only ones containing comments which could be interpreted as indicative of unrest in Palestine. A caravan master, who was also a messenger of Burnaburiash, had twice had his caravan plundered by Egyptian vassals, one of whom the Babylonian king identifies as 'the governor of a land belonging to you'. He demands that his own servant be compensated,[16] and the fact that this caravan master was alive and well to receive compensation strongly suggests that there had been no armed attack, and that the plundering was more the act of rapacious officials. At any rate Burnaburiash passed off the incident in ten lines of a long letter, without apparently attaching excessive importance to it.

A second incident brought a much more violent reaction. A caravan belonging to Burnaburiash was attacked near Hinnatuni in Palestine, and some of his merchants killed. He asks Ikhnaton to take action against the culprits, whom he names as Shumadda, the son of Balumme, and Shutatna, the son of Sharatum.[17] The identity of the former is not certain, but the latter was doubtless Zatatna, the son of Zurata, since both men are said to be princes of Acco. Hinnatuni is mentioned again in the letters in connection with Zurata, and this place was evidently reasonably close to Acco, Zurata's home.[18] However, the idea that the place name Hinnatuni contains the word Aton[19] lacks any supporting evidence beyond the fortuitous position of the letters of the word.

Burnaburiash says in comment on this disaster: 'Canaan is your land and its kings are your servants',[20] and this must indicate the actual state of affairs in the area at the beginning of Ikhnaton's reign. He also warns the Egyptian king to prevent a recurrence of such incidents, lest they weaken his hold on the area,[21] and in a subsequent letter recalls that during his own father's time a group of Canaanite rulers had proposed an alliance with Babylon in order to stage a joint attack on Egypt. Kurigalzu, however, had refused to entertain the notion on the ground of his alliance with Amenhotep III.[22] These are the only remarks by Burnaburiash on conditions in Egyptian-held territory, two of the incidents referred to being contemporary and the other having occurred some time in the past. It seems incredible that, if the Egyptian Empire were close to collapse, Burnaburiash should not have commented more fully. Instead, the last letters from him are concerned with another marriage negotiation, and although matters came to a temporary halt, as we have seen, over the question of an escort, the marriage must have eventually taken place. We know this from the inclusion in the collection of two tablets listing presents sent in either direction, most probably as bridal gifts.

Burnaburiash wrote five times to Ikhnaton, and mentions in his third letter that Ikhnaton's embassy had three times arrived at his court,[23] suggesting that Ikhnaton was in his third year of rule when this letter was despatched from Babylon. It seems then that most of the letters of Burnaburiash written during the sole reign of Ikhnaton have survived.

Burnaburiash provides one glimpse of his own problems when he requests Ikhnaton to have nothing to do with the Assyrians, whom he regarded as his own vassals,[24] but the Egyptians do not seem to have paid much attention to the hint, since two letters from the Assyrian king, Assur Uballit, are among the Tell el Amarna collection. And not only did embassies of Assyria[25] come to Egypt, but Egyptian embassies paid return visits. It is reasonably certain that Assur Uballit's letters were written to the Ikhnaton court, since they mention the subsidisation of the king of Mitanni by the father of the present king, who could only have been Amenhotep III.[26] The Assyrian ruler declares that he has never himself previously written to Egypt,[27] but that his father, Assur-Nadin-Ahe, had written and received from the king twenty units of gold.[28] Presumably the Egyptians had recognised the rising importance of Assyria for some time.

The journey from the Assyrian capital to Egypt was probably the longest overland trip which any ambassador of this period would have had to make, but the Assyrian king mentions no difficulties encountered by the embassy because of hostilities in Syria. He does note that the Egyptian envoy was delayed by

Sutu people, but this was within his own borders, and he took action against them as soon as he heard of the trouble. In consideration of his having shown such concern for the safety of the Egyptian embassy, he asks that his own messengers should not be detained in Egypt.[29] Unfortunately, his letters do not contain a great deal of useful information except the fact that his throne seems to have been subsidised by Egypt.

Equal in importance to the series of letters from the Babylonian court is the large group of documents from the court of Mitanni, which also cover the whole period of the Tell el Amarna correspondence. In his final letter, Tushratta notes that the messengers he sent on the death of Amenhotep III have been kept in Egypt four years,[30] and since they would probably not have arrived immediately on the new king's accession,[31] this letter must have been written in the later part of the sixteenth or in the early part of the seventeenth year of the reign of Ikhnaton.

Correspondence between the courts of Egypt and Mitanni went back at least as far as the reign of Artatama of Mitanni, Tushratta's grandfather, since it is recorded that Thutmose IV was forced to negotiate for a long time before this Mitannian king would give him his daughter in marriage.[32] In the next generation Amenhotep III, in the tenth year of his reign, married in his turn a daughter of Artatama's son, Sutarna, who had by then succeeded to the Mitannian throne.[33] On Sutarna's death, his elder son Artassumara came to the throne, but soon 'disappeared' and a noble called Tuhi, who was probably the assassin of the new king, may have been regent for Artassumara's younger brother, Tushratta.[34] We do not know how long Sutarna ruled Mitanni after the marriage of his daughter to Amenhotep III, nor how long Artassumara was king before his assassination, nor how long it was before Tushratta secured the execution of his brother's murderer. However, it is reasonable to suppose that such a series of events would take considerable time. Many scholars have thought that the first letter from Tushratta in the Amarna series was written soon after he assumed full power, but this does not appear to be the case, since he clearly speaks as if the events he is discussing were by now some time in the past. 'When I established myself upon the throne of my father,' he writes, 'I was still young and Tuhi committed an evil deed against my land in killing his lord. For that reason he did not permit me to cultivate friendship with those who wished me well. I, however, especially on account of those crimes which were perpetrated in my land, was not remiss [in my duty] and did not delay in killing the murderers of Artassumara, my brother, and [in confiscating ?] all their property [or perhaps "in killing the murderers of . . . and all their families"].' The phrasing here plainly points to Tuhi having held power for some time after his crime before Tushratta was able to avenge his brother's assassination, and Tushratta goes on to discuss a Hittite campaign[35] clearly subsequent to these events. Further confirmation that these letters do not come from the beginning of Tushratta's reign is the fact that the remainder are largely concerned with the marriage of his daughter to Amenhotep III,[36] though it is apparent that in such a purely political marriage the girl need not have been very old.

The Hittite attack which Tushratta goes on to describe to Amenhotep III may be the same one which is recorded in the preamble to a treaty between Tushratta's son Mattiawaza,[37] and the Hittite king, Suppiluliuma, who apparently came to the throne of Hatte about the year 20 of Amenhotep III. This preamble also records the series of events which led to Tushratta's fall from power and death, and it is important to note that if Tushratta was still writing to Ikhnaton close to the end of the latter's reign, then these events must have occurred after Ikhnaton's death.

It is interesting to see that Tushratta's downfall was brought about by the connivance of Assur Uballit, king of Assyria, who made use of a disaffected Mitannian prince, and had perhaps a silent partner in Suppiluliuma himself.[38] The plot had succeeded before Tutankhamen's death, since when this pharaoh died Suppiluliuma was besieging the north Syrian city of Karchemish, which was located in the Mitannian area. The siege belongs to the last six years of the Hittite king's reign,[39] when his troops were moving from victory to victory in north Syria. The point is, however, that such a series of victories had not always been unbroken, for at one point Tushratta wrote to Amenhotep III claiming defeat of a Hittite attack and sending part of his booty as a gift.[40] In this instance his defeated opponent is likely to have been Suppiluliuma himself, and not his predecessor, since Suppiluliuma ruled about forty years.[41] Since the Hittite king was still on the throne for a few years after Tutankhamen's death his reign commenced some time before the Amarna period began.

Scholars have often thought that the Hittites preserved peace during most of this period in northern Syria, but this impression is contradicted by the Amarna letters which give a picture of almost constant activity just north of the line of Egyptian control there. Tushratta's reference to a Hittite attack certainly comes from the earliest part of the correspondence; Akizzi, the ruler of the north Syrian city of Qatna, refers to a raid on his city[42] in the middle of the period; and Aziru,[43] the king of Amurru, refers to the Hittite menace in letters which are among the latest.

Tushratta's frequent intervention in the affairs of this area is apparent not only from his own letters but from those of Ribaddi. The last letter of Tushratta to Amenhotep III,[44] which differs from the rest in being written in the Hurrian language, deals most fully with the subject. Hurrian is still difficult to read, but difficulties of translation notwithstanding its information is important for the letter apparently says that Tushratta was defending Egyptian interests in north Syria in return for money payments. He writes of the division of the border area between Hurruhe and Mashriani[45]—once thought to be Syrian towns,[46] but now recognised as names for Mitanni and Egypt—and offers soldiers to Amenhotep III. We surely have here an offensive-defensive alliance,[47] such as we have already been led to suspect by Tushratta's constant requests for gold.[48] In this particular instance the Egyptian king had sent a great offering to Ihipe, a north Syrian city, apparently for Tushratta's use, and the Mitannian consequently writes: 'Because I fulfilled the desires of the land of my brother [Amenhotep III] because my brother fulfilled [his] promises concerning the oblation, then may Simigi, Aman, Easarri [gods of Egypt and Mitanni] permit my army [?] and the soldiers to bring victory to my brother as patron [?] and to his country.'[49] This is a curious passage, but clearly means that Amenhotep III was providing the money for troops and that

Tushratta was doing the fighting. Later there seems to be a reference to the determination of a frontier, but the state of the text does not permit an exact translation. Tushratta also goes on to say: 'Because my grandfather and my father have sent presents in exchange to your father, so do you commandeer these soldiers which are levied by me.'[50] In return for his defence of at least part of Egypt's Asiatic possessions, he was explicit in his demands for funds: 'To that which [i.e. gold] my brother sent in exchange for my father, let him add in proportion to the troops and to the subsidy . . .',[51] and twice more in this letter there are troop references: 'Furthermore, I shall add to your suggestions three . . . soldiers and border [?] lands . . . And my suggestions do you receive and my army do you take for thee and for me',[52] and 'While they are united may Tessupa and Aman, my kings, my fathers, be well pleasing-threefold to my gods. Then they the gods will protect them . . . They will always preserve this agreement with one another, that we may in brotherly and . . . manner be friendly with one another . . . One may demand from the other soldiers.'[53]

Although the translation of these two last references, and indeed of the rest of the letter, is occasionally obscure, the writer's intention is reasonably clear. Under a treaty between the two kings, Tushratta raised troops to protect the frontiers of both lands, and Amenhotep III made substantial payments in gold towards the cost of maintaining these forces. The letter also makes it evident, although the relevant section is obscure as well as broken, that the treaty also covered a demarcation of the frontier between the two powers. Tushratta had in fact assumed certain responsibilities towards Egypt and Egypt's sphere of influence in northern Syria, and in return Egypt recognised certain obligations towards him: this was the situation at least until the death of Amenhotep III.

Tushratta's letters to Amenhotep III must cover a comparatively short space of time, since from the third to the eighth and final one of the series, he was concerned with the negotiations for the marriage of his daughter, Tadukhepa, to the Egyptian king.

Under the new reign relations between the countries were less cordial, since Ikhnaton was not overly generous with the gold for which Tushratta was so anxious. The Mitannian king repeatedly requested Ikhnaton to consult his mother Tiy concerning the political agreements existing between himself and Amenhotep III.[54] In these letters to Ikhnaton the only indication of date is Tushratta's reference in the last of them to his messengers having been detained four years at the Egyptian court. Nowhere is there any indication that the embassies of Mitanni have suffered any trouble in reaching Egypt: all is peace and prosperity.

Only two letters are preserved from the king of the Hittites: one is directed to Ikhnaton, but the other is too badly broken for either salutation or context to provide a clue to the addressee. However, both indicate that relations between the two states have been uniformly good for some time, and the second refers in unambiguous terms to an alliance.[55]

The letters from Alashia and to (as well as perhaps from) Arzawa contain little positive information for the general conditions of the period, but it is interesting to see that Amenhotep's habit of diplomacy by matrimony extended as far as Arzawa.[56] One letter from Alashia gives advice that no treaties should be made by Egypt with the Hittites or the land of Sankhar,[57] but this is an isolated comment with no further references. With both these powers—Alashia and Arzawa—communication would have to be by sea, and transit seems to have been unhindered by hostilities here also.

In short, except for the remarks of Tushratta in what was obviously the earliest of his letters to Amenhotep III, there is no reference in the surviving royal letters indicating a state of war among any of the current great powers. All countries in correspondence with Egypt seem simply to have been in competition for gifts of gold, and the period seems to have been one of unparalleled prosperity with no hint of a collapsing Egyptian Empire.

# FIVE: The situation in Western Asia: the letters from subject princes

We now turn to the letters written to Egypt by various Syrian vassal princes, and the few remaining letters to them from the king or his officials.

The belief that the Egyptian hegemony in Western Asia was in the process of collapse derives largely from the study of these. The important letters are those from Ribaddi of Gubla, together with those from other princes whose names or activities are connected with him to a greater or lesser extent.

The majority of the letters of Ribaddi were in all probability written during the reign of Amenhotep III. It seems to me that any theory of the collapse of the Egyptian dominance in Western Asia during his reign is absurd, since both the Amarna letters and all the Egyptian evidence testify to the power of this king. When we add that the letters exchanged between the major powers contain almost no evidence of any unrest in Egyptian possessions in Syria-Palestine, then it is time to look again very closely at the situation as we find it described by Ribaddi and his colleagues.

Ribaddi was the prince of Gubla at the start of the period when the letters were written, and shortly before it closed he was ousted by a revolution and probably killed in the city of Sidon at the instigation of his bitter personal enemy Aziru,[1] the king of Amurru. Very few of the Tell el Amarna letters are demonstrably later in date than this assassination, so that the Ribaddi correspondence covers almost the whole of the period of the letters. Ribaddi represented himself as the pharaoh's most loyal servant in northern Syria,[2] an area which he declared had rapidly become very hostile to Egypt. His particular enemies were Abdi Ashirta,[3] of Amurru, and his sons, the most important of whom was Aziru.[4]

From a study of Ribaddi's letters we can easily see that not only were these people his enemies, but also any other person who associated with Abdi Ashirta, or his successors, was likewise classed as an enemy not only of himself but of Egypt, even if that person happened to be an official of the Egyptian crown.

People who have studied this age have, for the most part, tended to accept Ribaddi at his own valuation as a man who was maintaining his personal loyalty to his overlord in the face, not only of difficulties in his own territory, but also of opposition from the very Egyptian officials who should have helped him, and of indifference from the pharaoh himself. Are there any facts in the letters which contradict this romanticised self-portrait? Absence of any replies from the Egyptian ruler makes interpretation difficult, but the contrast between what Ribaddi asked for and what he said he received shows that the Egyptian court did not take him too seriously. Evidence in the letters also suggests that persons whom Ribaddi accused of treason were in communication with the Egyptian crown.

Can anything be found in Ribaddi's own letters to convict him of blatant exaggeration, if not lies? One piece of evidence that this correspondence cannot be taken at face value comes from the letter in which he reviews the general situation in his area for the benefit of the new king Ikhnaton. He recounts how Amenhotep III sent him a large number of soldiers when he asked for them,[5] and how on two other occasions when he sent people to Egypt to ask for troops a garrison was sent back.[6] These statements do not agree with his constantly reiterated demands in earlier letters for troops from Amenhotep III,[7] and his lack of reference to the arrival of such Egyptian military support, and since they occur chiefly in the letters directed to Ikhnaton, seem designed to shame the new monarch into sending him more troops.

A further circumstance arouses suspicion of Ribaddi's tales of woe. This series is the most numerous in the whole collection, extending from the beginning of the period covered by the letters until almost its end. In his first preserved letter, Ribaddi found himself in trouble: the SA·GAZ people were attacking the city of Sumur, and since Gubla was certainly close to Sumur, it was in danger.[8] In the next letter Ribaddi complained about rebellions among his own cities as well as his external enemies.[9] These wars and rumours of wars continued virtually without interruption throughout all his letters to the king of Egypt, until a rebellion in Gubla itself led by his brother surprised Ribaddi while he was out of the city[10] visiting Beirut. The chief difficulty in the way of accepting the truth of these reports is that no calamity ever overtook Ribaddi because of the attacks of these external enemies of whom he constantly expressed his fears. He was always tottering on the brink of disaster, constantly crying for help, and yet, after almost fifteen years of these pleas being ignored, the peril of his position never changed, until his own city got rid of him. It was a long time to walk a tightrope, and scholars who suppose the letters to cover a much longer period than fifteen years only make the situation more incredible.

The king of Egypt certainly did not believe him. Repeatedly Ikhnaton answered Ribaddi: 'Protect yourself'[11], but Ribaddi kept writing back with his tale of troubles, reciting in many cases virtually the same events as causes of new fears. When Ikhnaton wrote to Aziru, after Ribaddi had apparently come to his lifelong enemy and had been handed over by him to his enemies—and perhaps killed by them—the king of Egypt protested against this treatment of Ribaddi in these words: 'The following has been reported to the king, your lord. The prince of Gubla whom his brother has expelled has spoken to you thus: "Take me and lead me back into my city . . . and I will give it to you. Behold whatever is at hand in quantity which I do not have." He has spoken to you in this way. Do you [not] write to the king your lord thus: "I am your servant as all former regents who were in his [probably Ribaddi's] city." And still you have committed the sin of taking the regent whom his brother threw out of his city by the door. And when he found himself in Sidon you gave him [to] the regents according to your judgment. Know you not the hatred of the people? If you in truth are the servant of the king why have you not seen to it that he appeared before the king your Lord, when you are saying: "This regent has sent to me this information [request]. Take me and lead me into my city." And even if you have acted lawfully, still all the words are not true concerning which you have written, they are [not] trustworthy, so thinks the king", Everything is not right which you have said.'[12]

This was a rather severe rebuke. But the king's anger against Aziru arose from his action in handing over Ribaddi to his enemies instead of sending him to Egypt, rather than from his virtual seizure of Ribaddi's territory. The king's remarks were delivered, moreover, after Aziru had on Ribaddi's own admission conquered most of his territory by force of arms. This is not at all the kind of action which would have been expected from the king if Ribaddi were indeed his chief bulwark in north Syria.

We learn from the same letter that during Aziru's seizure of Sumur the city was completely or partially destroyed.[13] The king of Egypt merely insists that Aziru should rebuild it, but he does not seem to have objected to its seizure.

Nor was Aziru the only person whom Ribaddi vilified whose letters have been preserved. Letters survive from Aziru's father, Abdi Ashirta, who was similarly classed by Ribaddi as a villain.[14] Zimrida, the ruler of Sidon, was another person, some of whose letters remain, whom Ribaddi classes as pharaoh's enemy.[15] He also called the cities of Beirut[16] and Tyre[17] (and their rulers) enemies of pharaoh on more than one occasion, yet it was to Ammunira, the prince of Beirut, that Ribaddi went for help and an alliance immediately before his fall.[18]

Further doubt is cast on Ribaddi's veracity by his attitude to various Egyptian officials with whom he had come into contact. Often his comments on the Egyptian representative in the area were inconsistent. As long as these people did things of which he approved he wrote praising them, but if they acted in a fashion which he regarded as contrary to his own interests his disapproval amounted to libel. On one occasion he wrote 'by the representative of the king who was in Sumur Gubla has been saved. Lo Pahamanata, the king's representative, who is in Sumur is aware of the trouble which weighs upon Gubla',[19] but on another occasion he wrote: 'But Pahamanata did not listen to me, rather he behaved in a hostile fashion and indeed his son has looted Sumur.'[20] Ribaddi made this charge more specific. 'At the instance of Haib, his father has made the cities hostile [to Gubla]. Lo Haib has handed over Sumur.'[21] The remark 'Indeed, Haib is with you. Ask him',[22] regarding the doings of the sons of Abdi Ashirta, indicated another change of position. If Ribaddi indeed wrote letter number 101[23] as is generally believed, then Haia, whom Ribaddi had called a wise man and who was appointed by the king as deputy for the area,[24] was called in this place an enemy of the king.[25] Ribaddi had a law suit against another official, Iapa Addi,[26] against whom he evinced constant hostility and made various serious accusations,[27] including a charge that Iapa Addi had joined with Aziru against him. Iapa Addi was apparently in the royal service[28] and had something to do with the grain market in Iarimuta,[29] a place generally thought to be in the Delta. Against Bihuru, apparently the 'governor' of the northern Egyptian provinces,[30] Ribaddi also made charges: 'Bihuru also has greatly wronged me. He has despatched Sutu people and they have slaughtered men of Serdan, and he has deported three persons to Egypt. How many days has the town been stirred up against me?[31] The city has even said, "A deed which has not been committed previously from time immemorial has been done against us". Bihuru has sent, etc.'[32] This complaint involved an attack by one group of mercenaries in Egyptian pay on another group of mercenaries in the service of Gubla, and the capture and deporting of three people to Egypt. This latter action, especially, is not one that an official would take without authority. Even Ianhamu, the pharaonic deputy in Palestine,[33] was not exempt from Ribaddi's charges: 'Moreover, if now [the cities of] Sumur and Bit-Arha also are falling away then you [the king] have put me into the power of Ianhamu'.[34] Ianhamu had also apparently taken two persons of Gubla[35] whom Ribaddi wanted returned, and, according to Ribaddi, had not sent him grain to which he was entitled.[36] On other occasions, however, Ribaddi praised Ianhamu.[37] Thus it seems that Ribaddi quarrelled violently with every major Egyptian official in the area mentioned in the letters, with the possible exception of Amanappa who was probably a military man.

It is noticeable, and probably significant, that Ribaddi's language to the king from time to time lacked the form that one would expect would be required between lord and vassal: 'Send an answer to me. Otherwise, I will make a treaty with Abdi Ashirta as Iapa Addi and Zimrida have done',[38] and on another occasion: 'If my lord, the king, has written "Behold soldiers are indeed on the march" then you have [he has] written lies. There are no forces here, they have not marched forth.'[39]

This conglomeration of material makes a very strong case for doubting the sincerity of Ribaddi's professions of unique loyalty in north Syria, and we may take leave to doubt whether the term 'enemy of the king' which Ribaddi so often used had any real meaning as far as the Egyptian court was concerned.

The principal enemies of the king that Ribaddi named were Abdi Ashirta, the prince of Amurru; his sons, notably Aziru; and the SA·GAZ people. Among the lesser were the kings of Sidon, Beirut and Tyre, and Iapa Addi, a royal official. Letters from all of these people have survived, though not in nearly such quantity as those from Ribaddi. Whether this is a matter of chance, or whether Ribaddi was simply a very prolific writer, cannot be decided, perhaps a combination of both reasons is the answer. Can we find evidence in these letters to show that Ribaddi was pleading a cause rather than reporting facts?

Ribaddi claimed that Abdi Ashirta was an enemy of pharaoh, because he was in league with the SA·GAZ people to plunder and seize the king's land.[40] Among his specific crimes are his conquest of the city of Sigata; his advice to the people of the town of Ammia (Ambi) to kill their king and join the SA·GAZ;[41] his arrangement of the assassination of the king of Irqata[42] and his taking of the city with the help of the SA·GAZ people; his attempt to have Ribaddi assassinated;[43] and his capture of the city of Batruna.[44]

The letters from Abdi Ashirta[45] indicate a very different state of affairs. Abdi Ashirta claims to be a servant of the king appointed by him to rule the land of Amurru,[46] and writes that eleven of the kings of the area were trying to seize his lands.[47] The Egyptian overlord whom he names is Pahanate, the same man who is named in the Ribaddi correspondence as 'governor' of Syria,[48] and his letters are largely concerned with the defence of Sumur.[49] The name of Ribaddi is nowhere mentioned, but, like Ribaddi, Abdi Ashirta also stood constantly in need of pharaonic troops.[50]

Another letter seems relevant to this discussion, though the exact connection is difficult to establish. The writer (who is unknown) remarks that the Egyptians who lived in Sumur had had to leave and were at the time of his letter living in his own land: 'And he had made an alliance with the prince of Gubla and with the prince of . . . and all officials of your [pharaoh's] land and they stand in well with him, my lord. But now he is like the SA·GAZ [people] a run-away dog and he has captured

Sumur, etc.'[51] Whether all the actions of the unnamed malefactor were intended to be taken as crimes (thus classing Ribaddi and all the officers of the land as traitors), or whether the writer intended to convey a before and after picture of contrasted virtues and vice, is uncertain. Since Ribaddi never mentioned, in any case, that he made a treaty with either Abdi Ashirta or Aziru, this statement perhaps comes as further evidence of the unreliability of his letters.

It is unfortunate that the introduction of letter 101 has been broken. Some of the language suggests that the letter was written by Ribaddi, and it was almost certainly sent from Gubla, but the manner in which Abdi Ashirta is mentioned militates strongly against Ribaddi as the writer:[52] 'They [Mi-Lim people] have indeed killed Abdi Ashirta, whom the king placed over them and not themselves.' If the letter was indeed written by Ribaddi, this remark is of considerable importance in assessing the worth of his denunciations of Abdi Ashirta, for here Abdi Ashirta is classed as a royal appointee, as he himself claimed to be.

As far as Abdi Ashirta's son, Aziru, is concerned, not only Ribaddi but also Abimilki of Tyre[53] and Akizzi of Qatna[54] accuse him of anti-Egyptian activity. That this interpretation of Aziru's official acts was not accepted by the Egyptian crown is shown by a letter to him from the king: 'Now those who attract you to themselves seek to throw you into the fire. They, however, have [already] [burned or been burned] while you are in some ways very friendly. Indeed, if you bow down to the king, your lord, what is there which the king would not do for you? But if you for any purpose wish to do evil or if you store up evil and words of hatred in your mind, then you shall die by the axe of the king together with your whole family.'[55] These remarks of the king were followed by a reiteration of the demand that Aziru make his long delayed visit[56] to Egypt. Aziru had certain misgivings, but must have felt that he could be reasonably certain of a good welcome at court for he certainly made a visit to Egypt, since a letter mentioning his being there has been preserved.[57] Aziru apparently had had to ask the king's permission to enter Amurru[58] to take up his inheritance, and had also asked for investiture in his kingdom.[59] It is apparent from the king's letter wherein he called Aziru 'the man [prince] of Amurru'[60] that this was granted.

Ribaddi was not alone in speaking against Zimrida, the ruler of Sidon, for Abimilki,[61] the prince of Tyre, also accused him of helping Aziru. The case against him, however, is only as strong as the case against Aziru. In addition, Abimilki had a dispute of long standing with Zimrida over a town he alleged the latter took from him,[62] and this certainly did not make them friends.

And so, the two sides of the dispute are presented. It is evident that conflict on a minor scale was taking place in northern Syria between two groups, both nominally pharaonic vassals looking to Egypt for support, and claiming to be the bulwark of loyalty to the Egyptian crown in the north.

Is this consistent, however, with the idea that the Egyptian Empire was collapsing? At the time of the death of Thutmose III it was, to be sure, of somewhat greater extent than at the death of Amenhotep III. Yet the apparent decrease may have been due to policy rather than military defeat. We know that a definite agreement existed with Mitanni, which was concerned to a greater or lesser extent with frontier problems, and it will be shown that a similar treaty existed with Hatte. It is quite possible that at this period the limit of definite Egyptian control was a line to the north of Gubla on the coast, and passing inland to the south of the city of Kadesh on the Orontes. The existence of a flexible sphere of influence extending far north of this line, and fluctuating with the political conditions, also seems a reasonable assumption.

From this we can see that the maintenance of a state of unrest in north Syria which left the various princes too hostile towards one another to make a successful combination possible, and only required occasional Egyptian intervention to prevent a complete collapse of one or the other, could only work to the advantage of the Egyptian crown.

The Egyptians must have been aware of the situation in the north, since the names of many of their officials in the area from time to time are known, and it would be ridiculous to assert that all these men conspired to betray their country, and incidentally to deprive themselves of honour and livelihood. The picture painted by Breasted, Baikie, and far too many others, of a gentle mystical Ikhnaton sitting in Amarna as a resident missionary while his empire crumbled is equally false. The letters from the court of Ikhnaton show no lack of grasp of political reality. Apart from the quotations from the letter to Aziru already given, two other portions of the letter show the mind of the king: 'You surely know that the king does not wish to strike forcefully against the whole land of Canaan.'[63] This is an implied threat against Aziru if he does not visit Egypt, and the end of the king's letter is most explicit: 'Be sure that the king fares as well as the sun in heaven; his troops and his chariotry in multitudes from the Upper Land to the Lower Land, and from the rising of the sun to the going down of the sun are in good condition.'[64] No reasonable man could read this as other than a threat, and it was repeated in a second letter from the court, which may be to Aziru (it is very badly broken).[65] Another letter to Intaruda, the ruler of the city of Aksapa, written more probably by Amenhotep III than Ikhnaton, made a similar but less subtle threat: 'Prepare for the archers of the king, much food, wine and everything plentifully. Behold, he (Hani, son of Mairia) will find thee very quickly, and he will behead the enemies of the king. Know thou that the king is strong like the sun, which is in heaven, and that his troops and chariots are many and in good condition.'[66]

Threats, however, are not enough evidence with which to assault the long established, though inadequately based, premise that Ikhnaton's government was guilty of letting its hegemony in Syria-Palestine collapse through inactivity. The visit of Aziru, at the time probably the most powerful single Egyptian vassal, is important in this connection. The letter of Ikhnaton must have raised doubts in his mind as to the king's ultimate intentions. Nevertheless, he made the visit. Aziru was no fool, and asked for positive guarantees of safe conduct: 'Let the king, my lord, hear my words. My lord, I am afraid of the king, my lord, and of Dudu [an official, perhaps the vizier]. And behold, to my gods and to my messenger I have indeed sworn, O Dudu and you chief men of the king, my lord: Indeed I will surely come. And so O Dudu and the King, my lord, and the chief men [will you swear]: "Truly we will not plot anything that is not good against Aziru". So shall you indeed vow to my gods and to the god A.'[67] If the idea of Ikhnaton's government held by most Egyptologists were accurate, this fear on the part of Aziru would be ridiculous. The fact is that Aziru went to Egypt because he had no choice. The king might not want to go forth against the land of Canaan, but this didn't mean that he wouldn't or couldn't. Aziru went to Egypt as the lesser of two evils, because he felt certain that he would be attacked and destroyed if he did not go. It is evident from this that the king of the Hittites would not or could not help him.

The idea that Ikhnaton's military forces were not active in western Asia is also inaccurate. Ribaddi writes: 'Why has the king sent Sirma troops for archers, to take the cities? They have not the power to take them.'[68] Ammunira of Beirut writes: 'The king, my lord, my sun, has written to his servant and the dust of his feet: Make [everything] ready for the troops of the king your lord [of that] I have indeed heard. Now behold, I have prepared with my horses and with my chariots and with all that belongs, to me the servant of the king, my lord, for the troops of the king, my lord. May the troops of the King, my lord, my sun, my gods, crush the skull of his enemy.'[69] There were many other letters of this type wherein the writer acknowledged the receipt of a letter from the king regarding the troops and stated that all would be prepared for their arrival.[70] These letters from Ammunira were written about the time of Ribaddi's fall from power in Gubla. It is probable that at least some of the similar letters from other city rulers were written at the same time.

Abimilki of Tyre writes: 'Zimrida of Sidon and Azira, the enemy of the king, and the people of Arwada have sworn, and they have repeated the alliance among themselves, and they have assembled their ships, their chariots, their infantry to conquer Tyre, the handmaid of the king. [But] the powerful hand of the king has arrived and Tyre has smitten them. They were not able to conquer her. But Sumur they have conquered on the advice of Zimrida who brings the word of the king to Azira.'[71] In another letter Abimilki writes again: 'The king has turned his face towards his servant and given officers to protect the city of the king, my lord, and I am as such a one.'[72] Another example: 'And good it is that the infantry fear, my lord: they all fear.'[73]

Yet again: 'What the king, my lord, has said that I have done. The whole land fears before the soldiers of the king, my lord. I have allowed my people to board ships for the meeting of the soldiers of the king, my lord.'[74]

Striking additional confirmation is provided by a letter of Zatatna of Acco, defending his action in helping a servant who had asked him for protection from his master: 'He was with Suta, the servant of the king in the city of Un . . . [but] he [presumably Suta] did not say anything to him. The army of the king, my lord, marched off, etc.'[75] It is evident from this context that Ikhnaton had military forces in Palestine. Ribaddi notes in one of his frequent appeals to the king: 'Garrison troops of the kingdom are with him [the deputy], and royal provisions are in his possession. . . . Bihuru has committed a great wrong against me. He has sent people of Suta and they have killed men of Serdan, etc.'[76] This not only shows that there were pharaonic troops in north Syria at this time, but that the deputy used them against Ribaddi. The king may not have shared the poor opinion of certain of his vassals as to the adequacy of his military forces.

Mentions of the use of military force by Amenhotep III are not as frequent. In the correspondence of Ribaddi they occur when he comments on a past situation: 'I wrote to your father, and he listened to my words and sent troops',[77] or 'I sent a man to visit your father, when Amanappa came with a few soldiers, and I wrote to the palace: "So let the king send many soldiers", and the king sent a great army',[78] and again: 'Twice have I sent people to Egypt and a garrison was sent by them to me.'[79]

In the letters of Abdi Hiba of Jerusalem a reference is made to military operations. He notes that Ianhamu, the chief Egyptian official in Palestine, had taken away his garrison,[80] and another sent to him by Haia, the son of Miaria, was taken away by Addaia (other officials) and put in Gaza.[81]

The reference to military activity in the letters from vassal princes are not copious, but certainly sufficient to show that the armed forces of Egypt were not idle. A large number of letters also exist in which receipt of a royal command to prepare for the arrival of the king's archers is acknowledged, and it is improbable that all of them date from one single event.

Enough has been said to show that the correspondence from the subject princes is extremely contradictory, and cannot be accepted on its face value as a reliable guide to events in Syria-Palestine. However, individual facts mentioned are often very valuable in any attempt to reconstruct the real situation as distinct from the distortion mirrored in this section of the letters, especially with regard to the activities of Hatte and Mitanni.

Hatte is mentioned more often than Mitanni in the letters and then rather as a threat than as an active enemy. Various vassal princes accused enemies among their compeers of being Hittite agents, yet the long Ribaddi correspondence, wherein many references would be expected to the Hittite menace, lacks them. On one occasion Ribaddi wrote: 'Let the King, my lord, know that the king of Hatte has conquered all the lands which belonged to the king of Mitta or the king of Nahma, the land of their great kings.'[82] 'I have heard from the Hatte people that they [the sons of Abdi Ashirta?] burn the lands with fire',[83] and again 'Behold now they bring soldiers from the Hatte lands to conquer Gubla.'[84] The king of Hatte is named on two other occasions, once in a list of kings, and again in a broken context, probably another list.[85] The omission of much mention of the Hittites must be very significant, but it is very difficult to assess exactly what it means. The second passage seems to me to convey that Ribaddi had received the information concerned from Hittites visiting Gubla, which would seem to show some kind of friendly feeling between the Hittite people and Ribaddi. From this it is too much to say that Ribaddi was involved with the Hittites, yet his letters, undoubtedly written at the same time as those of Akizzi of Qatna, display no apprehension of Hittite aggression. It is, of course, also possible that those who write of Hittite menace could have been exaggerating greatly, but at the present time the problem is insoluble.

Mitanni played a more important role in the Ribaddi correspondence. Some scholars have thought that the words Mitanni, Mitta, Nahma and Subari all referred to Mitanni,[86] the words being used interchangeably by Ribaddi or his scribes. This is not impossible but it is difficult to accept, and it seems more likely that these words might refer to closely related but not identical lands.

In this case the section quoted would refer to a campaign of the Hittites against Mitanni, certainly close in time if not identical with the campaign acknowledged by Tushratta and reported by him as a Mitannian victory. In a later letter Ribaddi wrote: 'The king of Mitana has marched as far as Sumur, and wished to go as far as Gubla but there was no water for him to drink and so he has gone back to his own land.'[87] There is no indication that this expedition was hostile, and from the text I incline to think Ribaddi had no objection to it. In a letter of uncertain authorship the following passage occurs: 'Have not ships from the Mi-lim people penetrated into Amurru and killed Abdi Ashirta, because he had not sent to them either fine Kitu or Mar-stone so that payment could be made to the king of Mitana.'[88] The Mi-lim people appear to be soldiery,[89] and since Ribaddi was the bitter enemy of Abdi Ashirta, it is possible that he was at this time friendly to them, but in other letters he certainly regarded them as hostile.[90] At any rate, they were in the service of Mitanni. Both these passages mention massive Mittanian interventions in north Syria, clearly later than the letter in which Ribaddi reported that the Hittite king had seized all the Mitannian lands.[91] One must in this case conclude that all Ribaddi reported in the letter indicating a Hittite victory was the start of a campaign, and that either he did not report the Mitannian repulse of the Hittites, or that if he did do so the letter has not survived. It is quite probable that the Hittite activity noted in these letters, and the campaign reported by Tushratta in his first preserved letter to Amenhotep III, occurred at approximately the same time. This kind of intervention in Syria is precisely what would be anticipated from the agreement between Amenhotep III and Tushratta.

Other mentions of Mitanni made by Ribaddi are more obscure. In a letter to Amanappa (one of pharaoh's officials) he writes: 'Day and night there is unrest against you (Amanappa) and they the [regents?] have said [that] everything which has been taken from them to Mitana is very much.'[92] This may well relate to the agreement for the defence of Egyptian and Mitannian territories in the north, indicating the extension of Tushratta's authority over territory tributary to Egypt which he had contracted with Amenhotep III to defend. He also writes: 'Behold in Mitana is that . . . and his face is towards Gubla. Then what shall I do alone,'[93] and '. . . the king of Mitana looked at the land of Amurri and said "What land is this? Great is your land",'[94] but the significance of these latter two broken passages it is impossible to assess clearly.

It is also interesting that Abdi Ashirta, Ribaddi's early enemy, made no mention of either Hittites or Mitannians in his surviving letters. Surely some of the letters from Akizzi, the ruler of Qatna, were contemporary with some of those from Ribaddi and Abdi Ashirta. Why the Hittites were regarded by Akizzi as his chief enemy and not mentioned by Abdi Ashirta whose territory must have bordered fairly close on Qatna is inexplicable, unless Abdi Ashirta also had friendly contact with the Hittites.

Akizzi feared Aitugama, the king of Kadesh on the Orontes, whom he called an agent of the king of Hatte: 'But now Aitugama has marched out against me with the king of Hatte and he seeks my head. And now Aitugama has sent to me and said: "Come with me to the king of Hatte." But I said, "Even if I died I am not going to the king of Hatte. I am a servant of the king, my lord, the king of Egypt." I sent and so I spoke to the king of Hatte.'[95] In another letter he says: 'Arzawiya the prince of Rubizzi, and Teuwatti, the prince of Lapana, have united with Aitugama, the prince of Kinza [Kadesh] and with the king of Hatte they are involved,'[96] and in yet another: 'The gods and men of Qatna the king of Hatte takes.'[97] Aziru is also mentioned in the letter from which this last quotation comes, and a connection between him and the king of Hatte is very strongly suggested.

All the letters of Akizzi which are preserved, except the last, were concerned with the career of Aitugama, the prince of Kadesh on the Orontes. He was not the only person who wrote to the Egyptian court accusing Aitugama of being an enemy of the king and in league with the Hittites. Ilirabih of Gubla (perhaps the successor of Ribaddi) writes to the king: 'Aziru has committed an outrage. . . . He has sent his people to support Hakama [Aitugama] and he has smitten all the land of Amki, lands of the king, and now he has sent his people to conquer the lands of Amki and its inhabited places. Further let them not do [namely] the king of Hatte and the king of Narima and. . . .'[98] Abimilki of

Tyre writes: 'Etagama [Aitugama] lord of Kidsi [Kadesh] and Azira have begun hostilities against Namiawazi.'[99] Bieri, ruler of the city of Hasabu, writes: 'Behold we are in Amki, cities of the king, my lord, but Edagama [Aitugama] the man of Kinza [Kadesh] is gone against [in command of] the troops of Hatte and he has set on fire the cities of the king, my lord.'[100] These remarks were repeated almost identically by some other princes in letters to the king of Egypt.[101] Namiawaza writes: 'And Arzawiya has gone to Gizza [Kadesh] and he has taken the soldiers of Aziru and conquered Saddu and has given it to the SA·GAZ people, and he has not given it to the king, my lord. Now behold Atatkama [Aitugama] has destroyed Gizza [Kadesh] and behold Arzawiya together with Biridaswa have destroyed Abi.'[102] Earlier in this same letter he writes: 'When Biridaswa saw this deed then the city of Yanuamma arose against me and shut the door behind me. And he has taken chariots in Astarte and given them to the SA·GAZ people, but not to the king, my lord. When the king of Busruna and the king of Halunni saw they began hostilities together with Biridaswa against me and said: "Come we will kill Namiazawa and not let him come to Tahse". But I escaped out of their hands, and stand in Abi and Dimasqa—they said: "Servants of king of Hatte are we." '[103] Ikhnaton writes to Aziru: 'Indeed the king has heard that you have made an agreement with the prince of Kadesh [Aitugama] that you supply food and drink to one another. If this is really true, why are you doing thus? Why have you made an agreement with a man with whom the king has quarrelled?'[104] A letter from Aitugama also survives wherein he declares that Namiazawa had taken all his territory including Kadesh. In the course of this letter he affirms his loyalty to Egypt.[105]

It is evident that Aitugama of Kadesh was an opponent of Egypt, and that the king of Egypt recognised Aziru's involvement with him. There seems to be little doubt that Aitugama was also involved with the Hittite king. Aziru, however, maintained that he was opposed to the Hittites, and used the proximity of the Hittite king as an excuse not to go to Egypt. The letter written to Aziru in Egypt[106] by two of his henchmen mentions hostile activity in the land of Amki on the part of the Hittites,[107] but its date is uncertain. This is the only letter of the collection which seems to reflect the situation during the reign of Tutankhamen after the Hittites had begun to invade Egyptian territory, as the land of Amki must have been regarded. It is possible that Aziru managed to delay his visit to Egypt for a fairly long time, even until the reign of Ikhnaton was over, or almost over. Since we read in the letters that Tushratta complained regarding the long detention of his officials in Egypt when they came as ambassadors, it is also possible that Aziru—a potential trouble-maker—was held in Egypt for some years. In that case this letter written to Aziru was simply missed by those who sorted the contents of the records office when the court was leaving Akhetaton.

Since the career of Aitugama is mentioned both in connection with Aziru and independently, but not in connection with Abdi Ashirta, it could be maintained that Aitugama's active career as an anti-Egyptian focus began after Abdi Ashirta had passed from the picture. This would imply that the interference of the Hittite king in the affairs of the Qatna took place in the latest years of Amenhotep III. As we have seen the career of Aitugama is mentioned in the latest letters, but apparently it does not go back to the beginning of the correspondence. It is noted in the Hittite archives that Aitugama was captured by the Hittites when his father Sutarna, king of Kadesh, resisted the Hittite advance in the expedition designed to avenge the killing of the king of Nuhasse by Tushratta of Mitanni.[108] It is probable that during his captivity in Hittite lands Aitugama came to espouse their cause.

In the correspondence of Aziru the presence of the king of Hatte in Nuhasse was used by Aziru as an excuse for delaying his journey to Egypt 'The king of Hatte sits in Nuhasse and I am afraid of him. It is only two days' journey to where he stays from Tunip and I am afraid. Let him depart. Then I will come. If he only does not come here to Ammurri the land of my lord.'[109] This matter is raised by Aziru in identical terms in four different letters. It is evident that the city of Tunip at this period was held by Aziru for Egypt, but Nuhasse was recognised as the property of the Hittite king. There is no recorded objection on Egypt's part to Aziru's possession of Tunip, despite a letter of protest which its people wrote,[110] and if Aziru held Tunip, he probably exercised some control over Qatna, since these two centres must have been fairly near each other.

Mentions of Mitanni outside of the Ribaddi correspondence are rare. One important reference, however, comes from the correspondence of Akizzi of Qatna: 'And the messenger of my lord has come to me and has spoken thus: I have arrived in Mitanni and three or four kings are enemies of the king of Hatte who all serve me. And my lord has spoken to their messengers. . . .'[111] This passage occurs in two letters of Akizzi. In both, the contexts of these singularly important passages are broken. Another reference to Mitanni occurs in the letter of another Syrian prince to the Egyptian king, who writes: 'Furthermore know that the king of Mitan has marched out with chariots and with soldiers. . . . We have heard [that] to something . . . to submit; and they have submitted themselves . . . and of fear of him. . . .'[112] These documents certainly indicate that there was considerable activity on the part of the kings of Hatte and Mitanni in the northern part of the Egyptian sphere of influence in Syria.

The Ribaddi correspondence has been considered in detail as an example of a series within the Amarna letters, in order to ascertain whether or not the letters are an accurate reflection of the historical situation. It has been shown that the letters must be used with extreme care, and that on numerous occasions they were political polemics rather than reports. The same applies to the letters of Abdi Hiba of Jerusalem, but since we are concerned rather with assessing the position of Egypt at this period than attempting a reconstruction of the political situation in Palestine-Syria as it affected all parties, the correspondence from southern regents need not be considered in detail. It is obvious that if Egypt retained her position in the north she certainly retained it in the south.

We can now see from the letters that Egypt employed a definite policy of empire, suited to her needs and objects, and did not seek to Egyptianise the whole area or to integrate it with Egypt being satisfied with the more limited aim of ensuring the protection of her trade routes and protecting her tributary rights in the area. This was done by encouraging the quarrels of the various local rulers to the point of actual conflict between the vassals, such as that which existed between Ribaddi and the kings of Amurru, without permitting any regent to gain a complete victory. Egyptian troops were used, for example, both against Ribaddi and against Aziru. If the princes were kept constantly at odds, then Egypt would be able to maintain her interests without excessive effort, thus there were relatively few Egyptian armies and garrisoned bases in the area. At least until the death of Ikhnaton, the limits of Egyptian control in Syria were approximately those which existed at the beginning of the period covered by the letters. This includes territory north of Sumur on the coast. In the interior nominal control of the area of Kadesh and actual control of Amurru was in Egyptian hands during the period covered by the letters. The lands of Nuhasse and Ni were at this time definitely outside of the Egyptian sphere. Probably under the treaty with Amenhotep III, Tushratta of Mitanni protected the Egyptian frontier as far west as Kadesh.

# SIX: The Hittite material

No more than a century ago the only known references to the Hittites were a few scattered passages in the Old Testament, which indicated that they were another of the many peoples living in the land of Canaan. As further Egyptian texts became known, however, it was apparent that the Hittites of the Bible were only the remnants of a people whose original home had been far to the north of the biblical lands in Asia Minor.

The capital of the Hittite kingdom, known today as Boghaz Keuoi, was on the Anatolian plateau, and was discovered late in the nineteenth century when certain monumental remains still above ground attracted attention. Soon archaeologists came to excavate and a large store of cuneiform tablets was found, but the language conveyed by the script was not one hitherto translated. It provided much the same kind of challenge as the ancient Egyptian and Mesopotamian languages had previously done, but by 1917 the key to an understanding of Hittite had been discovered by the Czech scholar Beydrich Hrozny.

Since the first excavations at the site a great number of these clay tablets have been found, and large numbers published, though comparatively few have been translated. Among these last, however, are certain documents concerned with Egypt during the Amarna period. They are especially valuable because they refer to events immediately following those recorded in the Amarna letters. There is little material preserved on this period in Egypt itself, simply because of the thoroughness of the destruction of the monuments of the Amarna rulers by later Egyptian kings.

Particularly important for our purposes are: the annals of the reign of Suppiluliuma, the king of Hatte, as written by his son Mursilis II;[1] the preamble of the treaty we have already discussed between Suppiluliuma and Tushratta's son Mattiawaza;[2] the annals of Mursilis II himself;[3] and the so-called 'plague prayers' of Mursilis II.[4]

We begin with the quotation by Mursilis II of a letter from a queen of Egypt to his father, Suppiluliuma: 'While my father was in the land of Karchemish he sent Lupakkis and Tarhuntazalmas into the land of Amki, they went and fell upon the land of Amki and took prisoners, cows and sheep before my father, and when the Egyptians learned of the invasion of the land of Amki they were afraid and as their king Nibhururiya had just died, the queen of Egypt, Dahamunzu, sent a messenger to my father and wrote to him thus: "My husband is dead and I have no son. Well, everyone says that you have many sons, if you wish to give me one of your sons he could become my husband. Never shall I pick out a servant of mine and marry him . . . I am afraid."

'When my father learned of this he convoked the Hatte nobles in council, saying: "Such a thing has never happened to me in my whole life." He sent Hattusaziti, the chamberlain, to Egypt with these instructions: "Go and report to me true word, perhaps they wish to deceive me, perhaps they have a prince. You then report to me the true word."

'During the time until Hattusaziti returned from Egypt, my father finally conquered Karchemish.'[5] Suppiluliuma took the city in eight days. He respected the gods and temples, but deported the principal citizens, and made his own son Sarri Kusuh king of the city and country of Karchemish. After these things he returned to Hatte for the winter.[6]

'When it became spring Hattusaziti came back from Egypt, and a messenger from Egypt came with him, the great dignitary Hani. My father ordered when he sent Hattusaziti to Egypt as follows: "Perhaps they have a prince and wish [to deceive me], perhaps they have no need of one of my sons as king."

'The queen of Egypt replied to my father in the following letter: "Why did you say 'they may deceive me' in that way? If I had a son, would I indeed write abroad to publish the distress of myself and my country. And as for you, you did not believe me and you have even spoken thus. He who was my husband is dead and I have no son. Never shall I take a servant of mine and marry him. Now I have written to no other country but only to you. Everyone believes that you have many sons, give me one in order that he may be my husband and reign in Egypt." '[7]

A more recently discovered fragment of the annals continues the tale, the text beginning in the middle of a speech by Suppiluliuma to Hani, the Egyptian ambassador: ' "I myself was . . . friendly, but you, you suddenly did me evil. You came [?] and attacked the man [prince] of Kadesh whom I had taken away from the king of Hurri land. I, when I heard of this, became angry and sent forth my own troops and chariots and the lords. So they came and attacked your territory, the country of Amki. And when they attacked Amki which is your country, you probably were afraid; [therefore] you keep asking for a son of mine [as if it were my] duty. He will in some way become a hostage, but king you will not make him."

'Thus [spoke] Hani to my father: "Oh, my lord, this is . . . our country's shame! If we had [a son of the king] at all, would we have come to a foreign country and kept asking for a lord for ourselves? Nibhururiya who was our lord died, a son he has not. Our lord's wife is solitary. We are seeking a son of our lord [Suppiluliuma] for the kingship in Egypt and for the woman our lady, we seek him as her husband! Further we went to no other country only here did we come! Now oh our lord [Suppiluliuma] give us a son of thine!"

'So then my father concerned himself on their behalf in the matter of a son!

'Then my father asked for the tablet of the treaty again, in which there was told how formerly the storm god took the people of Kurustama, sons of Hatte, and carried them to Egypt and made them Egyptians, and how the storm god concluded a treaty between the countries of Egypt and Hatte, and how they were continuously friendly with one another. And when they had read aloud the tablet before them, my father then addressed them thus: "Of old Hatte and Egypt were friendly with each other and now this, too, on our behalf has taken place between [them]. Thus Hatte and Egypt will be friendly with each other continuously." '[8]

A further fragmentary section alludes to later happenings: 'When they brought this tablet they spoke thus. [The people of Egypt?] killed [Zannanza] and brought word: "Zannanza [died] . . ." When my father heard of the slaying of Zannanza he began to lament for Zannanza [and] to the gods he spoke thus: "Oh gods I did no evil, yet the people of Egypt did [this to me] they [also] [attacked] the frontier of my country." '[9]

These events and their sequel are also dealt with in the plague prayers of Mursilis II, son of Suppuliliuma. In these he tells how, the Hittite weather god having brought the people of Kurustama to the land of Egypt, a treaty was made and an oath sworn by the contracting parties. However, Suppiluliuma broke this oath when he 'sent out troops and chariots which suddenly attacked the border district of the land of Egypt, the land of Amki. And again he sent them out and again they attacked.'[10] It is at this point that the Egyptian pharaoh died, and his widow made her plea for a Hittite bridegroom, Zannanza, who was apparently done to death on his way to Egypt. In revenge, Suppiluliuma again attacked Egypt, and although the result of the campaign is not mentioned, it must have been at least partially successful since prisoners of war were brought back to Hatte. Unfortunately they were plague infected, and the disease ravaged Suppiluliuma's whole land for twenty years[11]—hence the 'plague prayers' of Mursilis, his son.

This Hittite material is of the utmost importance. In the first discovered fragments the pharaoh whose death precipitates these events is called Piphururiya, and in those published by Guterbock in 1956, Nibhururiya. His identity was in dispute as long as the name was read Piphururiya, but once the new fragments were published there was no longer room for doubt, he was obviously Tutankhamen, whose praenomen was Nebkheperure.

The similarity of names is not the only connection, for the name of the queen mentioned in the letter—Dahamunzu—evidently contains that of the god Amen. This particular combination did not occur between the time of Sitamen, the daughter-wife of Amenhotep III, and Ankhsenamen, the queen of Tutankhamen: the context rules out the first. Neither Nofretiti, nor Smenkhkare's wife, Meritaton, are known to have had other names compounded with Amen, and, as far as Nofretiti is concerned, the probability is that she predeceased her husband. Moreover, any queen of Egypt sending such a letter to the Hittite king would need to be the royal heiress, offspring of a marriage between a king and a queen, with a claim to the throne in her own right. This latter point would also rule out Nofretiti, though not Meritaton or Ankhsenamen. However, we have already eliminated Meritaton because, not only is her name not compounded with Amen, but the name of her husband, Ankhkheperure, in no way resembles Nibhururiya.

All the events we have been discussing are also obviously later than the situation apparent in the Tell el Amarna letters, because if the Hittite king had actually besieged Karchemish and attacked Egyptian forces in the land of Amki, some record of these activities would be expected in the letters. The only one giving any hint of such a situation as is described in the Hittite archives is the letter written to Aziru, while sojourning in Egypt, and here even the name of one Hittite commander is the same.

Despite all of this additional material bearing on the point at issue, however, the comparison of the names is so remarkable as to be conclusive, and we may take it as established that the pharaoh referred to is Tutankhamen. The course of events can hence be briefly summarised: While Suppiluliuma, the Hittite king, was besieging Karchemish in the far north of Syria, he sent two commanders, Lupakkis and Tarhuntazalmas, to attack the land of Amki. Just at this moment, or shortly before, Tutankhamen died. During the course of the attack ordered by Suppiluliuma on the Egyptian borderland the embassy of Queen Ankhesamen reached his court, perhaps arriving some months after the pharaoh's death, partly because of difficulties of communications and partly because of the probable reluctance of the queen's advisers to accept such a decision. Not surprisingly in the circumstances, Suppiluliuma refused to take the ambassadors at their face value and sent an embassy of his own to Egypt to find out the facts on the spot, returning himself to Hatte for the winter. In the spring his own ambassadors returned in company with the Egyptian envoy, Hani, and more discussion of the affair took place. Still more time elapsed before the princely Hittite bridegroom was despatched, and finally murdered, presumably while on the way to Egypt.

Such a course of events further vindicates the Egyptian historian, Manetho,[12] whose account, though badly garbled by his epitomists, still indicates the rule of a queen at the end of the Eighteenth Dynasty. Ankhsenamen must have ruled in her own right for at least a year and perhaps more, though the figure of three years given by Manetho seems too high.

We also learn from this material that the frontier of the Egyptian hegemony in Western Asia at the end of the reign of Tutankhamen remained the same as when the scene opened on the Tell el Amarna letters. This, of course, lays the ghost of the second part of the Amarna legend: the king can no longer be seen as a pacifist, who spent his time in Amarna composing hymns while his empire fell to pieces. As far as one can tell from the letter to Aziru in Egypt, Amki must be adjacent to Amurru, since apparently Hittite forces based in Nuhasse moved directly on it: 'Soldiers of Hatte and Lupakku have taken cities of Amki, and from the cities of Aaduma they have captured [some]. . . . Zitana is come and there are nine foot-soldiers who have come with him.'[13] In the Tell el Amarna letters there are no other references to Hittite forces under Hittite command active in Amki, though there is reference to activity in the Amki area by Aitugama, king of Kadesh, who had some Hittite troops under him.[14]

A provisional reconstruction would be as follows: Aitugama, who flourished from the reign of Amenhotep III on through the later period of the Tell el Amarna letters, had long been unfriendly to Egypt and had drawn the express disapproval of Ikhnaton, but it was not until some time after the Tell el Amarna correspondence closes that the Egyptians took decisive action against him.

Just preceding the report of Tutankhamen's death in the annals of Suppiluliuma is the passage: 'The country of Arziya, the country of Karchemish, made peace with my brother. The city of Murmuriga, the same city observed peace with him. Only the city of Karchemish in the land of Karchemish remained hostile to him and the priest my brother left to the land of Murmuriga 600 men, some chariots and Lupakkis the commander of the army. When the people of Harri saw the priest leave, the troops and chariots of Harri came towards Takuhsislis and they enveloped Murmuriga and to what was there of troops and chariots of Harri they were superior. . . . As my father had gone up from Kadesh, the troops and chariots of Egypt came and assailed the country of Kadesh. One sent a message to my father. "The troops and chariots which occupy Murmuriga the people of Harri surround and press them." My father mobilized troops and chariots and marched against the people of Harri and when he arrived at the country of Tegaramma he made a review of his troops and chariots at Talpa the rendezvous for the troops and chariots. Then he sent Arnuwandas his son and Zitas the "praetorian" from Tegarammu into the land of Harri. . . . When my father arrived in the lower land he did not meet the Harrian enemy, he descended to Karchemish and besieged it again.'[15] There follows a gap of twenty-three lines in which the copying scribe was apparently unable to read the original, after this comes the reference to the death of Tutankhamen.

This shows that some time not long before the death of Tutankhamen the Egyptians attacked and ravaged the area of Kadesh. The reprisal campaign for this attack was the one which was in progress at the time the Hittite king received the embassy from Ankhsenamen.

The facts, are however, more complicated. The Hittite king was apparently not only attacked by the Egyptians but had to defend himself against the people of Harri against whom he had been previously campaigning.

This material is fortified by a sentence from the speech of Suppiluliuma to Hani, the Egyptian envoy, already quoted: 'You came? and attacked the man of Kinza whom I had taken away from the King of Hurri land.'[16] Certainly at the beginning of the reign of Amenhotep III the territory of Egypt must have included, at least nominally, the area of Kadesh. It would not be surprising if such a remote area had been conquered by Suppiluliuma from the Egyptians, but this was not what Suppiluliuma said. He declared that he had taken the area from the king of Hurri land, and if this were so then it was the latter who had received control of the area from Egypt. This is confirmatory evidence of the existence of an agreement between Tushratta of Mitanni and Amenhotep III of Egypt regarding mutual defence of their frontier facing the Hittites. It is also evidence that this agreement was continued by the successors of Amenhotep III.

Taken in conjunction the material we have shows that at the time of these campaigns the fall of Tushratta of Mitanni had already occurred, and this is corroborated by another more badly preserved section of the annals which refers to the campaign of Arnuwandas against Egypt, and also to another campaign of Suppiluliuma against the lands of Harran and Mitanni. In this latter campaign Suppiluliuma's chief opponents were the men of Assur and Sutarna,[17] the son of a local king, who had apparently seized whatever power remained in Mitanni at Tushratta's death.

Tushratta's fall is recounted in the preamble of the treaty between Suppiluliuma and Mattiawaza, the son of Tushratta, who after marrying the Hittite king's daughter was restored to his throne by his father-in-law.[18] Unfortunately, this document is by no means clear, and does not observe a strict chronology. Suppiluliuma refers to a campaign in the course of which he reached the capital of Mitanni, Washshugganni, but Tushratta withdrew rather than give battle; on the way back from this campaign Suppiluliuma crossed the Euphrates and took the lands of Halpa (Aleppo) and Mukishi. At this time Takuwa, the king of the land of Niy, came in peace to meet Suppiluliuma, but an anti-Hittite party in Niy, led by the king's brother, Akitesub, rebelled at this friendly approach. Apparently Suppiluliuma was quick to suppress this move, captured the chief rebels and deported them to Hatte. At this time also he took the city of Qatna and partially plundered it. The king then told how he went on to Nuhasse and found that his ally Sarrupsi, the paramount king of the area, had been assassinated by a pro-Mittannian faction amongst his family. Suppiluliuma also mentions an attack on Kadesh, when he was forced to fight by the prince of that city, Sutarna. He was victorious and took Sutarna and his son Aitugama and other notables captive to Hatte.[19] A good many more less relevant details of the campaign are reported, but the king closed his narrative by saying that it was on account of the arrogance of Tushratta that he was led to plunder these lands for six years and carry their booty off to Hatte, commenting also that he had added the area from the Niblani (Lebanon) range and the west bank of the Euphrates to his realm. Following the close of this section, the next line mentioned the murder of Tushratta by his son and servants.[20]

These events can perhaps be approximately dated. The third letter of Akizzi of Qatna, which was certainly written close to the same time as his second letter, names Aitugama as the man (prince) of Kinza (Kadesh).[21] The preamble of the treaty between Suppiluliuma and Mattiawaza names Sutarna, the father of

Aitugama, as prince of Kadesh.[22] The events of the Qatna letters wherein Aitugama was called a Hittite agent must have been subsequent to the return of the converted Aitugama from his sojourn in Hatte. Akizzi also mentions an attack of the king of Hatte on his city.[23] Unfortunately, the time sequence in this letter (which also mentions Aziru) is rather confused: 'The gods and the men of Qatna the king of Hatte takes. My lord the people of Qatna, my servants that Aziru takes and he puts them out of the land of my lord, and now they dwell away from the land of my lord', and later 'but now the king of Hatte has taken from them the sun god the god of my father'. It is apparent that some time during the writer's relatively recent past Hatte forces had attacked Qatna. Since at the time of the Qatna letters Aitugama was the 'man' (prince) of Kinza (Kadesh) it seems likely that the attack on Qatna and on Kadesh, noted in the preamble to the treaty with Mattiawaza, occurred some time before the letters, preserved in the Tell el Amarna group were written. However, as the Hittite attack on Mitanni discussed here was apparently the last before the death of Tushratta, and probably occurred before the letters from Qatna were written, it follows that the campaign against Mitanni mentioned in the treaty and the attack by the Hittites about which Tushratta wrote to Amenhotep III were one and the same. Suppiluliuma himself noted that the campaigns summarised in the treaty took place over a period of six years, and the one against Mitanni could well have been at the beginning of that period and those against Qatna and Kadesh at the end, as the arrangement of the material in the treaty itself suggests. At any rate there were no further campaigns against Mitanni during the life time of Tushratta mentioned either by the letters from Tushratta to Egypt, or by the Hittite sources, and the treaty preamble noted the death of Tushratta in the next line after the conclusion of the description of the series of campaigns.

Tushratta, however, in his discussion of the campaign against him classed the result as a victory for his own troops, sending part of the booty and the prisoners to the Egyptian court. It is significant, as I have said above when discussing the Amarna letters, that, after this effort, Suppiluliuma made no active intervention south of Nuhasse until close to the death of Tutankhamen, though certainly Hittite activity in Nuhasse is amply indicated from Aziru's correspondence.

Since the Hittite king stopped his action in Syria for quite a considerable time, neither he nor Tushratta recording any further hostilities; since the campaigns of Tushratta in Syria are noted in the Ribaddi correspondence; and since Suppiluliuma speaks of taking Kadesh from the king of Hurri land, it appears that Suppiluliuma did not hold the area of Kadesh during the whole of this period, and that it was recaptured by the Mittanians, Egyptians or both acting together.

It is evident that the fall of Tushratta took place during the reign of Tutankhamen, and was brought about, according to Suppiluliuma, as a result of a palace conspiracy in which a son of Tushratta was involved,[24] without Hatte being concerned. At any rate Artatama, king of Harri, another Hurrian land, and the kings of Alse and Assyria profited. It is further apparent that Artatama, who perhaps had been excluded from the succession by Tushratta, became nominal ruler with his son Sutarna as regent.[25]

Another fragment of the annals of Suppiluliuma, placed by the editors after the attack on Egypt, noted another campaign in Mitanni in which the opponents of Suppiluliuma were the king of Assyria (either Assur Uballit or his immediate successor) and Sutarna, the regent of Artatama.[26] This happened despite Suppiluliuma's friendly relations with Artatama, the ruler of Harri. Possibly Artatama and his son had quarrelled, but Suppiluliuma had other reasons for intervention. The son of Tushratta, Mattiawaza, had fled to Hatte to seek refuge with the king because he found that his first haven, Babylonia, had become unsafe on account of growing Assyrian pressure for his assassination. The Hittite king received him well, married him to his daughter, and promised to restore him to his throne.[27] It is likely that the fragment already quoted came from the account of the campaign of restoration. In the treaty preamble it was apparent that Karchemish was used as a base of operations.[28] It is evident from this that the restoration of Mattiawaza must have taken place after the death of Tutankhamen, either in the reign of Eye or Haremhab.

Suppiluliuma's death was followed by the brief reign of his son Arnuwandas, who was then succeeded by a second son, Mursilis II. His annals survive to a far greater extent than those of his father, but references to Egypt are unfortunately very fragmentary. Once the king of Egypt is mentioned in connection with Karchemish,[29] and elsewhere the king records: 'When I arrived at Ziluna [in Hatte] the news was brought. The soldiers of Egypt he [the king of Karchemish] had fought them.'[30]

Aitugama, king of Kadesh, was killed by his son and the city rebelled against Hatte.[31] It seems that this event must have been supported by a pro-Egyptian party for the success of such a revolt even to be contemplated. It is evident, however, from the plague prayers of Mursilis II that the Hittites wanted peace with Egypt,[32] and from the absence of much material relating to Egypt we can see that peace was soon made, so that for the largest part of the reign of Haremhab there were no hostilities.

Egyptian sources bear this out. In the text of the treaty made by Ramesses II of Egypt, and Hattusilis II the son of Mursilis II, we find: 'As to the regular treaty that there was in the time of Suppiluliuma, the great chief of Hatte, and likewise the regular treaty that there was in the time of Muwatallis, the great chief of Hatte, my father, I take hold of it, etc.'[33]

Hattusilis, born before his father's tenth regnal year, was still young at his accession,[34] which followed the reign of his brother Muwatallis,[35] with possibly another short reign between. The remark as to the treaty cannot be accurate, since it would have been negotiated either with Mursilis II, the father of Hattusilis II,[36] or with Muwatallis, his brother. It is evident that the well known wars of Seti I and Ramesses II with Muwatallis were finally settled by the treaty of Hattusilis, rather than by a previous one dealing essentially with the same situation. It is preferable, though by no means definite, to correct the scribal error by changing Muwatallis to Mursilis rather than by changing 'my father' to 'my brother'. This second treaty, then, most probably closed the series of wars during the period of Tutankhamen and Eye.

# SEVEN: The Egyptian evidence

It is to be regretted that no comprehensive record of campaigns carved on tomb or temple wall by royal decree remains from this period. Surviving biographical inscriptions of pharaoh's servants are largely unconcerned with military affairs in Asia, except during the brief reign of Tutankhamen.

Under Amenhotep III we have only one badly broken record of a royal Nubian campaign from the fifth year of his reign.[1] As far as Asia is concerned there is no coherent account of military activity, although isolated references to Asia occur in various inscriptions. Speaking of the staff at the granary of his mortuary temple at Luxor, the king wrote: 'Its granary being full of male and female slaves from the children of the chief men of every foreign country which his majesty plundered',[2] chief's children could not be taken as booty unless real warfare was being carried on. In addition, a small stele has been found at Thebes in the temple of the Nineteenth Dynasty king Merneptah which commemorates Amenhotep III as the victor over Nubia and Asia,[3] and was probably set up originally to mark some successful military action. Such indefinite references as this could be multiplied, but are no substitute for a consistent hieroglyphic account of military operations. The Tell el Amarna letters are our only large source of information for this reign.

From Ikhnaton's reign we have only a fragmentary record of a Nubian campaign,[4] and the reliefs of the durbar of the year 12, recorded in the tombs of Huya and Meryre II at Amarna. The durbar reliefs show people from Asiatic areas as far away as Hatte attending a celebration which I believe marked Ikhnaton's assumption of sole power. Otherwise, the Tell el Amarna letters remain the only source of information as to Egypt's position in Western Asia.

The period of the Tell el Amarna letters, however, came to an end shortly before Ikhnaton's death. During the time of Tutankhamen the Hittite material is of assistance, but there are also more ample Egyptian sources. The tomb of Huy, the viceroy of Nubia, depicts Asiatic campaigning, and has a relief in which Huy presents the tribute of Syria before the king. Princes of Upper Retenu, who had not known Egypt since the time of the god, beg for mercy before his majesty and say: 'Give to us the breath of thy giving.'[5] This scene shows that tribute from Syria still flowed into the coffers of Egypt, but unfortunately it does not portray any actual warfare.

The tomb at Memphis of the general Haremhab, who later became pharaoh, was probably carved in Tutankhamen's time and originally had campaign references, but the monument has been completely destroyed and the scattered blocks now preserved in museums naturally provide only fragmentary material. It was decorated before Haremhab became king, and the uraeus (the mark of kingship) was added to his figure after the carving had been completed. An old copy of a now lost block reads: 'He (Haremhab) was sent as king's envoy to the region of the Aton's uprising [the word Aton used here indicates the god name] returning in triumph his [attack] having succeeded. No foreign land stood before him, he has despoiled them in the completion of a moment. His name was pronounced in . . . he did not delay in going northwards, and lo his majesty arose upon the throne of offering bringing. There were brought [the offerings] of the south and north while the hereditary prince Haremhab stood beside.'[6] Another reference to military activity comes from a doorpost of this tomb now in the Cairo museum: 'A [henchman] at the feet of his lord on the battlefield on this day of slaughtering Asiatics.'[7] In the reliefs preserved, Haremhab is shown accepting a royal reward while standing in front of long lines of manacled Syrian prisoners. There are also other warlike inscriptions from the tomb, but they do not give any more definite information.

A carved chest from the tomb of Tutankhamen shows the king in his chariot slaying Asiatics,[8] and a similar depiction of Eye on a small piece of gold leaf—found, together with other similar material from his reign and that of Tutankhamen, in a rock-cut chamber in the Valley of the Kings by the T. M. Davis Expedition—is the only evidence whatever from this latter reign of military activity.[9] Such a relief of the king standing in a chariot slaying enemies may well be significant indications that military activity on some scale was in progress during the reign concerned.

It should be mentioned here, however, that tomb evidence from the reign of Tutankhamen has been largely discounted as a repetition of the more substantial claims to power of other kings, which in this case were purely formal and possess little value as reliable historical evidence. Yet, the Hittite material shows that Egypt maintained her hold on the north during Tutankhamen's rule, and the tomb evidence from Egypt itself gains weight in consequence.

The reigns of Tutankhamen, Ankhsenamen and Eye constitute an extremely obscure period, not merely because the reigns were all quite short, but because Haremhab, and probably his successors, usurped their monuments. In the case of Tutankhamen this was probably done for political rather than personal reasons, but as we have seen, Haremhab obviously hated Eye, and tried to obliterate all traces of his predecessor's rule. Ikhnaton was treated in a similar fashion, and again there appears to have been personal enmity against the dead king, which must have first become predominant in the reign of Haremhab. It is only surprising that, considering the efforts made, the memory of the Amarna rulers was not entirely blotted out, but the demolition of Akhetaton—probably by Haremhab—was thorough and efficient, and as far as his own age was concerned doubtless achieved its purpose. It is only in modern times that the city has been rediscovered.

The material from the reign of Haremhab relative to Asia is little more significant than that from the reign of Tutankhamen. Most important is a relief of Asiatic tribute from the walls of the ninth and tenth pylons of the Karnak temple, the relevant portion of the inscription reading: '[Bringing] tribute by his majesty to his father Amen from that which he had brought from the land of Retenu.'[10] In the same place there is a relief of Haremhab leading Asiatic prisoners, and he also set up on the temple at Karnak a list of places which he claimed to have conquered, and which includes a number of Asiatic localities, as far away as the Hittite area.[11] All this strongly suggests that royal campaigns were made, but gives little definite material from which to draw conclusions, and foreign sources are also of little help. We have already seen that the annals of Mursilis II are most fragmentary in their references to Egypt, and the possible mention of a treaty between Haremhab and Mursilis II in the treaty between Hattusilis II and Ramesses II likewise is not very definite.

The situation becomes clarified only when the records of the campaigns of Seti I are considered. A stele discovered at Beth Shan, a city of Palestine, reads: 'year 1, third month of summer, day 10—This day one came to tell His Majesty that the vile foe who was in Hamath had collected to himself many men and was taking the town of Beth Shan, having made alliance with them of Pella [another town] and he would not permit the prince of Rehob to come out. And his majesty sent the first army of Amun, mighty of bows, to the town of Hamath and the first army of Pare, rich in valour, to the town of Beth Shan and the first army of Sutekh, victorious of bows, to the town of Yenoam. And it came to pass in the space of one day that they fell to the might of his majesty the king of Upper and Lower Egypt, Menmaatre, son of Re (Seti Merneptah) given life.'[12] This inscription certainly indicates that the suppression of a revolt was involved here, rather than a campaign of new conquest. Beth Shan was obviously held in the Egyptian interest. Indeed, very shortly after his reign began Seti was campaigning in the far north and fighting with the Hittites in about the same area as the fighting occurred in the time of Tutankhamen.[13]

# EIGHT: The archaeological discoveries from Syria-Palestine

Digressing for a moment to the archaeological material from Syria and Palestine from the period between the reigns of Amenhotep III and Ramesses I, it is a pity that the many sites excavated have yielded much important data bearing on local history, but little bearing upon the relations of the great powers of the day. In Beth Shan, the Palestinian city just mentioned, the Egyptian temple which was built in the reign of Amenhotep III was still apparently in use as late as the reign of Haremhab.[1] The only reasonable explanation is that Egyptian rule continued in the area during the obscure period, which would corroborate the material from other sources which points to the same conclusion. The temple in level VI of this site has foundation deposits of Ramesses I,[2] Haremhab's successor and the first king of the Nineteenth Dynasty, which would certainly indicate that he held power in the area. The presence of scarabs inscribed by various rulers of this period, however, need not necessarily mean that these Egyptian kings ruled the areas where they were found, though they are interesting as support of other more definitive data.

# NINE: The summing-up

The following conclusions may now be drawn: From the beginning of the period of the Tell el Amarna letters, which coincided with the year 29 (or slightly earlier) of Amenhotep III, until the end of the reign of Tutankhamen, the Egyptians held a large area of north Syria. Although there were boundary fluctuations from time to time, the land of Amki was regarded as so surely Egyptian that when Mursilis II wrote about it in the plague prayers he described it as the borderland of Egypt. Areas such as Amurru and Kadesh changed allegiance at least once during the period. We know that before the end of the reign of Suppiluliuma, Aziru had changed his master, and the evidence shows that late Hittite kings regarded the lords of Amurru as their vassals. We may even hazard a guess, impossible now to verify, that people such as Aziru and Akizzi of Qatna deliberately played Egypt and Hatte against one another. Existing data make it idle to attempt to demarcate the Egyptian frontier. Sumur, for example, was considered by Ribaddi as an Egyptian centre, but the pharaoh certainly did not seem to be too concerned that Aziru had taken possession of the district. Akizzi of Qatna claimed that Qatna and the lands of Nuhasse and Niy were loyal to Egypt, but there seems no reason to believe that the Egyptians had troops in this area during the Amarna period, and direct evidence that Nuhasse especially was involved with the Hittites is plentiful.

Nevertheless, it seems certain that Hittite influence replaced Egyptian in the very far north during the period, but how much Egyptian control there ever was except during an actual campaign in this remote region is uncertain. Another imponderable here is the effect of the Mittanian collapse on the balance of power. The Hittite campaigns against Egyptian-held territory do not seem to have had any effect, at least until after the death of Tutankhamen. The plague prayers of Mursilis show his strong desire for peace, and the absence of much reference to Egypt in his annals tends to prove generally peaceful relations between Egypt and Hatte. Further confirmation is provided by the most logical interpretation of the relevant remarks in the treaty between Hattusilis II and Ramesses II. The fact that Ramesses I was the founder of a new temple in Beth Shan, and that soon after the beginning of his reign Seti I was campaigning against the Hittites in the same area as was involved at the end of the reign of Tutankhamen, strengthens the case that the Egyptian collapse in the previous reign was a myth.

# Postscript

And so, the Ikhnaton legend—duly written as fact in the history books and solemnly taught in schools—disintegrates on steady analysis. For some this will be a matter for lament, just as there will be a sigh of regret for the 'Nofretiti' bust which might be taken as emblematic of this book's iconoclastic theme. Yet the work of art remains as beautiful, whatever the name of the queen depicted, and the events of the period, as the evidence suggests they really were, offer a greater challenge to the modern imagination than the romantic dreams of the nineteenth century.

[1] *Plaster mask of Ikhnaton, from the workshop of Thutmosis: Berlin Museum*

[II] *The mask of the preceding page in profile; the caricature head of Ikhnaton from one of the Karnak colossi in Cairo Museum; and a wooden statuette of the king from the Berlin Museum*

[III] *The limestone head, usually considered as that of Nofretiti, but more probably that of one of her daughters Ankhsenamen or Meritaton: Berlin Museum*

[IV] *Limestone stele showing Amenhotep III and Tiy, seated before a stand of offerings: British Museum*
*Caricature relief in limestone of Ikhnaton, Nofretiti and three of their daughters: Berlin Museum*

[v] *Limestone relief of Amenhotep III in the conventional style, from Thebes: Berlin Museum*

[VI] *Panel of wood, covered in thick gold foil, from the side of Tiy's sepulchral canopy. The photo is turned sideways to show the decoration more clearly: the Queen is to the right, and Ikhnaton (whose figure has been erased) is shown centre*

[VII] *The mummies of Iuya and Tuya, the father and mother of Tiy; the cover of an alabaster canopic vase found in the tomb of Tiy* (left) *on which the inscriptions have been erased, and* (right) *the fine soapstone head of the Queen found by* Flinders Petrie *at Sinai*

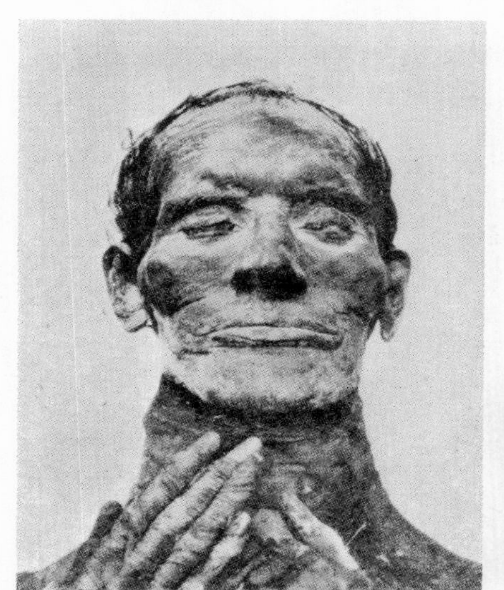

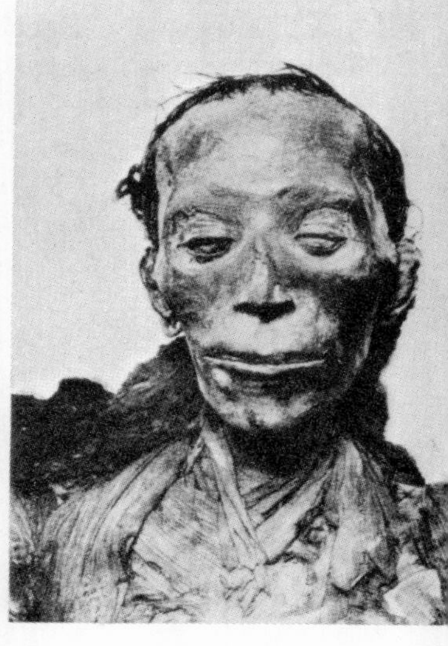

[VIII] *The limestone statue known as the 'Kissing King', representing Ikhnaton with either one of his daughters or Smenkhkare, now in Cairo Museum; and two limestone reliefs, one showing Ikhnaton wearing the double crown, sharing a meal with Smenkhkare* (left), *and the other showing Smenkhkare pouring the King's wine: both Berlin Museum*

[IX] *Limestone relief, most probably of Smenkhkare and Meritaton: Berlin Museum*

[x] *A limestone plaque from the Great Temple at Amarna, showing Ikhnaton* (left) *and Smenkhkare: Cairo Museum.*
*Chest lid inlaid with coloured ivory, showing Tutankhamen and Ankhsenamen*

[XI] *Head of a princess in brown sandstone from the workshop of Thutmosis in the Berlin Museum; a wooden bust of Tutankhamen in Cairo Museum; and two of the Amarna letters—Amenhotep III writes to Kadashman-Enlil, King of Karduniash* (left), *and Tushratta, King of Mitanni, writes to Amenhotep III: both in the British Museum*

[XII] *The central aisle o the hall of Eye's tomb a Amarna, and a close-up of Eye and his wife being rewarded with heavy gold necklets by Ikhnaton: Cairo Museum*

[XIII] *Haremhab shown as a scribe: Metropolitan Museum of Art.*

*Eye and his wife at prayer, from the tomb at Amarna. Eye's eventual tomb, as King, was in the Valley of the Kings*

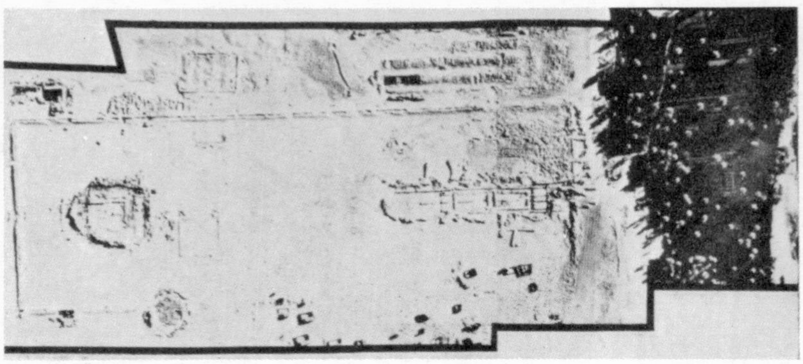

[XIV] *Aerial view of central Akhetaton showing the line of the* Royal Road. *Part of the ground plan of the Great Temple* (see also lower illus.) *is seen far left, next come its numerous storehouses, then the King's House, with the* Records *Office behind, and then the smaller temple and its subsidiary buildings. In the foreground the dark area of modern cultivation covers part of the area of the Great Official Palace*

[xv] *Perspective sketch of part of central Akhetaton. Above the Royal Road is the Window of Appearances, and the bridge leads down to the left into the garden of the King's House, and to the right into the Great Official Palace. Here the blocks on either side of the entrance from the road, in the foreground, are the north and south harems. In the middle distance is the smaller temple, with its magazines and priests' quarters lying beyond*

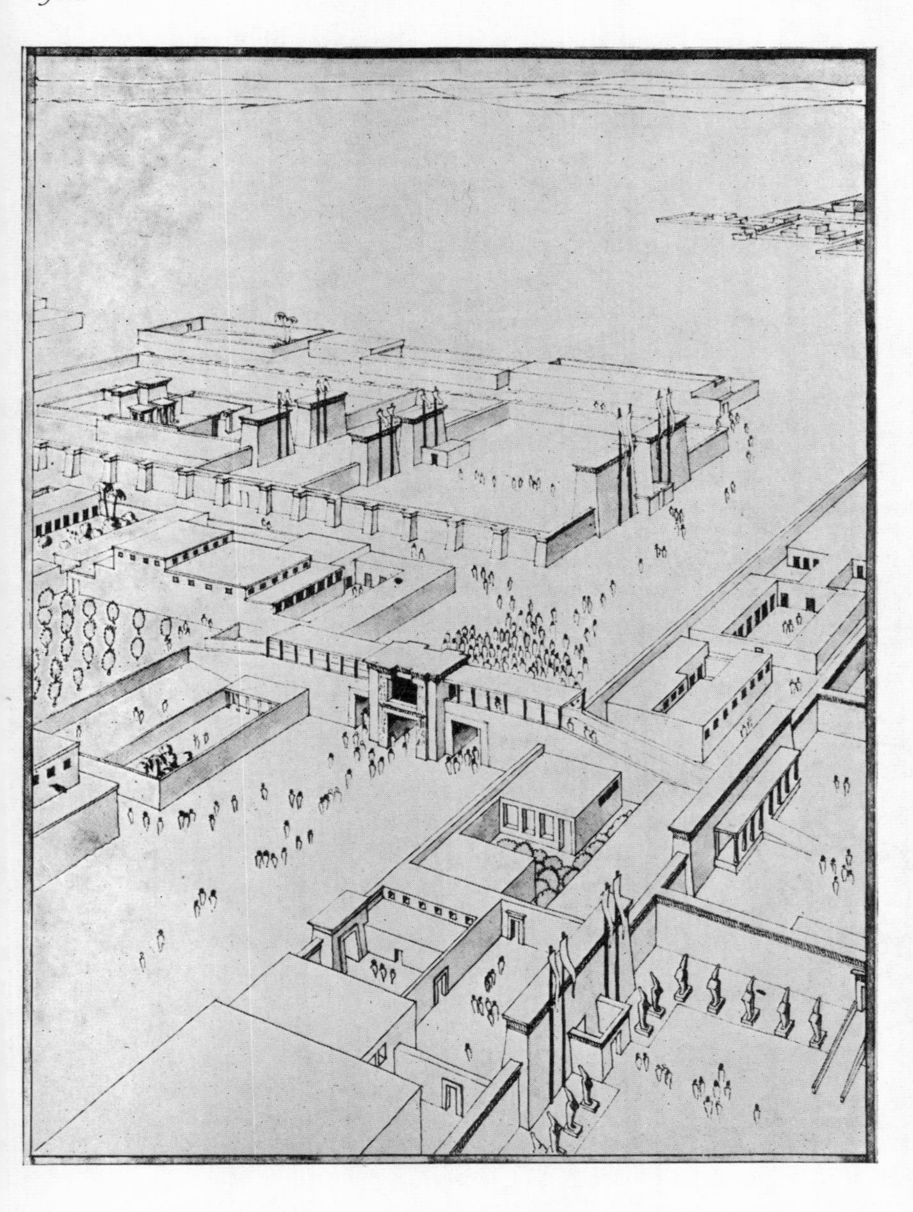

[XVI] *Representation of the sanctuary of the Great Temple in the tomb of Meryre I at Amarna, and a perspective reconstruction. There are offering tables in the outer court, and also in the inner one, where they almost surround the high altar, which has a small flight of steps leading up to it*

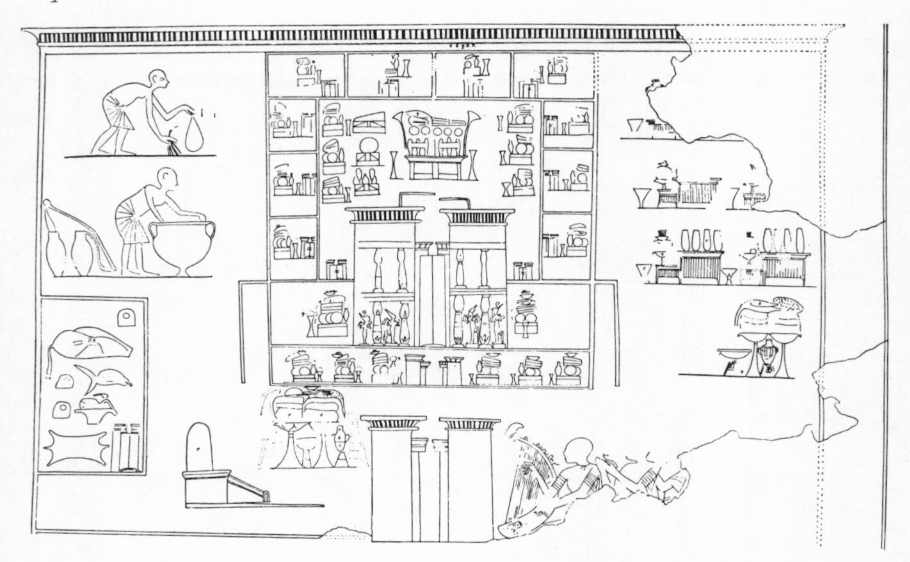

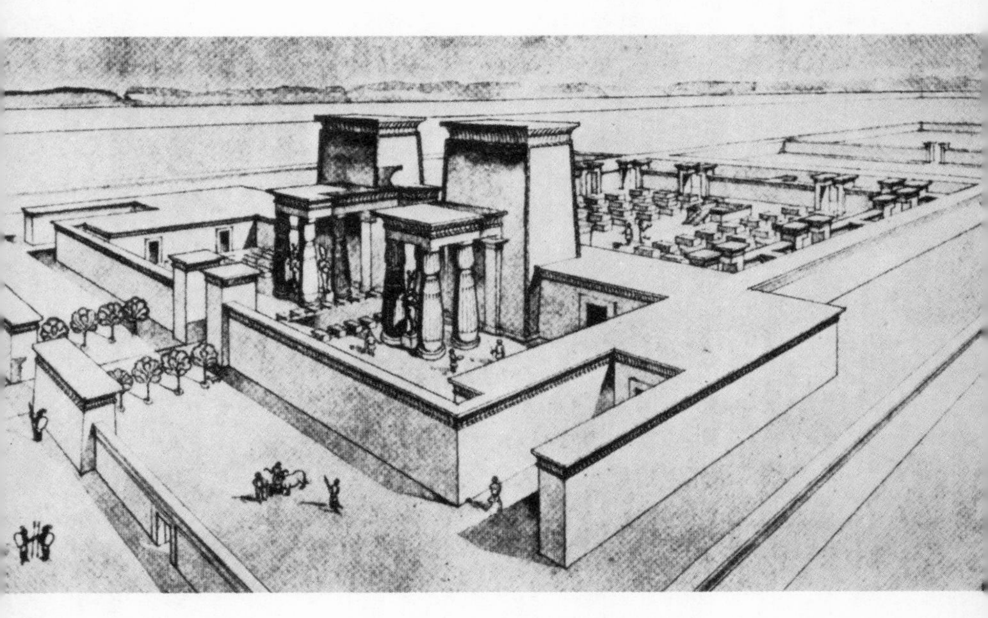

*The tomb of Huya: the Hymn to the Sun.*

*The royal family at dinner. To the left, Ikhnaton and Nofretiti with Meritaton and one of their younger daughters; to the right Tiy and Beketaton; and, lower centre, Huya serving as Tiy's chamberlain, receiving the dishes from the palace official.*

*Ikhnaton and Nofretiti, with Ankhespaaton and Meketaton, entertain Tiy and Beketaton to supper. Huya, lower centre, apparently directs the servants' operations with a wand.*

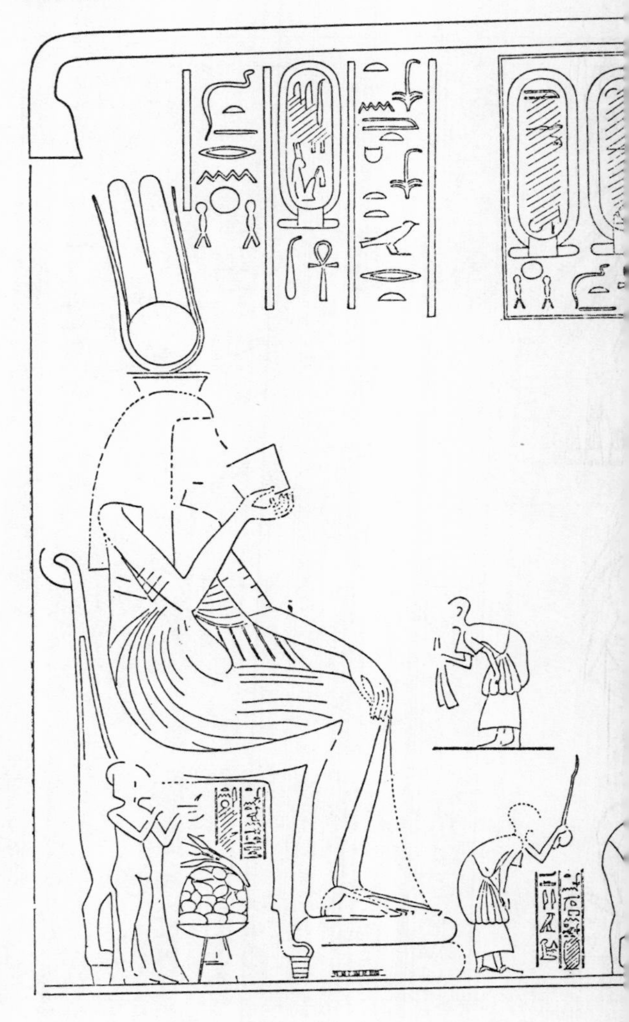

*Ikhnaton takes Tiy, in typical two-plumed headdress, to see the Sunshade of Tiy. His sister, Beketaton, follows with an altar gift, closely supervised by two nurses.*

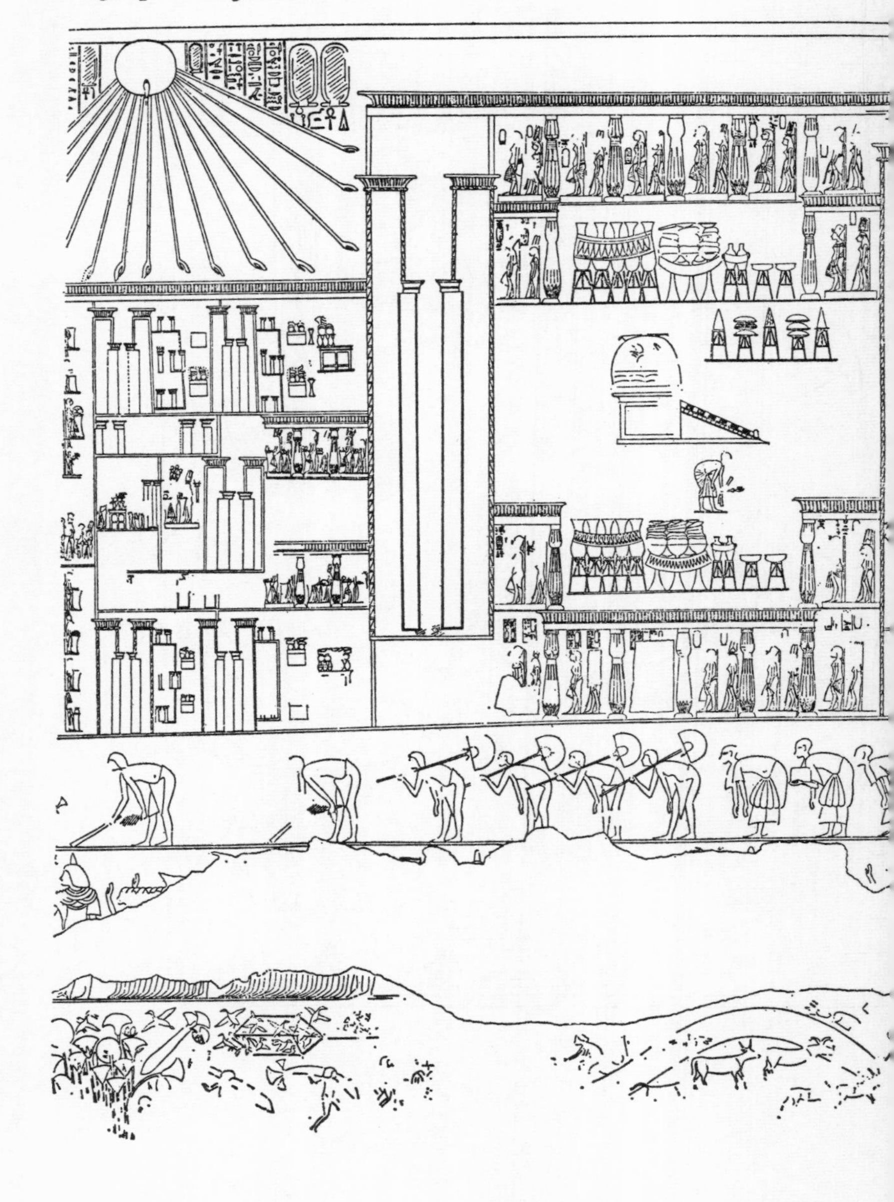

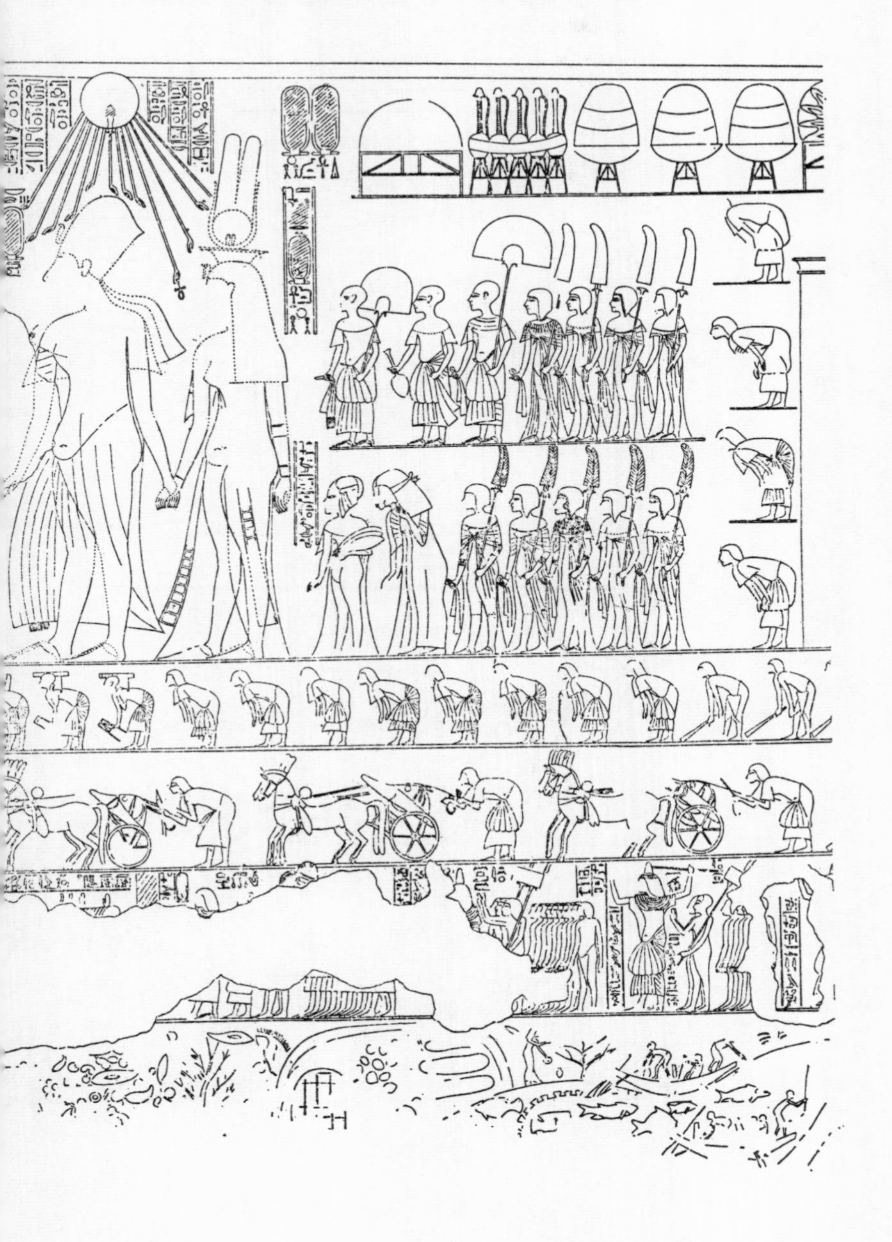

*Ikhnaton and Nofretiti are carried to the durbar on a palanquin, the two elder princesses walking behind with waiting women and two nurses.*

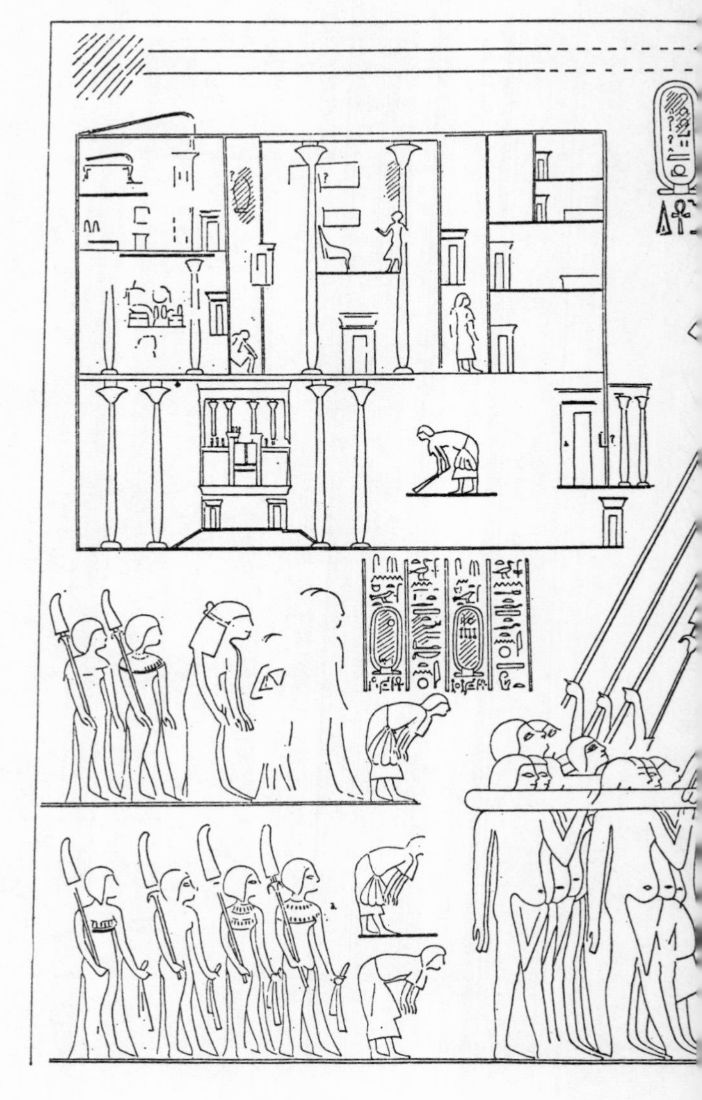

*Huya is honoured by the King and Queen, the two younger princesses, with their nurses, watching on the left. The scene marks Huya's appointment as 'Superintendent of the Royal Harem, Superintendent of the Treasury and Steward in the House of the Queen Mother', and a servant affixes a sash or some other insignia of office to his dress.*

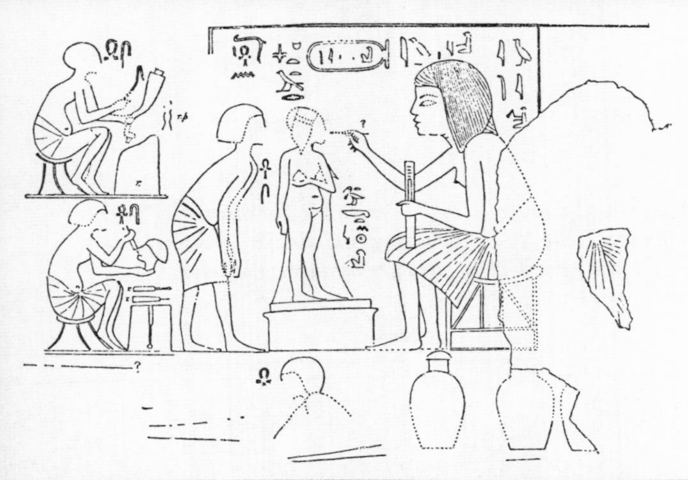

*a) Auta puts the finishing touches to a painted statue of Beketaton in his studio. The artist's assistants are engaged, one in shaping a chair leg, and the other on a portrait head.*

*b) The controversial lintel: the left-hand side* (above) *shows Ikhnaton and Nofretiti with four of their daughters, and the right-hand side, Amenhotep III with Tiy and Beketaton.*

*The durbar, as recorded in the tomb of Meryre II: Ikhnaton and Nofretiti enthroned, with the six princesses behind them, and three nurses beside the platform. On the right are the bearers of tribute, wrestlers, and so on.*

*Meryre II rewarded by Smenkhkare and Meritaton.*

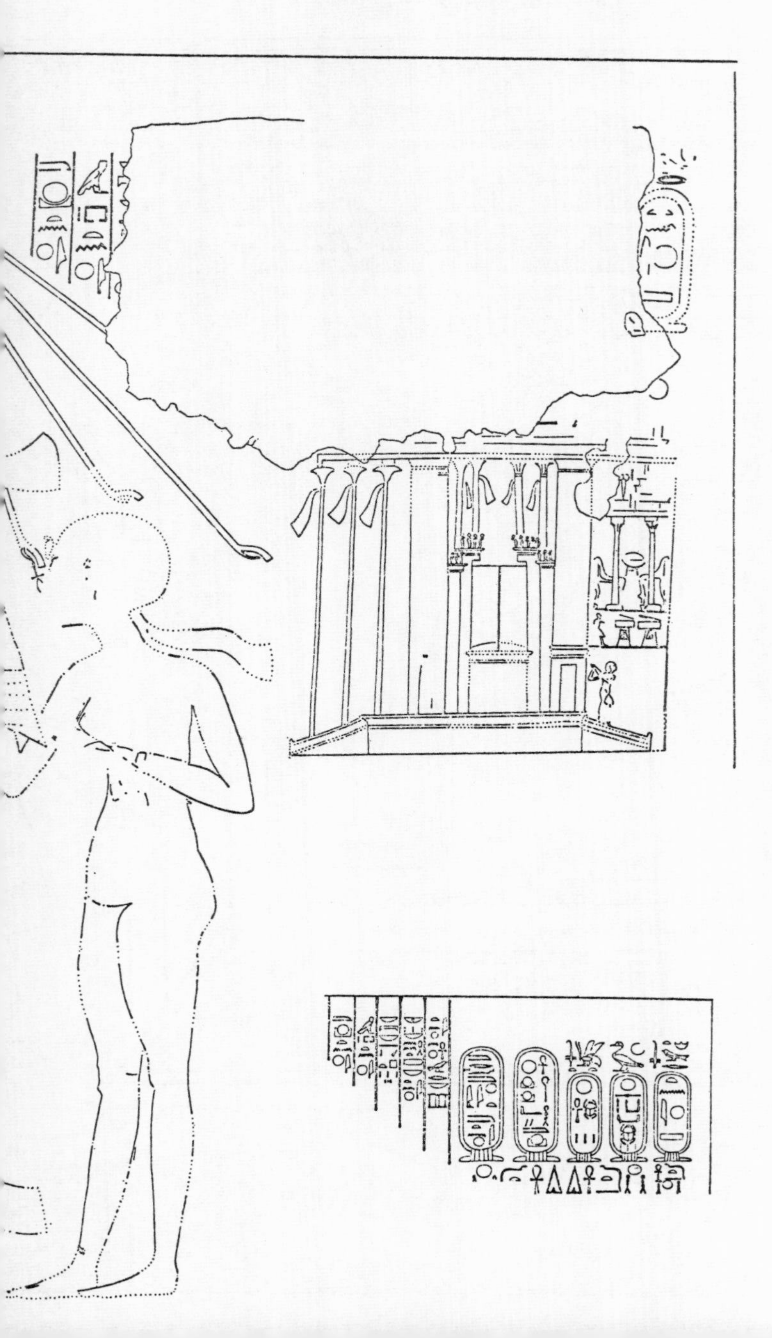

*Part of a scene from the northern portico of the tomb of Heruef at Thebes. Amenhotep III and Tiy are enthroned under a baldachin, the decoration on the side of Tiy's throne showing her as a human-headed lioness or sphinx. Heruef, most of whose figure has been erased by enemies, presents a decorated vase and box, necklaces and pectorals.*

# APPENDIX: Dating the Tell el Amarna letters

The letters to and from the southern area of Egyptian influence are 162 in number—1–16, 31A and 200–342, including the new letters added by Mercer—31A, 222A, 248A and 256A. Among these there are 65 reasonably complete letters which cannot be assigned to the reign of either Amenhotep III or Ikhnaton. These latter are for the most part notes requesting aid or confirming that their writers will obey instructions, and contain no names that can be cross-referenced with other letters.

Letters which can be assigned to the reign of Amenhotep III number 55, including the letters to and from the Babylonian court, namely 1–6, 31A, 222A, 232, 237, 242–6, 246A, 247–8, 252–6, 256A, 257–61, 264–71, 278–90, 290A, 329, and 333–5.

We have already discussed (p. 156) how letters 242–6 and 246A, although written by Biridya of Megiddo to an un-named pharaoh, can in fact be placed in the reign of Amenhotep III because they refer to Zurata. It follows that letters 247 and 248 from Jasdata, the brother of Biridya, must also belong to this reign. So also must the letters of Labaiya (252–4), the unfortunate captive of Biridya and Jasdata, and two other letters (249 and 250), written by a city-prince ADDU-UR-SAG (the name cannot be fully read)—in the first Labaiya is mentioned as living,[1] but in the second he is dead[2] and the depredations of his sons are described.

Letter 31A, which contains the name Amen,[3] must obviously have been written by Amenhotep III, and not the Atonist Ikhnaton. It is addressed to Milkili, a city-prince mentioned in 249 and 250 as an associate of Labaiya[4] and who, though he outlived Labaiya for some time, must therefore be a contemporary of Amenhotep III, to whom his letters (267–71) would have been written. The letters (264–6) to the Egyptian court of Tagi, father-in-law of Milkili, must also belong to Amenhotep III's time, additional confirmation being the mention of Tagi in connection with Labaiya and Milkili.[5]

Abdi-Hiba of Jerusalem, when writing to Egypt (289), condemns Milkili, Tagi, and Labaiya as alike enemies of the king and himself,[6] and accuses Milkili and his father-in-law of having combined to take the city of Rubuda.[7] In letter 290, however, he makes this same accusation, not against Milkili and Tagi, but against Milkili and another enemy of his, Suwardata.[8] By the time of letter 290A, however, written by Suwardata, he and Abdi-Hiba have apparently patched up their differences and together are making war on the SA·GAZ people, with the help of Zurata of Acco and Endaruta of Aksapa.[9] The introduction of Zurata's name again shows that Abdi-Hiba, Suwardata, and Endaruta are also contemporaries of Amenhotep III and that their letters (Abdi-Hiba 285–90 and Suwardata 278–84 and 290A) were addressed to him: consequently, letter 222A written to Intaruda of Aksapa (differences in the spelling of names in this appendix reflect differences in the sources themselves) was probably from Amenhotep III.

In Abdi-Hiba's letter 288 (probably from the reign of Amenhotep III) a reference to the death of three princes—Turbazu, Iaptih-Addu, and Zimridi of Lachish[10]—marks this event as belonging to the reign of Amenhotep III, so does letter 335,[11] which recounts the same event. Letter 329 written by Zimridi; and letter 333, which mentions Zimridi as still living,[12] must then also date from the reign of this king.

Ba'alu Mehir, yet another city prince of Palestine, wrote letters 257–61. He seems to have been a captive in the same way as Labaiya, and to have bribed Zurata to free him at about the same time,[13] so that his correspondence was probably with Amenhotep III's court. And so were the letters (255–6) which Labaiya's son, Mut-Ba'alu, wrote shortly after his father's death.[14] In 256 he mentions the escape of Aiab, king of Bihisi,[15] who is the writer of 256A, and this letter, too, most probably belongs to Amenhotep III's reign.

The names of Egyptian officials are also helpful from the point of view of ordering the letters. The most important official in the south throughout the period covered by the letters was Ianhamu. ADDU-UR-SAG mentions him in letter 249,[16] which means he held office before the death of Labaiya; he appears again in the Ribaddi correspondence (83),[17] not long after its beginning; and is last mentioned in letter 132,[18] not very long before Ribaddi's exile.

Addaia, who seems to have been one of Amenhotep III's officials, is mentioned by Labaiya,[19] and frequently by Abdi-Hiba.[20] And Pahanate,[21] whose name is mentioned in Ribaddi's very first letter, is also referred to in one of the latest of the series,[22] so that his career is another which must have covered almost the entire period. The same may have been true of Hania and Ha,[23] whose names are noted from time to time in the same way, but it is possible that here we are dealing with various officials whose names simply sounded alike to the Palestinians among whom they worked. Suta, whom we encounter in the letters of both Abdi-Hiba[24] and Zatatna of Acco,[25] is shown by this to have had a fairly long period of service in the area. Similarly, Maia[26] is named fairly frequently, but unfortunately only in letters which we are either unable to date or which belong to the later part of the period.

The rest of the Egyptians mentioned from time to time are of no help in dating the letters to a particular reign.

Coming to the next reign, there are 21 letters that can be assigned to the period of Ikhnaton—7–13 (from Burnaburiash), 209–10, 224–5, 233–5, 238, 273–4, 296, and 330–2.

When Burnaburiash writes to the king in letter 8, naming the culprits in the case of the robbed caravan as Sumadda the son of Balumme and Sutatna the son of Saratum,[27] we can be sure that these men were the contemporaries of Ikhnaton. Sutatna is readily identifiable with Zatatna the son of Zurata, the prince of Acco, so that his letters to the king (233–5) must be of this reign. The same applies to letters 244–5, probably written by the same Sumadda whom Burnaburiash accuses, but there is very little to go on. Suta the deputy of the king is mentioned,[24] but the only other reference to this man[25] occurs in one of Abdi-Hiba's letters which is manifestly earlier in date.

The son of Zatatna is mentioned as an enemy in a letter from Bajadi (238),[28] which may so be assigned to this reign, and letter 237, which mentions Labaiya in a broken context[29] (and is thought by Knudtzon[30] to be written by the same person as 238, by virtue of script, material, and content), seems to me to belong more probably to the reign of Amenhotep III than that of Ikhnaton. A reference to the sons of Milkili[31] in the first of the two letters (273–4) written to the king by the woman Ba'alat Nese, makes it likely that these also belong to the later reign.

Letter 296 from Iahtiri refers to his having been taken to Egypt when he was small by Ianhamu the king's deputy, since when he has been in the royal service.[32] Ianhamu first took office under Amenhotep III, and this allusion to the length of time he has held the post, probably dates the letter in the later reign.

Letters 330–2 are from Sipti Ba'alu the prince of Lachish, who is reported in 333 to be conspiring with Zimrida of Lachish. Sipti Ba'alu is quoted in this same letter as referring to Zimrida as his father,[33] and this seems to be meant literally, since in 332 Sipti Ba'alu refers to himself as the 'man' (Prince) of Lachish.[34] He must have succeeded on Zimrida's death at the hands of the rebels, as elsewhere reported by Abdi-Hiba.[35] These letters, therefore, are probably later than his accession and may be assigned to Ikhnaton's reign.

A fragmentary letter (210) is apparently addressed to Ikhnaton, and letter (209) from the same writer was probably intended for the same destination.

Of the remainder of the letters from the south, dividing the two groups for the sake of convenience at letter 200, letters 200, 208, 214, 219, 229, 236, 240, 291, 307–12, 327, 336, 338–42 (a total of 21) are fragmentary.

Altogether there are 185 letters from the north—16–199, 129A and 176A. Of these five are close to the change of reign—189 from Aitugama and 194–7 from Namizawa; eighty-three may be assigned to the reign of Amenhotep III—17–25, 31, 31A, 32, 51–9, 60–96, 99–100, 101–7, 109–15, 143–4, 155–7, 174–6, and 176A; and fifty-seven are from the reign of Ikhnaton—15–16, 26–30, 108, 116–38, 129A, 141–3, 146–54, 158–169, and 171. One letter—170—may possibly be later than the reign of Ikhnaton, and the remaining thirty-nine are too fragmentary, or contain insufficient information, to be dated.

There are various groups which, by their use of personal names, enable letters to be assigned to one reign or the other. However, one complication exists here which does not offer so much difficulty in the case of the analysis of the letters from the south. Quite a number of the leading protagonists, such as Namiazawa and Aitugama[36], and others of pharaoh's so-called enemies, had careers which began before the period of the letters and continued after its close.

The dominant group is the long series (68–96, 101–128) concerning Ribaddi the prince of Gubla. Letter 116 seems to have been written on the accession of a new king[37], and should probably have been closely followed by 108, which scholars have misplaced on account of the reference to the father of the addressee.[38] Consequently, letters 68–96 and 101–115 (except 108) will have been written during the reign of Amenhotep III.

Other useful groups are the letters of Akizzi of Qatna (52–5 and probably 56) and Tushratta of Mitanni (17–25), which are addressed to Amenhotep III by name. Two letters (31–2) concerning the land of Arzawa are also of his reign, the mention of Labaiya's name[39] in 32 making this certain even though the salutation is broken. Letter 53[40] from Addu-Nirari must also have been directed to Amenhotep III, since the grandfather of the king who is said to have interfered with the affairs of Nuhasse is far more likely to have been Amenhotep II than Thutmose IV.

The death of Abdi-Ashirta prince of Amurru[41] is first recorded in letter 101, emanating from Gubla, so that any other letters concerned with this man's activities can be placed similarly in the reign of Amenhotep III. Letter 116 of Ribaddi (with its reference to the accession of a new pharaoh) was written at about the time that Aziru, the son of Abdi-Ashirta, took the city of Sumur.[42] Events in Aziru's career previous to this conquest must, therefore, also belong to Amenhotep III's reign. Confirmation of this can be found in the correspondence of Akizzi of Qatna (directed by name to Amenhotep III), since in letter 55 he names his principal enemy as Aziru.[43] References to Abdi-Ashirta[44] in letters 58, 60–5, and 67 make them attributable to the reign of Amenhotep III, as does a reference to Akizzi of Qatna[45] in letter 57.

In letter 59 the inhabitants of Tunip mention that they have been in correspondence with the king for more than twenty years[46]—the only pharaoh of which this could be true would be Amenhotep III—and also express fears lest Aziru take their city.[47] Since we know from Aziru's own letters that he eventually did hold the city,[48] this is another reason for assigning the letter to the reign of the earlier king. Letters 99 and 100 are also from cities, in these instances Ammia and Irqata which Ribaddi recorded as having been taken over by Aziru before his attack of Sumur,[49] and so these, too, must date from the reign of Amenhotep III.

All the letters from the north so far dealt with can be ascribed with reasonable certainty to the reign of Amenhotep III, and we now come to those written principally during the reign of his son. Letters 26–9 from Tushratta of Mitanni were addressed to the latter by name, and Assur-Uballit of Assyria certainly sent letters 15 and 16 to him. Letter 30 refers to the death of an Egyptian ruler who must almost certainly be Amenhotep III; the series of letters from the king of Alassia begins with one mentioning the accession of a king;[50] and the two letters of the king of the Hittites are also directed to Ikhnaton.

In the Ribaddi series the accession of the new king is first noted in 116,[37] and is also indicated in 108 and 117.[51] Letters 108 (which, as I have already said, should closely follow 116) and 116–38 cover the later part of the career of Aziru until the disappearance of Ribaddi, and were certainly written during the reign of Ikhnaton. Letter 142 from Ammunira prince of Beruta (Beirut) mentions the exile of Ribaddi and his sojourn in his own city,[52] so that all three letters from this king are of the later reign.

The letters of Abimilki of Tyre (148–55) belong to the time when Aziru had become very powerful. Every letter, except 150, 153, and 155, dilates on the hostility of Zimrida of Sidon,[53] and most refer to Aziru,[54] his capture of Sumur[55] being mentioned in 149. Although the king of Tyre is not mentioned anywhere else, Ribaddi does thank the king of Egypt in one of his letters for having written to the kings of Tyre, Sidon and Beirut exhorting them to assist Ribaddi in protecting himself against the attacks of Abdi-Ashirta.[56] This situation seems to be reflected[57] in the last letter (155) of the series from Abimilki (as arranged by Knudtzon), for here also Sumur does not yet seem to have passed under Aziru's control,[58] and it would thus appear to be the earliest rather than the last of the series. Supporting this is the absence of reference to the enmity of Zimrida of Sidon (the only other letters omitting this fact so ever-present to Abimilki being, as we have seen numbers 150 and 153),[59] and despite the curious mention of someone called Salmaiati (conjecturally identified by Albright as Meritaton)[60] this letter appears to me properly to belong to the reign of Amenhotep III. In my opinion the name Salmaiati could be that of a god just as easily as a person, and I find its significance obscure.

The two letters from Zimrida himself (144–5) do not refer to Aziru, although he is mentioned as a friend of his in the latter part of the Abimilki series.[61] Zimrida is first mentioned, as an ally of Abdi-Ashirta, in letter 83[62] from Ribaddi, and his rule at Sidon covers the whole period of the Amarna letters. However, neither of his letters deals with the situation as it was in the time of Ikhnaton, so that they are best tentatively assigned to a date in the reign of Amenhotep III.

Aziru's letters are to be divided between the two reigns. Letter 157 specifically says that Sumur is hostile to him,[63] whereas in letter 159 he is promising to rebuild the city,[64] the implication being that he has in the meantime made it his own. The conquest having occurred at about the time of Amenhotep III's death, we can take it that 157 and also 156 (in which Aziru applied to Egypt's king for permission to enter Amurru)[65] belong to the preceding period, and that the rest (158–69 and 171) belong to the new reign of Ikhnaton.

Letter 170 appears to be a special case. It seems to have been written to Aziru[66] during his visit to Egypt by Ba'aluia and Battilo, who were either his brothers or other very close relatives.[67] It was not a normal item in the Egyptian archives, and could have been included because it was intercepted or because Aziru had submitted it to the pharaoh as evidence of the seriousness of the situation in Asia and the necessity for his own prompt return to Amurru. This letter is perhaps the latest of the series, and although its presence in the group shows that it must have been received by Aziru before the court left Amarna, the evidence it gives of renewed Hittite activity under specifically named generals[68] indicates that it marks the beginning of the events recorded in the Hittite archives. Not having been addressed to the Egyptian crown, it may have been overlooked by the officials sorting current documents for removal from Akhetaton. Probably it was written while

Tutankhamen was king, but such an attribution must still be tentative.

The real problem in placing the letters from the north arises when we come to an assessment of the careers of Aitugama of Kadesh, and his various allies and opponents. He is first mentioned in letters from Akizzi of Qatna to Amenhotep III,[69] and is described as a Hittite agent: Arzauis of Ruhizzi and Teuwatti of Lapana are named as his allies[70], and all three are said to be in league with the Hittites.[71] Letter 55, in which Akizzi mentions Aziru,[72] tells of an attack on Qatna by the Hittite king which caused the population of the city to flee and during which the Hittites removed a divine image:[73] by the time Akizzi came to write his letter, however, the image had been returned.[74] Letter 162 from Ikhnaton to Aziru was written fairly late in the Egyptian king's reign, since it refers to Ribaddi as having already been ousted from Gubla,[75] but it also refers to Aziru's connection with the king of Kadesh—'a man with whom the [Egyptian] king has disagreed'[76]—which indicates that Aziru and Aitugama continued their association over some period. Abimilki of Tyre also mentions it in letter 149,[77] the same in which he first refers to the conquest of Sumur,[78] and in letter 151 tells how the two men ḥave started hostilities against Namiazawa.[79] Akizzi refers in letter 53 to war between Aitugama and Namiazawa,[80] but omits any mention of Aziru although he does refer to the Hittites;[81] and letter 197 of Namiazawa, though omitting to mention Aitugama among his opponents, names Arzauia[82] as leading some of Aziru's troops. Assuming, as seems most probable, that the same campaign is involved in letters 151, 53, and 197, these events must have occurred when Amenhotep III died. This, of course, places some of the events in the letters of Akizzi of Qatna just before the Egyptian king's death, and those of Namiazawa and Aitugama relating the circumstances of this struggle close to the change of reigns. The letters written by various people about Aitugama's attacks on places in Amki (174–6 and 176A), seem to be tied more closely to the events related by Akizzi, and so are more probably to be dated to the reign of Amenhotep III. Still the relations of Aitugama, his friends and his opponents, are extremely complicated and obscure, and the reconstruction here set forth must be considered extremely tentative (see further pp. 100f and 192f).

# Notes

*Abbreviations*

A. du S. Annales du Service
J.E.A. Journal of Egyptian Archaeology
J.N.E.S. Journal of Near Eastern Studies
Z.A.S.A. Zeitschrift für Agyptische Sprache und Altertumskunde.
N.B. Unless otherwise stated the place of publication is London.

INTRODUCTION

1 W. M. F. Petrie, *Seventy Years in Archaeology*, Sampson Low (1931).
2 J. D. S. Pendlebury and others, *The City of Akhenaten*, 3 vols., 1923–51.

PART ONE THE IKHNATON LEGEND

*Chapter One Youth*

1 A. E. P. B. Weigall, *The Life and Times of Ikhnaton*, Blackwood (1910), p. 60.

*Chapter Two Religious Ideas*

1 Weigall, op. cit., p. 78.
2 J. H. Breasted, *A History of Egypt*, Hodder (2nd ed. 1941), p. 371.
3 Breasted, op. cit., p. 376.

*Chapter Four Foreign Policy*

1 Breasted, op. cit., p. 389

PART II EGYPT DURING THE AMARNA PERIOD

*Chapter One Two mummies*

1 G. Elliot Smith, 'The Royal Mummies', *Cairo Catalogue* (Imprimerie de l'Institut Français d'Archéologie Orientale, Cairo), p. 46 f., and G. Legrain, *Répertoire Généalogique*, etc. (Société Anonyme des Arts Graphiques) 220.
2 H. Carter, *The Tomb of Tutankhamen*, Cassell (1927), Vol. II, Appendix 1, D. E. Derry, 'Report on the Examination of Tutankhamen's Mummy', p. 148.
3 H. Gautier, *Le Livre des Rois d'Egypte* (Cairo, 1910), Vol. 2, p. 290, n. 3 and 4.
4 Smith, op. cit., p. 42 f.

*Chapter Two Amenhotep III and Tiy*

1 T. E. Peet, in *Kings and Queens of Ancient Egypt* (1926), ed. W. Brunton, p. 83 f.
2 H. Kees, *Der Götterglaube in Alten Aegypten* (Berlin, 1956), p. 367 f.
3 Luxor was left unfinished at the end of the reign, so that it must have been in the process of building during the period that this hypothetical power struggle was occurring.
4 See Part III.
5 W. Helck, *Urkunden IV*, Heft 20, No. 579C, p. 1739, ll.1–5.
6 W. C. Hayes 'Inscriptions from the Palace of Amenhotep III', *J.N.E.S.*, Vol. 10, pp. 37, 56 (fig. 16), 87.
7 H. Gautier, *Le Livre des Rois d' Egypte* (Cairo, 1910), Vol. 2, p. 290, n. 3 and 4.
Manetho gives 9 years, year 8 is the highest known from the monuments.
8 T. M. Davis, *The Tomb of Iouiya and Touiyou* (1907), p. XIII.
9 ibid., p. XIV f., the remarks on the titles were written by G. Maspero.
10 ibid., p. 37 f., pl. XXXIII, XXXIV, XXXVI.
11 *Urkunden IV*, p. 1738.
12 S. A. B. Mercer, *The Tell el Amarna Letters* (Toronto, 1951), Vol. 1, Nos. 19–21, 23–4.
13 C. Aldred, 'The End of the El Amarna Period', *J.E.A.*, Vol. 57, p. 32.
14 *Urkunden IV*, p. 1738, ll.6–11.
15 ibid., p. 1737.
16 ibid., p. 1741.
17 Examples: Tomb of Heruef, in A. Fakhry 'A Note on the Tomb of Kheruef at Thebes', *A. du S.* (Cairo, 1943), Vol. 42, p. 447 f. The Tomb of Surer, in T. Save-Söderbergh, *Four Eighteenth Dynasty Tombs* (Oxford, 1957), pp. 39–40, pl. 38–40.
18 J. Leibovitch, 'Une Nouvelle Répresentation d'une Sphinge de la Reine Tiy', *A. du S.*, Vol. 42, p. 93 f.
19 C. R. Lepsius, *Denkmäler aus Aegypten und Aethiopen* (Berlin, 1897–1913), Band 5, Abteilung III, pl. 83–8.
20 B. Porter and R. L. B. Moss, *Topographical Bibliography of Ancient Egyptian Hieroglyphic Texts, Reliefs and Paintings* (Oxford, 1951), Vol. VII, pp. 166–7.
21 S. A. B. Mercer, op. cit., No. 26.
22 Most recent copy, *Urkunden IV*, p. 1769, l.5 f., see also W. M. F. Petrie *Illahun Kahun and Gurob*, pl. 24, 7.

23 *Urkunden IV*, p. 1769, l.20 f.
24 A. E. P. B. Weigall, *Travels in the Upper Egyptian Desert* (1909), pp. 34–5 and C. R. Lepsius, op. cit., Band 6, Abteilung III, pl. 91, g.
25 W. M. F. Petrie, *Tell el Amarna* (1894), p. 4.
26 The latest objects relating to Tiy come from Gurob, see n. 22 and 23, and see G. Roeder, 'Thronfolger und König Smench-Ka-Re', *Z.A.S.A.* (Berlin, 1958), Vol. 83, p. 66c.
27 A. Rowe, 'Inscriptions of the Model Coffin Containing a Lock of the Hair of Queen Tiye', *A. du S.* (Cairo, 1940), Vol. 40, p. 625 f. and *Urkunden IV*, p. 1770, l.14 f.
28 A. Rowe, op. cit., p. 624.
H. R. Hall, *Hieroglyphic Texts from Egyptian Stelae, etc.* (1925), Vol. VII, p. 9, pl. XXI, No. 834.

## *Chapter Three Ikhnaton and his family*

1 N. de G. Davies, *The Rock Tombs of El Amarna*: Tomb of Huy, Vol. 3, pl. 13 and Tomb of Meryre II, Vol. 2, pl. 38.
2 K. Seele, 'King Ay and the Close of the Amarna Age', *J.N.E.S.*, Vol. XIV, p. 174, n. 44.
Seele discusses the death of Meketaton and her funeral. On wall A of Room γ of the Royal Tomb at Amarna is a relief, one of the figures of which is a nurse holding a baby, and breast feeding it. An inscription beside the figure is largely destroyed, and the words 'born to' and the name of Nofretiti being all that survives. Since the baby faces away from the inscription, Seele thinks that it must refer to the nurse and restores it almost entirely, only a lonely 't' sign remains readable from the whole of the first part of the inscription. He restores the inscription thus: [The king's daughter of his body his beloved Meri] t [aton] born to [the king's principal wife] (Nefernefruaton Nofretiti) may she live for ever and ever', and says 'There is no certain example in any Amarna tomb of a text naming a princess which faces opposite to both the head and the body of the princess. . . . Thus it appears virtually certain that the "nurse" with suckling child in this scene is . . . Meritaton with her new born child . . . who will then have been also the child of Smenkhkare. But if Meketaton is depicted alive in the year 12 (tomb of Meryre II) . . . ; it seems scarcely less certain that Meritaton was married to Smenkhkare in that year or shortly thereafter.' This will not do. The only reason the name of Meritaton stood in the lacuna is because Seele put it there. Seele has not

considered the evidence of Walls B and C of the same chamber where there is a depiction of Meritaton, standing behind her father and mother, still wearing the sidelock, and with an inscription written above her which needs no gratuitous restoration. Needless to say the idea of a marriage of Meritaton and Smenkhkare by year 12 appears without foundation.

3 H. W. Fairman, 'Once Again the So-called Coffin of Akhenaten', *J.E.A.*, Vol. 47, pp. 29–30.
4 H. Brunner, 'Eine Neue Amarna Princessin', *Z.A.S.A.*, Vol. 74, p. 104 f.
5 ibid., p. 105.
6 S. A. B. Mercer, op. cit., letters Nos. 7, 26, 27, 28, 33, 34, 41.
7 C. Aldred, 'The Beginning of the Amarna Period', *J.E.A.*, Vol. 45, p. 24 f.
8 T. E. Peet and C. L. Woolley, *The City of Akhetaten* (1923), Vol. 1, p. 123 f.
9 J. D. S. Pendlebury, 'Preliminary Report of Excavations at Tell el Amarna, 1930–1', *J.E.A.* (1931), Vol. 17, p. 243.
10 W. von Soden, 'Zu den Amarna Briefen aus Babylon und Assur', *Orientalia* (Rome, 1952), Vol. 21, p. 432. If von Soden is right here, Knudtzon reads otherwise in the relevant letters (No. 10, l.44, No. 11, reverse 26, J. S. Knudtzon, *Die El Amarna Tafeln*). The issue is by no means decided.

*Chapter Four The co-regency: the case against*

1 Sir A. H. Gardiner, 'The So-Called Tomb of Queen Tiy', *J.E.A.* (1957), Vol. 43, p. 13.
2 S. A. B. Mercer, *The Tell el Amarna Letters*, Vol. I, No. 41, ll.14–20.
3 ibid., No. 26.
4 ibid., No. 27, after l.114, copy in *Urkunden IV*, p. 1995.
5 ibid., No. 27, ll. 89–90, 99–105; No. 41, ll. 14–20; No. 33, ll.1–14.
6 A. Erman, in *Z.A.S.A.* (Leipzig, 1889), Vol. 27, p. 63.
7 W. Helck, 'Die Sinai Inschrift des Amenmose', *Mitteilungen des Instituts für Orientforschung* (Berlin, 1954), Vol. 2, p. 196 f.
8 ibid., p. 196.
9 H. W. Fairman (editor), J. D. S. Pendlebury, *The City of Akhenaten* (1951), Vol. 3.
10 V. Loret, 'La Grande Inscription de Mes à Saqqarah', *Z.A.S.A.* (Leipzig, 1901), Vol. 39, p. 10, l.8.

The date from his statue in the mortuary temple at Medinet Habu of year 27 contains a king's name, but is a graffito.

11 W. Helck, op. cit., p. 197.

12 See also *Urkunden IV*, p. 1748, l.8, 'which he made as his monument for his divine essence living upon earth (Nebmaatre) lord of Nubia' shows that this cult was connected with the divinity of Amenhotep III while alive.

13 W. Helck, loc. cit.

14 *Urkunden IV*, p. 1747, l.1.

15 W. Helck, loc. cit.

16 id. loc. cit.

17 id., op. cit., p. 198.

18 id., loc. cit., his No. 7.

19 id., loc. cit., his No. 8.

20 id., op. cit., p. 199.

21 id., loc. cit.

22 id., loc. cit., his Nos. 2, 3, 5.

23 id., loc. cit., his Nos. 4, 5. See also E. Chassinat, 'Une Statuette d'Amenothes III', *Bulletin de l'Institut d'Archéologie Orientale*, Vol. 7, p. 167. This piece is a headless statuette of Amenhotep III in the Amarna style. The erasure of the second cartouche indicates that this art style was not an innovation of Ikhnaton.

24 W. C. Hayes, 'Inscriptions from the Palace of Amenhotep III', *J.N.E.S.*, Vol. 11, p. 178.

*Chapter Five The co-regency: the case for*

1 H. Frankfort and J. D. S. Pendlebury, *The City of Akhenaten* (1933), Vol. II, pp. 102, 108.

2 H. W. Fairman, *The City of Akhenaten*, Vol. III, p. 155 and p. 81, No. 570.

3 F. Ll. Griffith, 'Stela in Honour of Amenophis III and Taya from Tell el-Amarnah,' *J.E.A.* (1926), Vol. 12, p. 1 f.

4 H. R. Hall, 'An Egyptian Royal Bookplate, The Ex-Libris of Amenhotep III and Tiy', *J.E.A.* (1926), Vol. 12, p. 30 f.

5 N. de G. Davies, *The Rock Tombs of El Amarna* (1908), Vol. 5, p. 32, l.5, pl. 27, l.5. The Egyptian word *ỉmw* usually meant a tent and can perhaps be extended to refer to other buildings of a temporary character. The section as a whole seems to be describing a visit of the king to the area rather than an incident during his permanent occupation of the city.

6 It is interesting to note in this connection the hieratic docket noted above, pp. 60–61. Very few of the letters have such dockets and one can only conclude that the docket concerned indicated some unusual circumstance connected with the receipt of the letter. In this case either the letter had to be sent on from Amarna to the king who was in Thebes, or else the docket was intended to remind the official in charge of correspondence that the letter was received while the king was in Thebes and should be drawn to his attention on his return. I do not read the boundary stele to mean that the king took a vow never to leave the precincts of Akhetaton. The earlier version of the boundary stele (Davies, op. cit., p. 30) makes it quite clear that the section usually so interpreted as a vow of the king actually refers to his promising not to enlarge his city beyond its boundary stele, and not to change its location. The oath on the later boundary stele in all probability records the same intention, though the wording is much less clear. (Davies, op. cit., p. 32–3.)

7 H. W. Fairman, op. cit., p. 199 f.

8 ibid., p. 199 f.

9 N. de G. Davies, op. cit., Vol. 4, p. 22, pl. 35.

10 W. C. Hayes, 'Inscriptions from the Palace of Amenhotep III', *J.N.E.S.*, Vol. 10, p. 56, fig. 16, and p. 82 f.

11 ibid., Vol. 10, p. 56, fig. 16. The matter of the location of the royal residences is one which has intrigued me for some time. All too often Thebes is called the capital of Egypt during the Eighteenth Dynasty. It is by no means certain that Egypt possessed a capital in the sense that we would use the term today. It is far more likely that there were a number of royal residences in Egypt among which the king travelled. Certainly Thebes was the permanent centre of the Amen cult and Heliopolis the permanent centre of the Re cult, but whether or not there was a permanent administrative centre at this period is an open question. Thebes, for example, would be an exceedingly inconvenient location from which to control Syria—Palestine, and Memphis was a very long way from Nubia. In addition the idea of Upper and Lower Egypt even at this late date seems to pervade Egyptian thinking. Both Amenhotep II and Thutmose IV had spent a good deal of time at Memphis as crown princes and possibly even lived there as children. It is certain that Amenhotep III had a mortuary temple in Memphis (*Urkunden IV*, p. 1795, l. 5 f.), a statue of the Chief Overseer of the House of Amenhotep reads: 'He promoted me to control works in his new mansion of millions of years, which his majesty built anew in the

cultivated land to the west of Hikaptah [Memphis] on the banks of Ankhtawy'. In a stele of King Eye (G. Daressy, *Receuil de Travaux*, Vol. 16, p. 23) there is mentioned the 'house' [per] of (Aakheperkare) and the 'house' [per] of (Menkheperure), both at Memphis. In the tomb (originally at Abusir), of a man called Amenemone, who was, among other things, 'first prince of Memphis', is mentioned his office of 'Overseer of the house in the mansion [hwt] of (Menkheperure), (H. Ranke, *Z.A.S.A.*, Vol. 67, p. 78). Apparently Amenhotep III did not reside in the Malqatta palace except during the jubilee periods. Certainly the Nineteenth Dynasty had residences at least at Thebes and Tanis, and probably Memphis as well. The idea that in the Eighteenth Dynasty the kings did not spend all their time in any one residence seems persuasive.

12 R. Engelbach, 'Material for a Revision of the History of the Heresy Period of the Eighteenth Dynasty', *A. du S.* (Cairo, 1940), Vol. 40, p. 134 and n. 3.

13 U. Bouriant, G. Legrain, and G. Jequier, *Monuments pour Servir à l'Étude du Culte d'Atonou en Egypte*, Vol. I, *Les Tombes de Khouitatonou* (Cairo, 1903), p. 15.

14 N. de G. Davies, op. cit., Vol. 3, pl. XVIII, The Lintel, third figure from the left.

15 Most recent copy *Urkunden IV*, p. 1942 f.

16 T. M. Davis, *The Tomb of Queen Tiyi* (1910), p. 13 f., pl. 27–9, 31–3. The object study was actually made by G. Daressy.

17 id., op. cit., p. 13.

18 B. Gunn, 'Notes on the Aten and His Names', *J.E.A.* (1923), Vol. 9, section II, p. 170 f.

19 P. E. Newberry, 'Akhenaten's Eldest Son-in-law Ankhkheperure', *J.E.A.* (1928), Vol. 14, p. 6. See also Sir A. H. Gardiner, 'The Graffito from the Tomb of Pere', *J.E.A.* (1928), Vol. 14, p. 10 f.

20 N. de G. Davies, op. cit. Vol. 3, p. 8, pl. XII.

21 ibid., pp. 1–25, pl. I–XXIV, and XXXVI, XXXVII.

22 ibid., p. 9 f., pl. VII and XIII–XV.

23 ibid., pp. 4–9, p. 15 f., pl. IV–XII and XVIII.

24 ibid., p. 12 f., pl. XVI and XVII.

25 ibid., p. 3 f., p. 17 f., pl. II and III.

26 ibid., p. 4 f., pl. IV and V.

27 ibid., p. 7, pl. VI and VII.

28 ibid., p. 7 f., pl. VIII–XII.

29 ibid., pl. XVII detail, pl. XVIII sculptor's studio.

30 ibid., pl. XVIII, lintel.
31 ibid., p. 15 f.
32 ibid., Vol. 3, pl. XVIII lintel.
33 ibid., Vol. 3, pl. XVIII lintel.
34 ibid., Vol. 3, pl. IV, VI, VIII, IX, and XVIII, both parts.
35 It would seem to me that such an age would be the absolute minimum that would fit the circumstances. She was probably older.
36 N. de G. Davies, op. cit., Vol. 3, p. 7 f., pl. VIII, p. 19 f.
37 ibid., Vol. 3, p. 15, pl. XXI door jambs.
38 ibid., Vol. 3, pp. 1–25, pl. I–XXIV, XXXVI, XXXVII, The Durbar Relief pl. XIII–XV, p. 9 f.
39 ibid., Vol. 2, pp. 33–45, pl. XXVIII–XLI, pl. of the Durbar Relief XXIX inscription E. Wall and XXXVII–XL, p. 38 f.
40 ibid., Vol. 2, pl. XXXVII and XXXVIII. In this tomb varying numbers of princesses are shown with the king and queen. Pl. XXXIV shows five, pl. XXXII shows three, and here a definite gradation by size is noticeable. Pl. XXXVII and XXXVIII make no difference in size, though manifestly the youngest princesses are still very young. All the figures wear the sidelock, indicating that all were children at the time of the carving.
41 E. Naville, *The Festival Hall of Osorkon* (1892). The plates show the customary dress of the king while celebrating this festival.
42 *Urkunden IV*, p. 79, l. 1. Coronation decree of Thutmose I, and *Urkunden IV*, p. 291, l. 3.
43 N. de G. Davies, *The Tomb of the Vizier Ramose* (1941).
44 A. Fakhry, 'A Note on the Tomb of Kheruef at Thebes', *A. du S.* (Cairo, 1943), Vol. 42, p. 447 f.
45 N. de G. Davies, *The Tomb of the Vizier Ramose*, p. 14, pl. XIII, 2.
46 ibid., pl. XXXIII and LIII.
47 W. C. Hayes, op. cit., p. 48, fig. 8, no. 92.
48 C. Aldred, 'Two Theban Notables During the Later Reign of Amenophis III, *J.N.E.S.* (Chicago, 1959), Vol. 18, p. 117, n. 32.
49 ibid., p. 118.
50 ibid., p. 120.
51 A. Fakhry, op. cit., first jubilee pl. XL, p. 489–500; third jubilee pl. XXXIX, p. 468–88.
52 id., op. cit., p. 463, note 1.
53 I do not consider myself an archaeologist, but I have thoroughly discussed this problem with Professor W. B. Emery and Dr. R. Faulkner, and have found them in substantial agreement on this point. Fakhry (op. cit., p. 455) says: 'The tomb was not finished,

the work was begun at the entrance and the Eastern wall of the first court, but all the other parts are uninscribed'. There was, however, a second court completely uninscribed, likewise work on the façade was unfinished. The work on the entrance hall was completed and this appears to be the earliest work in the tomb. It is quite possible that work on the façade was commenced first, and that the artist later left the façade to concentrate on the tomb's interior. At any rate, that the method outlined in the text was the one used is shown by the fact that not only is the inscribing of the tomb incomplete, but its cutting is unfinished. There is apparently no burial chamber. (See the plan in L. Habachi, 'Clearance of the Tomb of Kheruef at Thebes, 1957–1958', *A. du S.* (Cairo, 1958), Vol. 55, p. 325 f., plan pl. I.). It, however, includes a pillared hall, and a longitudinal hall, beyond the decorated court. Regarding tomb construction at Amarna, see Davies, Vol. 4, p. 9 f.

54 F. Ll. Griffith (ed.), *Hieratic Paypri from Kahun and Gurob*, *Gurob II*, (1898), 1, 2, 3, p. 92 f.

55 Sir A. H. Gardiner, 'Four Papyri of the Eighteenth Dynasty from Kahun', *Z.A.S.A.* (Leipzig, 1906), Vol. 43, p. 27 f.

56 ibid., p. 28 f.

57 ibid., p. 35 f.

58 ibid., p. 38 f.

59 C. R. Lepsius, *Denkmäler aus Aegypten und Aethiopen* (Berlin, 1897–1913), Band 6, Abteilung III, pl. 110 K.

60 H. Frankfort, *Kingship and the Gods* (Chicago, 1948), p. 134 and pl. 32.

*Chapter Six The co-regency: final remarks*

1 The idea that Amenhotep III abdicated his functions and lived in retirement has been put forward by J. Vandier (*Manuel d'Archéologie Egyptienne II*, p. 850, n. 2) and more recently taken up by W. C. Hayes (*The Sceptre of Egypt*, Cambridge, 1959, p. 280) and D. R. Redford (*J.E.A.* 45, p. 35). I find it difficult to accept the idea of an abdication at this period, in view of the divinity of the king.

2 H. W. Fairman, 'A Block of Amenhotep IV from Athribis', *J.E.A.* (1960), Vol. 46, p. 80 f.

3 id., 'The Supposed Year 21 of Akhenaton', *J.E.A.* (1960), Vol. 46.

*Chapter Seven Ikhnaton and Smenkhkare*

1 J. E. Samson, *The City of Akhenaten*, *Part III*, p. 231 f, U.C. 410.

2 Sir A. H. Gardiner, 'The Graffito from the Tomb of Pere', *J.E.A.* (1928), Vol. 14, p. 10.
3 N. de G. Davies, *The Rock Tombs of El Amarna*, Vol. 2, p. 45, pl. XLI.
4 *Urkunden IV*, p. 2024, l. 7 f.
5 P. E. Newberry, op. cit., p. 7.
6 G. Roeder, 'Thronfolger und König Smench-Ka-Re', *Z.A.S.A.*, Vol. 83, p. 47, C III 3.
7 P. E. Newberry, op. cit. p. 8.
8 J. D. S. Pendlebury, *The City of Akhenaten,* Vol. III, p. 194 f.

*Chapter Eight The reign of Ikhnaton: a reconstruction*

1 A. Rowe, op. cit., p. 623 f.
2 I. E. S. Edwards 'The Prudhoe Lions', *Annals of Archaeology and Anthropology* (Liverpool, 1939–40), Vol. XXVI, p. 5.

*Chapter Nine Smenkhkare*

1 H. Frankfort and J. D. S. Pendlebury, *The City of Akhenaten* (1933), Vol. II, pl. 50, No. 29, and N. de G. Davies, *The Rock Tombs of El Amarna* (1905), Vol. II, pl. XLI.
2 Sir A. H. Gardiner, 'The Graffito from the Tomb of Pere', *J.E.A.*, Vol. 14, p. 10, ll. 1 and 2 of inscription.
3 P. E. Newberry, 'Akhenaten's Eldest Son-in-law Ankhkeperure', *J.E.A.* (1928), Vol. 14, p. 7.
4 G. Roeder, 'Thronfolger und König Smench-Ka-Re', *Z.A.S.A.* (Berlin, 1958), Vol. 83, p. 50, C V 1.
5 P. E. Newberry, op. cit., p. 7.
6 H. W. Fairman, *The City of Akhenaten,* Vol. III, p. 159.
7 K. Seele, 'King Ay and the close of the Amarna Age', *J.N.E.S.,* Vol. XIV, p. 172.
8 H. Frankfort and J. D. S. Pendlebury, *The City of Akhenaten,* Vol. II, p. 104, n. 1, and p. 103, n. 3.
9 T. E. Peet and C. L. Woolley, *The City of Akhenaten,* Vol. I, (1923), p. 165, n. 1.
10 G. Daressy, 'Le Cercueil de Khu-n-Aten', *Bulletin de l'Institut d'Archéologie Orientale* (Cairo, 1916), Vol. 12, p. 150, Inscription D, and R. Engelbach, 'The So-called Coffin of Akhenaten', *A. du S.* (Cairo, 1931), Vol. 31, p. 100, Inscription D.
11 D. E. Derry, 'Note on the Skeleton Hitherto Believed to be that of King Ikhnaton', *A. du S.*, Vol. 31, p. 115 f.

12 G. Roeder, op. cit. p. 60, D V 7.
13 H. Carter, *The Tomb of Tutankhamen* (1927), Vol. II, report by D. E. Derry, Appendix I, p. 143 f. and p. 158 f.
14 H. Carter, op. cit. (1933), Vol. III, p. 21 f. and p. 147 f.
15 A. Erman, 'Geschichtliche Inschriften aus dem Berliner Museum', *Z.A.S.A.* (Leipzig, 1900), Vol. 38, p. 113.
16 T. M. Davis, *The Tomb of Queen Tiyi* (1910), p. 1 f.
17 P. E. Newberry, op. cit., p. 8 f. The relief is broken. The crown cannot definitely be determined, but one of the territorial crowns seems likely.
18 H. W. Fairman, *The City of Akhenaten* (1951), Part III, p. 164, No. 8, pl. LXXXVI, 35.
19 G. Roeder, op. cit., p. 55, D III 4.
20 ibid., p. 63, D VII 1.
21 U. Bouriant, G. Legrain and G. Jequier, *Monuments pour Servir à l'Étude du Culte d'Atonou en Egypte* (Cairo, 1903), Vol. 1, plate X.
22 N. de G. Davies, op. cit., Vol. 2, pl. XXXIV and XXXVIII.
23 J. D. S. Pendlebury, *The City of Akhenaten,* Part III, pp. 60–1, and p. 80.

*Chapter Ten The burial of Smenkhkare?*

1 G. Daressy, op. cit., p. 145 f.
2 R. Engelbach, 'The So-called Coffin of Akhenaten', *A. du S.* (Cairo, 1931), Vol. 31, p. 98 f.
3 Sir A. H. Gardiner, 'The So-called Tomb of Queen Tiy', *J.E.A.* (1957), Vol. 43, p. 11 f.
4 G. Roeder, op. cit., p. 65 f., E.
5 H. W. Fairman, 'Once Again the So-called Coffin of Akhenaten', *J.E.A.* Vol. 47, p. 25 f.
6 C. Aldred, 'The Tomb of Akhenaten at Thebes', *J.E.A.*, Vol. 47, p. 41 f.
7 T. M. Davis, op. cit., p. 19.
8 ibid., p. 10.
9 ibid., p. 26 f., number 19, etc.
10 Eye had himself shown performing the funeral rites for Tutankhamen, on the wall of the latter's tomb. This ritual was probably performed by each monarch for his predecessor where possible. See H. Carter, op. cit., Vol. 2, p. 26 f.
11 T. M. Davis, op. cit., p. 9.
12 ibid., p. 10.

13 ibid., p. 4 f.
14 H. Carter, op. cit., Vol. II, p. 113; Vol. III, p. 133, 147, and 17 f.
15 R. Engelbach, 'Material for a Revision of the History of the Heresy Period of the Eighteenth Dynasty', *A. du S.* (Cairo, 1940), Vol. 40, p. 137 f.
16 H. W. Fairman, op. cit., p. 39.
17 T. M. Davis, op. cit., p. 13 f.
18 ibid., p. 1.
19 C. Aldred, op. cit., p. 49 f.
20 ibid., p. 51–2.
21 ibid., p. 56.

*Chapter Eleven Tutankhamen and Eye*

1 W. M. F. Petrie, *Tell el Amarna*, p. 29.
2 see p. 189.
3 P. E. Newberry, 'King Ay the Successor of Tutankhamen', *J.E.A.* (1937), Vol. 18, p. 50.
4 *Urkunden IV.*, p. 2110, l.13.

PART THREE THE ORIGIN, NATURE, AND DISTRIBUTION OF THE ATON CULT

*Chapter One The Background*

1 M. and J. Doresse, 'Le Culte d'Aton sous la XVIII Dynastie', *Journal Asiatique* (Paris, 1941–2), Vol. 223, p. 181 f.
2 H. R. Hall, 'Yuia the Syrian', *Proceedings of the Society of Biblical Archaeology* (1913), Vol. 35, p. 63 f.
3 W. M. F. Petrie, *A History of Egypt* (1899), Vol. II, p. 229 f.
4 M. and J. Doresse, op. cit., p. 82.
5 A. Erman and H. Grapow, *Worterbuch* I, p. 145.
6 W. C. Hayes, 'Inscriptions from the Palace of Amenhotep III', *J.N.E.S.* Vol. 10, p. 94, n. 149, and Sir A. H. Gardiner, *Ancient Egyptian Onomastica*, Vol. I, No. 118, p. 36 f.; and Vol. 2, p. 267 f.
7 N. de G. Davies, *Amarna*, Vol. I, pl. XXXIII.
8 H. M. Stewart, 'Some Pre Amarna Sun Hymns', *J.E.A.*, Vol. 46, p. 83 f.
9 M. and J. Doresse, op. cit., p. 184.

10 ibid., p. 185, see also *Urkunden IV*, p. 1276f. and p. 1285 f.
11 *Urkunden IV*, p. 1540 f., especially p. 1542, l.17 f.
12 ibid., p. 1962, l.10.
13 The fact that the jubilees of Ikhnaton were either simultaneous with, or identical to the jubilees of the Aton further supports this view. See B. Gunn, 'A Note on the Aton and his Names', *J.E.A.*, Vol. 9, p. 168 f.

*Chapter Two The inscriptional evidence*

1 A. M. Blackman, 'Middle Egyptian Stories', *Bibliotheca Aegyptica* II (Brussels, 1932), Part 1, p. 3 R, l.6 f.
2 ibid., loc. cit.
3 *Urkunden IV*, p. 16, 1.7.
4 ibid., p. 19, l.6 f.
5 ibid., p. 54, l.15 f.
6 ibid., p. 59, l.13 f.
7 ibid., p. 82, l.13.
8 ibid., p. 266, l.4 f.
9 ibid., p. 332, l.10 f.
10 ibid., p. 341, l.11 f.
11 ibid., p. 348, l.9 f.
12 ibid., p. 490, l.7.
13 ibid., p. 520, l.2 f.
14 ibid., p. 575, l.11 f.
15 ibid., p. 582, l.16 f.
16 ibid., p. 887, l.14 f.
17 ibid., p. 896, l.1 f.
18 ibid., p. 1183, l.15.
19 ibid., p. 1293, l.6.
20 ibid., p. 1512, l.19.
21 S. Hassan, 'A Representation of the Solar Disk', *A. du S.*, Vol. 38, p. 53 f.
22 ibid., p. 55.
23 ibid., p. 61, l.8 and pl. IX.
24 A. Bey Kamel, 'Rapport sur les Fouilles du Comte de Galarza', *A. du S.* (Cairo, 1910), Vol. 10, p. 117.
25 W. C. Hayes, op. cit., p. 178 f. and p. 97 f., and G. Legrain, 'Fragments de Canopes', *A. du S.* (Cairo, 1904), Vol. 4, p. 138 f.
26 ibid., fig. 4, No. 9, following p. 40.
27 A. W. Shorter, 'Historical Scarabs of Tuthmosis IV and

Amenophis III', *J.E.A.* (1931), Vol. 17, p. 23 f.

28 J. D. S. Pendlebury, *The City of Akhenaten*, Vol. III, p. 200.

29 M. and J. Doresse, op. cit., p. 191.

30 W. M. F. Petrie and G. Brunton, Sedment II, pl. LIII, base of stela, l. 1, *British School of Archaeology in Egypt, Twenty-seventh year, 1921* (1924).

31 *Urkunden IV*, p. 1635, l. 14.

32 ibid., p. 1016, l. 3.

33 T. E. Peet, 'The Problem of Akhenaton', *Journal of the Manchester Egyptian and Oriental Society* (Manchester, 1921), Vol. IX, p. 42.

34 *Urkunden IV.*, p. 1664, l. 18 f.

35 ibid., p. 1667, l. 7 f.

36 ibid., p. 1670, l. 7 f.

37 ibid., p. 1696, l. 20.

38 ibid., p. 1697, l. 6.

39 ibid., p. 1737, l. 16.

40 ibid., p. 1754, l. 6.

41 ibid., p. 1761, l. 6.

42 ibid., p. 1767, l. 10.

43 ibid., p. 1819, l. 13 f.

44 ibid., p. 1833, l. 11 f.

45 ibid., p. 1830, l. 19.

46 ibid., p. 1847, l. 7 f.

47 ibid., p. 1923, ll. 12 and 18.

48 ibid., p. 1935, l. 18.

49 ibid., p. 1945, l. 2.

50 W. Helck, 'Inhaber und Bauleiter des Thebanischen Grabs 107', *Mitteilungen des Instituts für Orientsforschung* (Berlin, 1956), Vol. 4., p. 13, long inscription col. 2; p. 17 cols. 1, 7, 10; p. 18 col. 16.

All of these examples are written ⊙ .

51 S. R. K. Glanville, 'Notes on Material for the Reign of Amenophis III', *J.E.A.* (1929), Vol. 15, p. 6. n. 1.

52 W. Helck, op. cit., p. 18, cols. 5 and 8.

53 G. Legrain, 'Notes d'Inspection', *A. du S.* (Cairo, 1902), Vol. 3, p. 265.

54 U. Bouriant, 'À Thebes', *Recueil de Travaux* (Paris, 1885), Vol. 6, p. 52 f.

55 A. Wiedemann, 'Notes on Some Egyptian Monuments', *Proceedings of the Society of Biblical Archaeology* (1913), Vol. 35, No. 17. See W. M. F. Petrie, *Historical Scarabs* XVIII, No. 1261.

56 G. Legrain, 'Fragments de Canopes', *A. du S.*, Vol. 4, p. 138 f.
57 W. C. Hayes, op. cit., p. 96 f.
58 ibid., p. 178 f.
59 See above p. 122.
60 M. F. L. Macadam, *The Temples of Kawa* (1955), Vol. 2, ch. 4.
61 E. A. W. Budge, *The Book of the Dead* (1898), Text Vol., p. 61, l.7 f.
62 ibid., p. 112, l.8 f.
63 ibid., p. 138, l.5 f.
64 E. Naville, *Das Aegyptische Todenbuch* (Berlin, 1886), Vol. 1, Introduction, p. 29 f. A.

*Chapter Three Interpretation of the inscriptions*

1 B. Gunn, 'Notes on the Aton and his Names', *J.E.A.*, Vol. 9, p. 173.

*Chapter Four The priests and the king*

1 M. and J. Doresse, op. cit., p. 184 f.
2 ibid., p. 185 f.
3 ibid., p. 190 f.
4 For the titulary of this man see *Urkunden IV*, p. 1594, l.7 f.
5 N. de G. Davies, *Amarna*, Vol. 5, p. 30 f., l.20.
6 He does hold the title 'Greatest of Seers' in 'Hetwer' but it seems most likely that this office also is connected with Upper Egypt, though admittedly 'Het Wer' usually means the Heliopolis temple. See *Urkunden IV*, p. 1894, l.11, and M. and J. Doresse, op. cit., p. 194.
7 M. and J. Doresse, op. cit., p. 195.
8 ibid., loc. cit.

*Chapter Five The distribution of the Aton cult*

1 Or less probably the ' Harim of the Aton', a structure which would also have a religious purpose.
2 M. F. L. Macadam, op. cit., Vol. 2, ch. 4, p. 12.
3 A. M. Blackman, 'Preliminary report on the Excavations at Sesebi', *J.E.A.* (1937), Vol. 23, p. 148.
4 J. H. Breasted, 'A City of Ikhenaton in Nubia', *Z.A.S.A.* (Leipzig, 1902–3), Vol. 40, p. 112.
5 G. Legrain, 'Fragments de Canopes', *A. du S.*, Vol. 4, p. 148.
6 N. de G. Davies, 'Akhenaten at Thebes', *J.E.A.* (1923), Vol. 9, p. 141 f.
7 G. Legrain, 'Notes d'Inspection', *A. du S.*, Vol. 3, p. 263.

8 See the various reports of the work at Karnak from 1926 forward in the *Annales du Service*.
9 A. Fakhry, 'Blocs Décorés Provenant du Temple de Louxor', *A. du S.* (Cairo, 1935), Vol. 35, p. 7.
10 ibid., p. 42 f.
11 G. Legrain, 'Fragments de Canopes', *A. du S.*, Vol. 4, p. 147, n. 2.
12 G. Maspero, 'Notes sur Quelques Points de Grammaire et d'Histoire', *Z.A.S.A.* (Leipzig, 1881), Vol. 19, p. 116, No. XVII.
13 J. H. Breasted, op. cit., p. 112.
14 R. Engelbach, 'Riqqeh and Memphis VI', p. 17 and pl. XV 1, *British School of Archaeology in Egypt Nineteenth Year* (1913).
15 J. G. Wilkinson, *The Manners and Customs of the Ancient Egyptians* (3rd ed. 1878), Vol. 3, p. 52, n. 3.
16 S. Gabra, 'Un Temple d'Amenophis IV à Assiout', *Chronique d'Egypte* (Brussels, 1931), Vol. 6, p. 238.

### *Chapter Six The Aton after Amarna*

1 U. Bouriant, op. cit., p. 54.
2 M. F. L. McAdam, op. cit., pp. 32 and 37.
3 ibid., p. 35.
4 *Urkunden IV*, p. 2035, l.4 and p. 2036, l.8.
5 ibid., p. 2039, l.8 f.
6 ibid., p. 2052, l.12.
7 ibid., p. 2054, l.16.
8 ibid., p. 2055, l.16.
9 ibid., p. 2063, l.6.
10 ibid., p. 2089, l.4.
11 A. Wiedemann, 'Beitrage sur Aegyptischen Geschichte', *Z.A.S.A.* (Leipzig, 1885), Vol. 23, p. 81.
12 T. M. Davis, *The Tomb of Harmhabi and Touatankhamanou*, p. 28 f.
13 P. Lacau, 'Steles du Nouvel Empire', *Cairo Catalogue* (Cairo, 1909), No. 34175, pl. LXV.

## PART FOUR

### *Chapter One The historical setting*

1 This method of dividing Egyptian history into periods called dynasties was invented by an Egyptian priest-historian named

Manetho who lived in the third century B.C. It is often purely arbitrary in its application. The succession of Ahmose is a case in point. This king succeeded his brother Kamose, who also had a great deal of success in battle against the Hyksos, but had the misfortune to die prematurely. It was this brother Ahmose who finished the job that Kamose had begun and with his reign Manetho declared the Eighteenth Dynasty began.

*Chapter Two The Tell el Amarna letters*

1 S. A. B. Mercer, *The Tell el Amarna Letters* (Toronto, 1951), No. 23, l.33 f.

*Chapter Three The date of the letters*

1 S. A. B. Mercer, op. cit., No. 26; No. 27, ll. 38 f., 89 f.,; No. 28 l.13 f.; No. 33, l.9 f.; No. 41, l.7 f.; and No. 116, l.63 f.

2 E. Edel, 'Neue Keilschriftliche Umschreibungen Ägyptischer Namem aus den Bogazkoy Texten', *J.N.E.S.* (Chicago, 1948), Vol. 7, p. 15. Edel thinks that the king's name in the salutation of letter No. 9 should be read Ni-ib-hu-ur-ri-ri-ia instead of Ni-ip-hu-ur-ri-ri-ia, which both Mercer (No. 9, l.1) and J. A. Knudtzon (*Die El-Amarna Tafeln*, Leipzig, 1907, No. 9, l.1.) adopt. The letter, says Edel, was written to Tutankhamen. Burnaburiash in all probability outlived Ikhnaton, hence there is no reason why this letter could not have been written to Tutankhamen. In the other letters to Egypt from Babylon mentioning the name of Ikhnaton, an 'a' vowel occurs in the first syllable, but this is the only evidence to justify the reading, since the body of the text gives no indication one way or another. If this letter was indeed written to Tutankhamen, it provides strong evidence that relations between Egypt and Babylon were still normal. It also makes more certain my idea that the group of letters was sorted when the administrative offices of the government left Akhetaton; and the latest, and most significant letters removed. It must be emphasised, however, that the assigning of this letter to the reign of Tutankhamen is by no means proven. The strongest argument against this view is No. 9, l.30, where a king certainly Amenhotep III, is called the father of the king to whom the letter is addressed. It is clear that Burnaburiash's father was contemporary with Amenhotep III (see note 9) and was dead when Ikhnaton began to reign. If this letter

were actually addressed to Tutankhamen, the 'father' here would have to be Ikhnaton. I believe this to be quite possible, but the contemporaneity of Kurigalzu and Ikhnaton seems beyond acceptance. I suspect that letter 170, however, may be assigned to the reign of Tutankhamen.

3 S. A. B. Mercer, op. cit., No. 29, l. 113; No. 27, l. 89 f.
4 ibid., Nos. 7–11.
5 *Urkunden IV*, p. 1738, l. 6 f.
6 S. A. B. Mercer, op. cit., No. 17, l. 11 f.
7 ibid., Nos. 19–23.
8 ibid., Nos. 1–5.
9 ibid., No. 6; No. 11 l. 5, notes a complaint of Amenhotep III (the 'father' of Ikhnaton) sent to Burnaburiash. This certainly proves that the two kings were contemporaries for a short time.
10 P. Van der Meer, *The Chronology of Ancient Western Asia and Egypt* (2nd ed., Leiden, 1955), Table 3, p. 15 f.
11 ibid., No. 1, l. 62 f.
12 ibid., No. 10, l. 8 f. Evidently the first king in the series contemporary with Amenhotep III in whose reign relations between Egypt and Babylon were first instituted. No. 1, l. 63 f. indicates that the reign of the father of Kadashman Enlil overlapped that of Amenhotep III's father.
13 S. A. B. Mercer, op. cit., No. 9, l. 19 f.
14 ibid., No. 1, l. 11 f.
15 ibid., No. 8. l. 13 f.
16 Knudtzon's numbering (followed by Mercer) will be adopted unless I have strong reasons for changing it.
17 ibid., from Zurata, No. 232; from Zatatna, Nos. 233 and 234.
18 ibid., No. 245.
19 ibid., No. 250, l. 16 f.
20 ibid., No. 116, l. 63 f. See also note 16.

*Chapter Four The situation in Western Asia: the royal letters*

1 S. A. B. Mercer, op. cit., Nos. 2–4.
2 ibid., Nos. 6–11, 13.
3 ibid, Nos. 17–29.
4 ibid., Nos. 15–16.
5 ibid., Nos. 41–2.
6 ibid., perhaps No. 32.
7 ibid., Nos. 33–9.

8 ibid., No. 11, l.19 f.
9 ibid., No. 3, l.9 f.
10 ibid., No. 1, l.11 f.
11 ibid., No. 1, l.62 f.
12 ibid., No. 10, l.11 f.
13 ibid., No. 2, l.10 f.; No. 2, l.6 f.; No. 3, l.7; No. 4, l.4 f.
14 ibid., No. 2, l.13 f.; No. 4, l.36 f.
15 ibid., No. 3, l.13 f.
16 ibid., No. 7, l.73 f.
17 ibid., No. 8, l.13 f.
18 S. A. B. Mercer, op. cit., No. 245, l.30 f.
19 J. H. Breasted, 'A City of Ikhenaton in Nubia', *Z.A.S.A.*, Vol. 40, p. 108.
20 S. A. B. Mercer, op. cit., No. 8, l.25 f.
21 ibid., No. 8, l.30 f.
22 ibid., No. 9, l.19 f.
23 ibid., No. 10, l.12 f.
24 ibid., No. 9, l.31 f.
25 ibid., No. 16, l.6 f.
26 ibid., No. 16, l.22 f.
27 ibid., No. 15, l.9.
28 ibid., No. 16, l.19 f.
29 ibid., No. 16, l.37 f.
30 ibid., No. 29, l.113 f.
31 ibid., No. 27, l.97 f.
32 ibid., No. 24, col. 3, l.52 f.; No. 29, l.16 f.
33 *Urkunden IV*, p. 1738, l.6 f.
34 S. A. B. Mercer, op. cit., No. 17, l.11 f.
35 ibid., No. 17, l.31 f.
36 ibid., No. 19, l.18 f.; No. 20, l.8 f.; No. 21, l.13 f., etc.
37 E. F. Weidner, 'Politische Dokumente aus Kleinasien', *Boghaz-Koi Studien* (Leipzig, 1923), Heft 8, No. 1, l.25 f.
38 E. Cavaignac, *Subbiluliuma et son Temps* (Paris, 1932), p. 61 f.
39 E. Cavaignac, 'Piphururiyas= Ay', *Kemi* (Paris, 1930), Vol. 3, p. 33.
40 S. A. B. Mercer, op. cit., No. 17, l.30 f.
41 E. Cavaignac, *Les Hittites*, Table of Chronology, pp. 52–3; see also pp. 26 and 30 for dates of start and end of reign.
42 S. A. B. Mercer, op. cit., No. 55, l.43.
43 ibid., No. 164, l.21 f.; No. 165, l.18 f., 34 f.; No. 166, l.21 f., etc.
44 S. A. B. Mercer, op. cit., No. 24.
45 ibid., No. 24, col. 2, l.68 f.

46 J. A. Knudtzon, op. cit., p. 1056, n. 1 and 2.
47 S. A. B. Mercer, op. cit., No. 24, col. 3, l. 58 f., and l. 123.
48 ibid., No. 24, col. 3, l. 66 f., especially l. 71 f.
49 ibid., No. 24, col. 1, l. 84 f., ll. 96–103 quoted.
50 ibid., No. 24, col. 3, l. 58 f.
51 ibid., No. 24, col. 3, l. 71 f.
52 ibid., No. 24, col. 3, l. 119 f.
53 ibid., No. 24, col. 4, l. 117 f.
54 ibid., No. 27, l. 71 f.; No. 28, l. 42 f.; No. 29, l. 6 f.
55 ibid., No. 42, l. 19.
56 ibid., No. 31, l. 12 f.
57 ibid., No. 35, l. 49 f.

*Chapter Five The letters from subject princes*

1 S. A. Mercer, op. cit., No. 162, l. 9 f.
2 ibid., No. 70, l. 10 f.
3 ibid., No. 71, l. 16 f.
4 ibid., No. 104, l. 18 f.
5 ibid., No. 117, l. 21 f.
6 ibid., No. 117, l. 48 f.; No. 108, l. 28 f.
7 ibid., No. 88, l. 23 f.; No. 87, l. 25; No. 83, l. 21 f., etc.
8 ibid., No. 68, l. 12 f.
9 ibid., No. 69, l. 12 f.
10 ibid., No. 136, l. 33 f.
11 ibid., No. 117, l. 83 f.; No. 119, l. 8 f.; No. 121, l. 7 f., etc.
12 ibid., No. 162, l. 2 f.
13 ibid., No. 159, l. 12 f.; No. 160, l. 26 f.; No. 161, l. 35 f.
14 ibid., No. 71, l. 16 f.; No. 76, l. 7 f.; No. 88, l. 9 f.
15 ibid., No. 118, l. 24 f.; No. 114, l. 10 f.; No. 83, l. 24 f.
16 ibid., No. 118, l. 24 f.
17 ibid., No. 89, l. 10 f.
18 ibid., No. 136, l. 24 f.; No. 137, l. 14 f.
19 ibid., No. 68, l. 19 f.
20 ibid., No. 131, l. 34 f.
21 ibid., No. 132, l. 40 f.
22 ibid., No. 133, l. 9 f.
23 J. A. Knudtzon, op. cit., p. 1197, n. to No. 101.
24 S. A. B. Mercer, op. cit., No. 71, l. 7 f.
25 ibid., No. 101, l. 1 f.
26 ibid., No. 117, l. 64.

27 ibid., No. 83, l.24 f.; No. 105, l.83 f.; No. 113, l.7 f.; No. 114, l.15 f.
28 J. A. Knudtzon, op. cit., p. 1168 f.
29 ibid., p. 1153 f.
30 S. A. B. Mercer, op. cit., No. 117, l.59 f., he seems to have an equivalent office to Ianhamu, No. 122, l.22 f.; No. 123, l.9 f.
31 ibid., No. 122, l.31 f.
32 ibid., No. 123, l.9 f.
33 J. A. Knudtzon, op. cit., p. 1169 f., n. to l.31.
34 S. A. B. Mercer, op. cit., No. 83, l.27 f.
35 ibid., No. 83, l.38 f.
36 ibid., No. 85, l.23 f.
37 ibid., No. 106, l.35 f.; No. 118, l.55 f.
38 ibid., No. 83, l.23 f.
39 ibid., No. 129, l.34 f.
40 ibid., No. 71, l.17 f.
41 ibid., No. 74, l.24 f.
42 ibid., No. 75, l.25 f.
43 ibid., No. 81, l.14 f.
44 ibid., No. 87, 1.18 f.
45 ibid., Nos. 60–5.
46 ibid., No. 60, l.6 f.
47 ibid., No. 60, l.13 f.
48 ibid., No. 60, l.10 f.; No. 68, l.22 f.
49 ibid., No. 60, l.21 f.; No. 62, l.9 f.
50 ibid., No. 60, l.10 f.; No. 64, l.10 f.
51 ibid., No. 67, l.10 f.
52 ibid., No. 101, l.29 f.
53 ibid., No. 149, l.57 f.
54 ibid., No. 55, l.23 f.
55 ibid., No. 162, l.30 f.
56 ibid., No. 164, l.27 f.
57 ibid., No. 169, l.17 f.
58 ibid., No. 156, l.13 f.
59 ibid., No. 159, l.45 f.
60 ibid., No. 162, l.1.
61 ibid., No. 149, l.57 f., 67 f.
62 ibid., No. 149, l.47 f.
63 ibid., No. 162, l.40 f.
64 ibid., No. 162, l.78 f.
65 ibid., No. 163, l.6 f.

66 ibid., No. 222A, l. 15 f.
67 ibid., No. 164, l. 27 f.
68 ibid., No. 124, l. 50 f.
69 ibid., No. 141, l. 18 f.
70 ibid., Nos. 191, 193, 195, 199, etc.
71 ibid., No. 149, l. 57 f.
72 ibid., No. 150, l. 4 f.
73 ibid., No. 151, l. 68.
74 ibid., No. 153, l. 6 f.
75 ibid., No. 232, l. 13 f.
76 ibid., No. 122, l. 24 f.
77 ibid., No. 108, l. 28 f.
78 ibid., No. 117, l. 21 f.
79 ibid., No. 117, l. 48 f.
80 ibid., No. 286, l. 26 f.
81 ibid., No. 289, l. 30 f.
82 ibid., No. 75, l. 35 f.
83 ibid., No. 126, l. 51 f.
84 ibid., No. 126, l. 58 f.
85 ibid., No. 116, l. 71; No. 129, l. 76.
86 J. A. Knudtzon, op. cit., p. 1071 f.
87 S. A. B. Mercer, op. cit., No. 85, l. 51.
88 ibid., No. 101, l. 3 f.
89 J. A. Knudtzon, op. cit., p. 1197 f., note to No. 101, l. 4.
90 S. A. B. Mercer, op. cit., No. 126, l. 62 f.
91 Letter 101 is written after the death of Abdi Ashirta.
92 ibid., No. 86, l. 8.
93 ibid., No. 90, l. 19 f.
94 ibid., No. 95, l. 27 f.
95 ibid., No. 53, l. 8 f.
96 ibid., No. 54, l. 26 f.
97 ibid., No. 55, l. 42 f.
98 ibid., No. 140, l. 20 f.
99 ibid., No. 151, l. 59 f.
100 ibid., No. 174, l. 8 f.
101 ibid., No. 175, l. 7 f.; No. 176, l. 7 f.; No. 176A, l. 7 f.
102 ibid., No. 197, l. 26 f.
103 ibid., No. 197, l. 7 f.
104 ibid., No. 162, l. 22 f.
105 ibid., No. 189, l. 6 f.
106 ibid., No. 165, l. 18 f.; No. 166, l. 21 f.

107 ibid., No. 170, l.14 f.
108 E. Cavaignac, *Subbiluliuma et son Temps*, p. 20.
109 S. A. B. Mercer, op. cit., No. 167, l.20 f.
110 ibid., No. 59, l.4 f.
111 ibid., No. 54, l.38 f.; No. 56, l.36 f., the salutation of the latter letter is broken.
112 ibid., No. 58, l.4 f.

*Chapter Six The Hittite material*

1 E. Cavaignac, *Les Annales de Subbiluliuma* (Strasbourg, 1931), and H. G. Güterbock, 'The Deeds of Suppilulima as Told by his Son, Mursilis II', *Journal of Cuneiform Studies* (New Haven, 1956), Vol. X.
2 E. F. Weidner, op. cit.
3 E. Cavaignac, 'Les Annales de Mursile II', *Revue d'Assyriologie* (Paris, 1929), Vol. 26, p. 145 f.
4 A. Götze, 'Die Pestgebete des Mursilis', *Kleinasiatische Forschungen* (Weimar, 1929), Vol. I.
5 E. Cavaignac, op. cit., p. 20 f., (a), and H. G. Güterbock, op. cit. p. 94 f., (b).
6 ibid., (a) p. 21; (b) p. 95.
7 ibid., (a) p. 22; (b) p. 96 f.
8 H. G. Güterbock, op. cit., p. 97 f.
9 ibid., p. 107/8.
10 A. Götze, op. cit., p. 209 f.
11 ibid., p. 207 f.
12 E. Waddell, *Manetho*, p. 101 f.
13 S. A. B. Mercer, op. cit., No. 170, l.14 f.
14 ibid., Nos. 174–6, and 176A.
15 H. G. Güterbock, op. cit., p. 92 f.; and E. Cavaignac, op. cit., p. 16 f.
16 H. G. Güterbock, op. cit., p. 97.
17 ibid., p. 111.
18 E. F. Weidner, op. cit., No. 1.
19 ibid., No. 1, ll.27, 30 f.
20 ibid., No. 1, l.48.
21 S. A. B. Mercer, op. cit., No. 54, ll.22, 28.
22 E. F. Weidner, op. cit., No. 1, l. 40 f.
23 S. A. B. Mercer, op. cit., No. 55, ll.42 f. and 56 f.
24 E. F. Weidner, op cit., No. 1, l.48 f.

25 E. Cavaignac, *Subbiluliuma et son Temps*, p. 61 f.
26 H. G. Güterbock, op. cit., p. 111.
27 E. Cavaignac, op. cit., p. 61 f.
28 E. F. Weidner, op. cit., No. 2, l. 35 f.
29 E. Cavaignac, *Les Annales de Mursile II*, p. 161, l. 64.
30 ibid., p. 162, l. 70.
31 ibid., p. 169, l. 89.
32 A. Götze, loc. cit.
33 S. Langdon and Sir A. H. Gardiner, 'The Treaty of Alliance', etc., *J.E.A.* (1920), Vol. 6, p. 189.
34 E. Cavaignac, *Les Hittites*, p. 34.
35 ibid., p. 39.
36 S. Langdon and Sir A. H. Gardiner, op. cit., p. 202; it is evident from this letter that there was active war between Egypt and Hatte during the reign of Hattusilis II.

*Chapter Seven The Egyptian evidence*

1 J. H. Breasted, *Ancient Records of Egypt* (Chicago, 1906), Vol. 2, p. 844.
2 *Urkunden IV*, p. 1649, l. 8 f.
3 ibid., p. 1658, l. 9 f.
4 ibid., p. 1963, l. 1 f.
5 ibid., p. 2070, l. 5 f.
6 Sir A. H. Gardiner, 'The Memphite Tomb of General Haremhab', *J.E.A.*, Vol. 39, p. 3.
7 ibid., p. 4.
8 H. Carter, *The Tomb of Tutankhamen*, Vol. 1, pl. LIII.
9 T. M. Davis, *The Tomb of Harmhabi and Touatankhamanou*, p. 127, No. 3.
10 *Urkunden IV*, p. 2126, l. 17 f.
11 R. O. Faulkner, 'The Wars of Sethos I', *J.E.A.* (1947), Vol. 33, p. 34.
12 ibid., p. 36.
13 ibid. There are no dates on these campaigns other than the year 1. The entire inscription may well represent a short period. The fighting in the south seems to have taken up a rather short time. Seti himself declares that he took his objectives in one day.

## *Chapter Eight The Archaeological discoveries from Syria-Palestine*

1 A. Rowe, *Topography and History of Beth Shan* (Philadelphia, 1930) p. 19.
2 ibid., p. 24.

## *Appendix Dating the Tell el Amarna letters*

1 S. A. B. Mercer, *The Tell el Amarna Letters*, No. 249, ll. 17 f. and 29.
2 ibid., No. 250, ll. 4 f. and 16 f.
3 ibid., No. 31A, l.28.
4 ibid., No. 249, ll. 16 f. and 29 f.; No. 250. l.35 f.
5 ibid., No. 249, l.8 f.
6 ibid., No. 289, ll. 5–29.
7 ibid., No. 289, l.11 f.
8 ibid., No. 290, l.5 f.
9 ibid., No. 290A, l.20 f.
10 ibid., No. 288, l.43 f., the comparison of No. 285, l.5 f.; No. 286, l.9 f.; No. 287, l.25 f.; No. 28, l.9 f., all very similar, shows that these letters constitute a closely related group. The enmity of Ilimilku (Milkili) to the king is noted in No. 286, l.36 f., and in No. 287, l.29 f. This establishes the connection of this group of letters with the reign of Amenhotep III.
11 ibid., No. 335, l.7 f.
12 ibid., No. 333, l.4 f.
13 ibid., No. 245, l.41 f.
14 ibid., No. 255, l.14 f.
15 ibid., No. 256, l.4 f.
16 ibid., No. 249, l.20.
17 ibid., No. 83, ll.31, 39, 40.
18 ibid., No. 132, l.29.
19 ibid., No. 254, l.37.
20 ibid., No. 285, l.24; No. 287, ll. 46, 49; No. 289, l.32.
21 ibid., No. 68, l.22.
22 ibid., No. 131, l.34.
23 ibid., p. 887 for list of places where these names appear.
24 ibid., No. 288, ll.19, 22.
25 ibid., No. 234, ll.14, 23.
26 ibid., p. 888 for occurrences of this name.
27 ibid., No. 8, l.18 f.
28 ibid., No. 238, l.23.

29 ibid., No. 237, l.2.
30 J. A. Knudtzon, *Die Tel El Amarna Tafeln*, p. 1304, n. 1.
31 S. A. B. Mercer, op. cit., No. 273, l.22 f.
32 ibid., No. 296, l.24 f.
33 ibid., No. 333, l.5 f.
34 ibid., No. 332, l.3.
35 ibid., No. 288, l.43 f.
36 ibid., pp. 884 and 889 for occurrence of these names.
37 ibid., No. 116, l.63 f.
38 ibid., No. 108, l.28 f.
39 ibid., No. 32, ll.1, 4, 10.
40 ibid., No. 51, l.4 f.
41 ibid., No. 101, l.4 f.
42 ibid., No. 116, l.8 f., but see No. 116, l.17 f.
43 ibid., No. 55, l.23 f and l.45 f.
44 ibid., No. 58, reverse l.3. Letters 60–5 were written by Abdi-Ashirta; No. 87 refers either to Abdi-Ashirta or Aziru, however it is quite certain that Aziru never made a treaty with Ribaddi. The conquest of Sumur mentioned in l.17 f. was probably that of Abdi-Ashirta, but it is impossible to be certain in this case.
45 ibid., No. 57, obverse l.2.
46 ibid., No. 59, l.13 f.
47 ibid., No. 59, l.34 f.
48 ibid., No. 161, ll.12 f., 32 f.
49 ibid., No. 104, l.6 f. and No. 103, l.11 f. There is no further mention of Irqata by Ribaddi, but in Nos. 139 and 140 the writer notes that the city also has been taken by Aziru (No. 139, l.14 f. and No. 140, l.10 f). No. 109 l.58 f. indicates that only Sumur is left under Ribaddi's control.
50 ibid., No. 33, l.9 f.
51 ibid., No. 117, l.21 f.
52 ibid., No. 142, l.15 f.
53 ibid., No. 146, l.14 f.; No. 147, l.66 f.; No. 148, ll.24 f., 39 f.; No. 149, ll.49 f., 57 f., 67 f.,; No. 151, ll.10 f., 64 f.; No. 152, l.7 f.; No. 154, ll.14 f., 22 f.
54 ibid., No. 147, l.66 f.; No. 149, ll.35 f., 57 f., 67 f.; No. 151, l.59 f.
55 ibid., No. 149, ll.57–70.
56 ibid., No. 92, l.30 f.
57 ibid., No. 155, l.67 f.
58 ibid., No. 155, l.66 f.

59 ibid., No. 150 is badly broken and No. 153 is almost a note.
60 W. F. Albright, op. cit., p. 191, the name is used in No. 155, ll.9, 15, 22, 26, 42, 50, and 62.
61 S. A. Mercer, op. cit., No. 151, l.59 f.
62 ibid., No. 83, l.24 f.
63 ibid., No. 157, l.10 f.
64 ibid., No. 159, ll.11 f., 43 f.
65 ibid., No. 156, l.13 f.
66 See note 67. The salutation is very different from the heading on letters sent to the king of Egypt. The greeting to various persons in l.36 f. would certainly not be added to a letter to pharaoh. The connection of the two senders with Aziru is amply shown in the letters. He is known to have sojourned in Egypt (No. 169, ll.12 f., 16 f., 24 f.). The conclusion that he is the addressee of the letters is inescapable.
67 ibid., No. 161, l.20 f.; No. 165, l.9 f.
68 ibid., No. 170, l.14 f.
69 ibid., No. 53, ll.8 f., 24 f., 28 f., 35 f., 56 f.; No. 54, ll.22 f., 26 f.
70 ibid., No. 53, l.35 f.
71 ibid., No. 54, ll.26 f., 31 f.
72 ibid., No. 55, ll.23 f., 27., 44 f.
73 ibid., No. 55, ll.42 f., 56 f.
74 ibid., No. 55, l.59 f.
75 ibid., No. 162, l.2 f.
76 ibid., No. 162, l.22 f.
77 ibid., No. 149, l.30 f.
78 ibid., No. 149, ll.57 f., 67 f.
79 ibid., No. 151, l.59 f.
80 ibid., No. 53, l.28 f.
81 ibid., No. 53, l.24 f.
82 ibid., No. 197, l.23 f.